ANXIETY AND DEPRESSION IN THE CLASSROOM

Norton Books in Education

Anxiety and Depression in the Classroom

A Teacher's Guide to Fostering
Self-Regulation in Young Students

Nadja Reilly

W. W. NORTON & COMPANY
New York • London

For information about permission to reproduce selections from this book,
write to Permissions, W. W. Norton & Company, Inc.,
500 Fifth Avenue, New York, NY 10110

For information about special discounts for bulk purchases, please contact
W. W. Norton Special Sales at specialsales@wwnorton.com or 800-233-4830

Manufacturing by Edwards Brothers Malloy
Production manager: Christine Critelli

ISBN 978-0-393-70872-1 (pbk.)

W. W. Norton & Company, Inc.
500 Fifth Avenue, New York, N.Y. 10110
www.wwnorton.com

W. W. Norton & Company Ltd.
Castle House, 75/76 Wells Street, London W1T 3QT

1 2 3 4 5 6 7 8 9 0

I dedicate this book to my children,
Christopher and Michael.
They are my forever love, light,
and inspiration.

Contents

Acknowledgments

The completion of a project like this is never a solitary endeavor. It is fueled by the help, encouragement, and guidance of many generous individuals. I would like to thank A. Deborah Malmud at W. W. Norton & Company, Inc. for inviting me to write this book, and especially for her patience in reading the manuscript and offering such valuable suggestions.

Throughout my career, I have had the honor of learning from many gifted colleagues. I am grateful to Dr. Annette LaGreca, Dr. Gerald Koocher, Dr. David DeMaso, Dr. Eugene D'Angelo, and Dr. Caroline Watts. Despite how much time may pass between opportunities to see each other, your influence is felt daily. A special thank you to all my friends and colleagues at Boston Children's Hospital and the Williams James College (formerly Massachusetts School of Professional Psychology).

To my colleague, mentor, and friend, Margaret Hannah, I offer my heartfelt thanks. Your generosity is boundless, and I thank you for your gifts of knowledge, love for our work, encouragement of ideas, leadership, strength, and compassion. Thank you for reminding me to dream and play.

I am also immensely fortunate to work with passionate individuals who continuously find ways to promote the emotional health and wellness of children. Mr. Robert Anthony has been such an advocate, and I am grateful for his interest in the book and for his tireless efforts to unite individuals whose impact in this field will be significant and long lasting. My sincere gratitude to the teachers, school staff, parents, and students with whom I've worked over the years. They have shared their stories, offered ideas and suggestions, and have been invaluable advocates for children's mental health.

It is true that words of comfort and love can lift one's spirit even in the toughest of moments. Throughout my life, my parents have always been that source of comfort and love and I thank them with all my heart. My husband and sons offered patience, understanding, and encouragement, and I thank them for their endless cheering and never wavering belief that "you can do it mommy!"

I am grateful indeed for all these people, gifts, opportunities, and dreams yet to come.

ANXIETY AND DEPRESSION IN THE CLASSROOM

Introduction

IT'S 10 IN THE morning, and Charlie has already visited the nurse's office twice. During the first visit, she said her tummy hurt and that she needed to rest. Shortly after she returned to class, Charlie left again, saying she had a headache and needed medicine. The nurse, after giving her some water and much gentle reassurance, sent Charlie back to class, where she joined her peers in time to go to art class. Charlie cried throughout art class, saying in between sobs, "I'm no good at this. My project is terrible. I can't do anything right."

Charlie's second-grade teacher, Ms. Renato, is worried, and frankly, frustrated. Charlie is a smart, gentle girl and a good student, yet these emotional difficulties are becoming increasingly disruptive to her learning and functioning. She leaves the classroom, cries, or isolates herself from her peers almost every day; this has especially been the case over the past month. Ms. Renato cannot figure out the reason for Charlie's distress. Ms. Renato is also struggling with how to effectively keep the classroom routine for her other students when she has to step out of the room with Charlie so often.

It is not unusual for elementary school children to have minor behavioral or emotional difficulties in response to adjusting to the school environment. For example, some fidgetiness, reluctance to leave home in the morning, worries, talking out of turn, or brief falling out with a peer are not uncommon. Such difficulties are generally transient and are successfully addressed through redirection, emotional support, and

1

reinforcement of positive behaviors. In some instances; however, as seen in Charlie's story, children may experience more notable distress that is indicative of a diagnosable emotional disorder. The disturbance in overall functioning and self-regulation caused by these disorders can take a significant toll on children's emotional, social, and academic development.

Understanding the nature of students' emotional and behavioral dys-regulation can be a challenge for teachers, yet it is of utmost impor-tance. Approximately 1 out of 10 youth (birth to age 18) have mental health problems severe enough to impair how they function at home, in school, or in the community. Furthermore, major mental illnesses may begin quite early in childhood, as early as 7 to 11 years of age (Stagman & Cooper, 2010).

What triggers the worries, sadness, and acting out in such young chil-dren? How does one differentiate the typical behaviors associated with developmental changes from symptoms of a mental health disorder? How do the symptoms associated with mental health disorders impact learning? And finally, how is it possible to support students' emotional health in the context of the classroom? This book offers responses to these questions with a specific focus on anxiety and depression, two mental health disorders that may have their onset during the elemen-tary school years.

The book is divided into three main sections, each offering informa-tion and practical tips based on a variety of case studies, frameworks, research, and clinical practices. The first section focuses on under-standing the connection between children's development, self-regula-tion (emotional and behavioral), and academic learning (Chapter 1). The second section focuses on two diagnoses that significantly impact regulation and learning: anxiety and depression (Chapters 2 and 3). The third section focuses on specific tools and activities that teachers may use in the classroom to support students' emotional needs (Chapters 4 and 5), and in fostering communication with parents around chil-dren's emotional functioning (Chapter 6). Chapter 7 concludes the book with a broad view of how to use the information, frameworks, and tools listed in the first six chapters to promote schoolwide programming and advocacy efforts focusing on child mental health.

Frameworks

Addressing children's emotional and academic functioning is a complex endeavor that requires exploration and intervention at multiple levels of the child's life and experience. This book relies on a set of frameworks that guide the multifaceted approach required to most appropriately foster children's mental health, learning, and self-regulation. Each framework is listed below.

THE 4 RS OF LEARNING: READING, WRITING, ARITHMETIC, AND REGULATION (OF BEHAVIOR AND EMOTIONS)

The transition from preschool into the more structured learning environment of elementary school presents a significant time of adjustment and change for children. Influences that facilitate a positive transition include environmental factors, such as supportive caretakers, enriching opportunities, and positive modeling, and individual factors, such as readiness to learn and self-regulation. In the 4 Rs of learning framework, the first three Rs, reading, writing, and arithmetic, refer to the fundamental tools for children's readiness to learn and academic success. Through scaffolding and practice, children use these skills to understand and master increasingly complicated material. The fourth R, *self-regulation*, is posited to be an equally fundamental tool for children's academic success. Self-regulation refers to the interaction of processes at the biological and behavioral levels that allow children to understand and manage their emotions, behaviors, and thoughts in order to appropriately respond to their environment (Neuenschwander, Röthlisberger, Cimeli, & Roebers, 2012). Self-regulation is a crucial process in the emotional, social, and academic development of children (see Figure I.1). It is a critical component of school readiness as well as an important predic-

FIGURE I.I. Self-regulation is critical to the emotional and social development of children as well as to their academic success.

tor of academic and social competence into adulthood. Self-regulation is therefore presented in this book as key to our understanding of the link between children's emotional and academic functioning.

Successful self-regulation can be seen in the classroom when children are able to follow classroom routines, maintain attention during a lesson, use learned information to solve new problems, and interact well with teachers and peers. When a child experiences emotional difficulties, however, all the processes associated with self-regulation are affected. For example, Annie, a 7-year-old, is struggling with an anxiety disorder. Annie is unable to maintain attention appropriately during class, as her thoughts are consumed by worry over whether her mother will be able to pick her up from school. She begins to think about different negative scenarios that might prevent her mom from being there after school, despite this never having actually occurred. Because of these persistent worries, Annie does not complete her classwork. At recess, she is worried about her unfinished work, isolates herself from her peers, and does not engage in play. Annie's difficulties with self-regulation interfere with her emotional, social, and academic development.

THE DEVELOPMENTAL APPROACH

Following a developmental approach means understanding what is occurring for children neurobiologically, cognitively, socially, and emotionally during distinct developmental phases. For example, a fifth-grade student's cognitive understanding of abstract concepts is sufficiently developed to allow her to understand emotions and how they impact her thoughts and behavior. She can independently use this information to develop new ways of coping, modifying social emotional skills she has learned in one setting to use in a different setting or context. In contrast, a kindergarten student will need more concrete examples, reminders, and scaffolding in order to use context-specific skills.

Similarly, the diagnoses of anxiety and depression are discussed from a developmental psychopathology perspective. That is, children are not merely little adults. An appropriate understanding of how mental illness impacts children's cognitive and social emotional development, as well as of how appropriate interventions are developed under optimal conditions, must be acquired through a developmental lens. It is this lens that guides the activities found in Chapters 4 and 5.

CULTURAL SENSITIVITY

Cultural factors significantly influence attitudes about and responses to mental health. Within schools, programs addressing mental health cannot follow a "one-size-fits-all" model, as such an approach does not consider the differences in conceptualization, understanding, acceptance, and utilization of mental health services found among different cultures. It is also important to create a definition of cultural diversity that is broader than simply racial or ethnic differences. Cultural diversity is seen across multiple domains, including race, ethnicity, gender, socioeconomic status, country of origin, religion, sexual orientation, age, physical and mental ability, language, and learning styles. Throughout the book, specific information related to cultural differences in mental health conceptualization and communication is offered. Finally, the culture of the school is also of critical importance. This will be further discussed in Chapter 7.

PREVENTION AND SOCIAL EMOTIONAL LEARNING

Given the significant number of children struggling emotionally, approaches that address mental health issues before they develop into diagnosable disorders are critical. Prevention science is a "multidisciplinary field devoted to the scientific study of the theory, research, and practice related to the prevention of social, physical, and mental health problems" (O'Connell, Boat, & Warner, 2009, p. xxvii). There are two main concepts of prevention science that are highly relevant to children's emotional health and well-being: prevention and mental health promotion.

Prevention refers to "interventions that occur prior to the onset of a disorder that are intended to prevent or reduce risk for the disorder" (O'Connell et al., 2009, p. xxvii). Prevention happens at three different levels, each defined by the degree of risk in the population (Domitrovich et al., 2010).

- *Universal prevention* strategies target the general public or an entire population that has not been identified on the basis of individual risk. For example, a universal prevention program can be used with an entire class or grade without requiring identification of children who may be struggling.

- *Selected prevention* strategies target individuals or subgroups that are identified as being at elevated risk for a disorder. The individuals or groups are chosen not because they are demonstrating symptoms of a disorder, but because their circumstances place them at higher risk for disorders—for example, children of recently divorced parents, children with chronic illnesses, or children who recently emigrated from another country.

- *Indicated prevention* strategies target individuals who are identified as having some initial symptom presentation related to mental disorders but who do not yet meet full criteria for a diagnosis.

Mental health promotion refers to strategies that "focus on well-being rather than prevention of illness and disorder, although it may also decrease the likelihood of disorder" (O'Connell et al., 2009, p. 65). Mental health promotion strategies aim to enhance individuals' ability to achieve developmentally appropriate tasks; aid them in acquiring a positive sense of self-esteem, mastery, and well-being; and strengthen their ability to cope with adversity (O'Connell et al., 2009). Mental health promotions strategies are typically used with a whole population (e.g., an entire class, the whole grade), so they are particularly well suited for use in the classroom.

Social emotional learning (SEL) is an approach that "integrates competence promotion and youth development frameworks with the goals of reducing risk factors and fostering protective factors for positive adjustment" (Durlak, Weissberg, Dymnicki, Taylor, & Schellinger, 2011, p. 406). SEL is a perfect combination of prevention and mental health promotion that is particularly developed for the school setting. By participating in SEL activities, "students feel valued, experience greater intrinsic motivation to achieve, and develop a broadly applicable set of social-emotional competencies that mediate better academic performance, health-promoting behavior, and citizenship" (Durlak et al., 2011, p. 407).

The Collaborative for Academic, Social, and Emotional Learning

(CASEL) is the nation's leading organization around social emotional learning. CASEL has identified five core competencies to be addressed in SEL programs. The definitions below are from the CASEL website and resources (http://www.casel.org/social-and-emotional-learning/core-competencies). The activities found in this book each target one or more of the core competencies.

- *Self-awareness:* The ability to accurately recognize one's emotions and thoughts and their influence on behavior.
- *Self-management:* The ability to regulate one's emotions, thoughts, and behaviors effectively in different situations.
- *Social awareness:* The ability to take the perspective of and empathize with others from diverse backgrounds and cultures, to understand social and ethical norms for behavior, and to recognize family, school, and community resources and supports.
- *Relationship skills:* The ability to establish and maintain healthy and rewarding relationships with diverse individuals and groups.
- *Responsible decision making:* The ability to make constructive and respectful choices about personal behavior and social interactions based on consideration of ethical standards, safety concerns, social norms, the realistic evaluation of consequences of various actions, and the well-being of self and others.

THE ECOLOGICAL APPROACH

Children's development can best be understood from a human ecological systems theory, which posits that development is influenced by the interaction of the contexts in which children live, study, and play (Atkins, Hoagwood, Kutash, & Seidman, 2010; Bronfenbrenner, 1977). The child is at the center of this series of nested systems, contributing individual factors that include temperamental qualities and cognitive abilities (Bronfenbrenner, 1977). The interactions between individual child factors; the quality of the child's relationships with family, teachers, and peers; and broader ecological factors (e.g., school quality, neighborhood safety) collectively have a significant impact on children's emotional and behavioral regulation (Greenberg, 2006). The ecological approach further accounts for the impact that broader organizations, policies, and culture have on child mental health outcomes (e.g., mental health disparities, lack of access to services due to lack of insurance; Espelage, Hong, Rao, & Low, 2013).

Notice, Give, and Nurture: Active Tools for Teachers

An underlying structure that weaves together the frameworks identified above and how they impact child functioning is *relationships*. The power of relationships is crucial in children's successful development. In this book, teachers can learn how to engage the power of their relationships with students to promote children's self-regulation and, therefore, their emotional, social, and academic success.

A "Notice, Give, and Nurture" structure is embedded throughout the book. Each chapter will inform you of how to intentionally *notice* the behaviors, words, and interactions of your students. The *notice* sections will also outline a process of self-reflection, encouraging you to examine the factors you contribute to your relationships with your students. The *give* sections share skills, support, and responses to use with students to foster their self-regulation. Finally, the *nurture* sections provide guidance in maintaining the relational and emotional safety students need for successful emotional and academic growth.

I recognize that the notice, give, and nurture sections may raise sensitive issues for you as a teacher, as well as require you to practice a potentially new set of skills. Therefore, I want to emphasize that the goal of this section is not to ask you to assume the role of a mental health practitioner. My expectation is not that you will become a diagnostician or clinician. Instead, my goal is to offer supporting materials that will promote your support of student emotional well-being.

While this book is primarily written for teachers, it is also a valuable resource for all school personnel. Fostering emotional and academic success requires a supportive school culture, and this entails a schoolwide effort. Focusing on the enhancement of social emotional learning for all students will help in developing a safe, supportive environment that will benefit all students.

CHAPTER ONE

What Is Self-Regulation?

Do you know how hard it is to read when Ryan is sticking his pencils in his mouth and singing, "I'm a walrus!"?
—Christopher, first-grader

IT WAS THE ONLY the second week of school, but Ms. Thompson, the kindergarten teacher, had already identified three students who would likely have a hard time during the year. Brendan was a kind and polite boy, but he struggled with communicating his needs and thoughts. It took a significant amount of time and reassurance to gently coax him to speak in class, and it was clear that his peers did not have the patience to encourage this in their interactions. As a result, Brendan was usually alone during recess and overlooked in games and conversations. In contrast, Charlotte, a lively and energetic girl, seemed to absorb all the attention. She frequently required redirection and reminders not to distract her peers as well as reminders of how her words and behaviors impacted others. Then there was Andrew, a shy boy who seemed to struggle with every aspect of learning. He was easily distracted, hardly demonstrated enthusiasm for learning, and seemed generally fearful of approaching anything new, either academically or socially.

Ms. Thompson's concern for these students was not driven by their academic performance and test scores, but rather by the children's inability to modify or regulate their behavior in a way that would allow them to be successful socially, emotionally, and academically in the classroom. Her experience is consistent with results from a nationally representative study involving 3,000 kindergarten teachers, who reported that more than one in three students had difficulty following directions, working in a group, or interacting with others (Valiente, Swanson, & Lemery-Chalfant, 2012).

Children's ability to communicate, to engage in and be curious about learning, to follow directions, to modify their actions and feelings based on particular situations, and to be sensitive to others' feelings are all related to a larger construct known as *self-regulation*. Self-regulation refers to the ability to control and direct one's attention, thoughts, emotions, and actions to achieve particular goals (Blair, 2002; McClelland & Cameron, 2012; Zelazo & Lyons, 2012). Imagine Michael, a second-grade student who in math class is learning how to "carry over" when adding. He first needs to focus his attention while attempting to put aside his worry that math is too hard for him. Next, he has to intently listen to the teacher while she explains this new skill. This means ignoring the person mowing the grass outside the window as well as the child behind him who is kicking the back of the seat. He will also need to keep in mind several rules at once—you add the first two numbers in the right column, then put the first number of that total next to the first number of the left column. After that, he will need to remember his math facts to successfully complete the equation. If he completes the math problem incorrectly, he will have to refrain from yelling or throwing the paper to the floor. He will need to refocus, ignore this perceived evidence that math is too hard for him, and try again. In a span of just a few minutes, Michael has to significantly rely on self-regulatory processes to be able to engage in his academic work.

Self-regulation skills develop rapidly during early childhood, with a large burst of skill development around 30 months of age (Zelazo & Lyons, 2012). However, it is once children enter formal schooling that the engagement of these skills will significantly impact their adjustment and success. While school readiness as associated with the traditional three Rs (reading, writing, and arithmetic) is certainly important and facilitates adjustment into the school setting, without the fundamental skills of the fourth R—regulation—students will likely struggle both academically and socially. Indeed, childhood regulation is so critical that it predicts multiple outcomes well into adulthood, including those of physical health, substance dependence, socioeconomic status, and likelihood of criminal conviction at age 32 (McClelland & Cameron, 2012; Moffit, 2011, as cited in Zelazo & Lyons, 2012). Importantly, these results were true after controlling for class and IQ (Zelazo & Lyons, 2012). Other studies have confirmed that self-regulation is distinct from intelligence, indicating that high levels of motivation and self-regulation are associated with academic achievement independent of IQ (Blair, 2002). From a social perspective, better self-regulation in childhood has been associated with increased social competence, more intimate interpersonal relationships, and higher self-esteem and self-efficacy (McClelland & Cameron, 2012).

Emily is a fourth-grader who moved to her new school just one month ago. Emily and her mother relocated from a different state seeking distance from the mom's abusive ex-partner. They have no family in the area and are living in a shelter until they find more permanent housing. Emily is very quiet and afraid of loud noises, and when the teacher offers gentle feedback or correction, Emily bursts into tears. She has told the teacher that she does not have any friends and that everyone stares at her and makes fun of her. Emily's academic history is poor and she is barely able to grasp new material, even though it is already being presented at a much lower level than would be expected for a fourth-grader.

Michael, the second-grader learning math, and Emily, the fourth-grader, have very different presentations, yet their eventual academic and emotional success largely depends on their ability to self-regulate. Michael's temperament likely impacts his self-regulation, while Emily's history of trauma and current stressors impact her self-regulation. The next sections of this chapter will further define self-regulation, address the neurobiology associated with it, and describe the environmental factors influencing its development.

Self-Regulation

Regulation enables children to make plans, choose from alternatives, control impulses, inhibit thoughts, and regulate social behavior (Fjell et al., 2012). Historically, regulation has been studied as a two-sided coin, with behavior on one side and emotion on the other. The behavior side allows children to make plans, choose from alternatives, control impulses, and inhibit thoughts (Fjell et al., 2012). The emotion side allows children to regulate social behavior and modify their emotional reactions in response to a particular context or situation (Denham et al., 2003; Dennis, 2010; Röll, Koglin, & Petermann, 2012; Shaffer, Suveg,

Thomassin, & Bradbury, 2012). While cleanly separating these two sides is quite difficult, we will briefly discuss behavioral regulation and emotional regulation separately to better understand each component. Next, we will discuss the more current view of regulation as an integration of the behavioral and emotional components yielding the broader concept of self-regulation.

BEHAVIORAL REGULATION

Cognitive psychologists and neuroscientists study regulation from a cognitive/neural systems approach, and focus on the prefrontal cortex and *executive functions* as the key cognitive structures related to behavioral regulation (Diamond, 2010; Liew, 2012). The prefrontal cortex in found in the frontal lobe of the brain and is associated with core executive functions, which are a set of cognitive functions involved in the top-down control of behavior with the purpose of achieving a particular goal (Diamond, 2010). These executive functions include attentional and behavioral inhibition as well as working memory (Diamond, 2010; Liew, 2012). Remember Michael's experience with learning math? He demonstrated attentional inhibition when paying attention to the teacher only and ignoring the mowing outside the window. He also demonstrated behavioral inhibition when refraining from turning around and yelling at his peer who was kicking the back of the chair. Michael also used his working memory to hold multiple rules in mind, relate the math facts he had learned earlier to this new task, and perform mental arithmetic. Collectively, these executive functions allowed him to stay focused and learn a new task.

Executive functions develop significantly during the period between birth and age 5. Five-year-olds, for example, are able to spend a longer amount of time working on tasks than 3-year-olds, and exhibit less difficulty waiting and focusing (Kalpidou, Power, Cherry, & Gottfried, 2004). During this same period, children demonstrate increased accuracy in their working memory. This allows them to remember specific instructions that lead to better behavioral control. In class, for example, children use working memory to remember instructions not to speak while a classmate or the teacher is speaking, and therefore they are able to inhibit the impulse to shout out responses or speak out of turn (Blair

& Razza, 2007; Tominey & McClelland, 2011). These core executive functions form the foundation for the more complex executive functions that develop later in elementary school, including planning, critical thinking, creative problem solving, and insightful reasoning. For example, fifth-graders who participate in an "invention convention" are encouraged to think critically about what inventions would be helpful and how they might creatively develop their invention as well as to engage in more in-depth reasoning regarding the social and emotional impact of their invention on prospective consumers.

Developmental researchers study behavioral regulation from a temperament-based approach. Temperament is the "relatively consistent basic inherent dispositions in a person that underlie and modulate the expression of activity, reactivity, emotionality, and sociability" (Lonigan & Phillips, 2001, p. 62). Temperament-based factors include how reactive a child is to change or novelty, how intense his or her reaction may be to that change, and how physiologically aroused he or she may become. With respect to regulation, researchers focus on the temperamental traits of *negative affectivity* and *effortful control* (Bridgett, Oddi, Laake, Murdock, & Bachman, 2013; Liew, 2012; Valiente, Swanson, & Lemery-Chalfant, 2012). Negative affectivity refers to a tendency toward negative emotions and reactions (e.g., fear). Effortful control refers to the ability to voluntarily inhibit a dominant response (e.g., run and hide) in order to perform a subdominant response (e.g., walk into a new classroom; Posner & Rothbart, 2000). This control happens through attentional and inhibitory control mechanisms that are also used to regulate emotional arousal, motivation, and behavior (Liew, 2012; Valiente, Swanson, & Lemery-Chalfant, 2012; Zhou, Chen, & Main, 2012). Effortful control is shaped by heredity and environmental factors, appears early in life, and shows some continuity across the life span (Liew, 2012). Effortful control continues to develop steadily through early elementary school and is further refined as the child matures (Dennis, 2010; Liew, 2012; Valiente, Swanson, & Lemery-Chalfant, 2012). In combination, temperamental traits can impact child regulation, with low negative affectivity and high effortful control leading to better regulation, and conversely, high negative affectivity and low effortful control leading to poor regulation.

Emily, the fourth-grader who was new to her school, had been described by her mom as a reserved baby who shied away from novelty and change. This withdrawal tendency to shy away from novelty continued as she matured. After her exposure to domestic violence, Emily became further reserved and had difficulty shifting her attention from worries and fears related to the home environment. She also had difficulty activating behaviors or coping skills to help her decrease her sense of anxiety and worry. In school, Emily hesitated to participate in small-group activities and learning centers. She became very distraught when new material was presented, worrying that it would be too hard for her and that she would fail. Emily's difficulty with all these aspects of negative affectivity and effortful control significantly interfered with her self-regulation.

EMOTIONAL REGULATION

Work derived from developmental and clinical psychology highlights the role of emotional regulation on child functioning. Emotional regulation is defined as the ability to modify one's emotional reactions in response to a particular context or situation. Calkins and Hill (2007) describe this regulation as a result of "behaviors, skills, and strategies, whether conscious or unconscious, automatic, or effortful, that serve to modulate, inhibit, and enhance emotional experiences and expressions" (p. 229). When a child is successfully able to regulate her emotions, she is able to (a) understand and label the emotion she experiences (e.g., I am feeling sad because I had an argument with my best friend), (b) use a specific coping skill to manage that emotion (e.g., reach out to the friend and apologize), and (c) not allow the emotion to interfere with appropriate behavior (e.g., even though she feels sad, she is able to pay attention in class and wait until recess to apologize to her friend). If she expresses the emotion, it is proportionate to the situation (e.g., is sad but not overly tearful) and appropriate to the context (e.g., remains more quiet and reserved in the classroom), and her emotions do not change too abruptly or too slowly (e.g., remains sad until she is able to apologize to her friend and talk about what happened, then experiences more positive mood) (Herts, McLaughlin, & Hatzenbuehler, 2012; Röll et al., 2012).

Directly related to emotional regulation is the notion of how *controlled* a child is when responding to a particular emotion-laden situation. The child may respond with withdrawal (over-controlled) or impulsivity (under-controlled). If a child is too controlled, she will be more reticent to speak, will internalize emotions, will experience them intently but might not share them, and may not have the appropriate skills to shift from that intense internal experience to a more neutral one. What might this look like in a classroom? A child struggling with overcontrol may be shy and withdrawn, will be reticent to try new things and fear failure. She may interpret failure as due to her own shortcomings, and interpret others' reactions as criticisms. She may also not have the appropriate skills to manage her feelings. A simple task like being asked to deliver a note to a teacher in a different room may evoke questions for the child such as "what if I don't find the room? What if other kids are in the hallway and they look at me? What if the teacher is not there and I can't give her the note—my teacher will not like me anymore." While the child may accept the task of delivering the note, the anxiety that it produces may likely continue to interfere with her ability to focus on classroom material, even if she has successfully delivered the note.

For a child struggling with under-control, behavior will be very different. In a classroom setting, the child's behavior is likely to be much more impulsive. For example, if she finds something funny, she may not be able to inhibit the impulse to burst out laughing or to distract classmates while the teacher is talking. If feeling misunderstood, criticized, or judged, she may react aggressively, such as by pushing or yelling at a peer. Over time, such extremes of control impede appropriate regulation and may lead to anxiety or mood related disturbances. Chapters 2 and 3 of this book will discuss how these extremes of control are manifested in children struggling with anxiety and depression.

In contrast, healthy emotional regulation is related to flexibility, where the child is able to respond flexibly "to the varying demands of experience with a range of responses that are socially acceptable but also allow for spontaneity" (Eisenberg, Hofer, & Vaughan, 2007, p. 290). When children demonstrate flexibility in their emotional responses, they are able to inhibit behaviors in order to be focused and reach a goal, but can also be more spontaneous and less controlled when appropriate. Ideally, children will develop this flexible, more balanced approach that allows them to have control when the situation demands (e.g., focusing while taking a test prior to recess) but also allows them more freedom and spontaneity when such control is not required (e.g., playing and talking loudly during recess). As children mature, this flexibility further enhances emotional regulation by allowing them to choose which coping skill will be most helpful to use in a particular context or situation. For example, a fifth-grader may feel discouraged and upset after failing a test. If he demonstrates healthy regulation and flexibility, he is able to manage his initial upset, analyze the situation, and realize that there are active steps he can take to change the outcome of the next test. He can use problem-solving skills and determine a plan of action (e.g., studying with a buddy or taking practice tests) as ways to cope emotionally and remedy the situation. If the same fifth-grader is sad, angry, and frustrated after learning that his parents are divorcing, he will need to choose a different set of coping skills that will help him cope with a situation that is not within his control to change. He might decide to talk to friends, listen to music, and play basketball as ways to help him relieve the feelings related to his parents' divorce. It is this flexible shifting in coping and all the attentional control, working memory, and inhibitory control associated with it that lead to more successful emotional regulation (Dennis, 2010; Eisenberg et al., 2007).

During infancy and toddlerhood, there is a significant and dramatic increase in the development, control, and use of emotional regulation skills. Infants rely primarily on caretakers' actions (e.g., holding, rocking, gentle soothing) for emotional regulation. Toddlers are increasingly able to develop their own actions for emotional regulation, including finding a favorite stuffed animal or blanket to hold when upset, or using distraction by finding another playmate or toy. While during this period of maturity we see children acting more independently and developing their own ways to regulate, the quality and breadth of the repertoire of emotional regulation skills are heavily dependent on what children observe and integrate from relationships with others. For example, children who observe adults who use deep-breathing exercises and take a break when facing a stressful situation may also use these techniques in their own attempts to regulate their emotions. Conversely, children who witness emotional volatility, screaming, or lack of coping skills may also use these behaviors in their own attempts to self-regulate (Calkins & Hill, 2007).

SELF-REGULATION: AN INTEGRATION OF COGNITION AND EMOTION

As we can see, there is significant overlap between the factors associated with behavioral and emotional frameworks of self-regulation. Therefore, it is more useful to adopt an integrated approach that examines "multiple levels of analysis of self-regulation rather than isolating emotion regulation from related" behavioral regulation (Calkins & Hill, 2007, p. 231). Self-regulatory processes can thus be conceptualized as an interconnected system that may be observed at the physiological, attentional, behavioral, emotional, cognitive, interpersonal, and social levels (Calkins & Hill, 2007). Within the rest of the book, when self-regulation is discussed, it refers to this broader conceptualization.

Exciting new developments in neuropsychology offer an explanation of how these interconnected systems are physically manifested (Dennis, 2010). The anterior cingulate cortex (ACC) is a brain structure located in the medial frontal cortex. It serves as an intermediary between the ventral and dorsal systems, and appears to be the structure that bridges

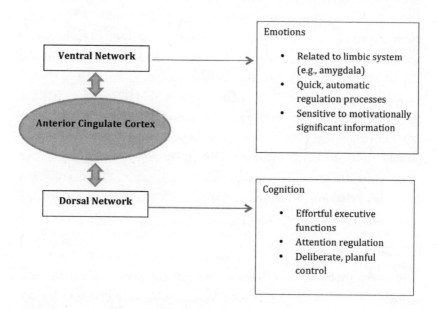

FIGURE 1.1. The function of the anterior cingulate cortex.

emotion and cognition, respectively, in regulation (Calkins & Hill, 2007; Dennis, 2010; see Figure 1.1). The ACC supports the structures that identify and regulate emotional reactions as well as structures that focus on controlling attention, decision making, and other cognitive processes (Dennis, 2010).

The integrated view of self-regulation supports the understanding that emotion and cognition cannot be fully understood in isolation, as one clearly impacts the other. As Diamond (2010) indicates, "our thinking and our brains suffer if we are lonely or feeling socially isolated, and that is particularly true of executive functions and the prefrontal cortex on which they rely" (p. 2). If a child feels rejected by his peers, that emotional experience will impact his cognitive experience. He will likely demonstrate difficulties in problem solving (e.g., he will not know how to best ask the teacher for help), decreased persistence on difficult problems (e.g., he will give up when trying to learn new spelling words), and impaired selective attention (e.g., he may become easily distracted by sounds and activities in the classroom).

In contrast, when a child feels a strong sense of safety and comfort in the classroom, this positively impacts his executive functions and cognitive experience. He will demonstrate more focused attention to the teacher's instructions, he will use working memory and problem solving to approach new tasks (e.g., he will remember that when he raised his hand quietly and waited for the teacher to acknowledge him, he was able to ask for help), and he will be able to ignore distracting stimuli in the classroom (e.g., even though two peers are talking to each other, he will remain focused and on task). Therefore, when the emotional experience can assist and support the "processes of attention, memory, inhibitory control, and problem-solving, it promotes self-regulation and optimal functioning" (Blair, 2002, p. 118). Simply stated, children's emotions, behaviors, learning, and regulation are inextricably tied and cannot be considered separately.

It Takes a Village

Teachers are familiar with the whole-child approach, where the educational focus is on multiple facets of the child, including social, emotional, and physical domains. However, even that more expansive view is too narrow in scope when examining the factors that influence a child's self-regulation and readiness for school. Self-regulation skills are developed in the context of neurobiology, developmental maturation, individual child factors, relationships, training, and specific environments (e.g., school). Researchers focusing on school readiness recognize that an exclusive look at cognitive skills in the assessment of readiness is only of limited value. Understanding readiness as a "socially constructed phenomenon" has led researchers to focus on teachers, schools, and educational policies as key determinants of children's school readiness. This conceptualization includes the impact of self-regulation on readiness as mediated by social relationships (Blair, 2002, p. 122). As Blair (2002) indicates,

> the emotionally reactive and poorly regulated but otherwise typically developing child in an environment that cannot optimize and support the child's regulatory capability is likely at risk for an atypical trajectory toward the development of executive function skills and school readiness. However, the same child in a supportive environment will be less likely to develop reactive forms of regulation and will exhibit greater propensity toward effortful regulatory skills (p. 119)

The R That Ties It All Together: Relationships

Humans are social beings. There is very little, if any, development and learning that occurs in isolation, and therefore, the quality of relationships has an incredible impact on long-term outcomes. This is especially true in relation to children's self-regulation. One of the most impactful relationships is that of parent or caretaker and child. The research literature defines this early relationship as attachment. Attachment describes the "interactions between children and their caregivers that have a longstanding impact on the development of identity and personal agency, early working models of self and other, and the capacity to regulate emotions" (Kinniburgh, Blaustein, & Spinazzola, 2005, p. 426). John Bolwby's seminal work on attachment argued that by the end of the first year of life, the interactions between child and caregiver produce an attachment relationship that provides a sense of security for the child and significantly influences the child's subsequent adaptation to other relationships and developmental challenges (Calkins & Hill, 2007). Mary Ainsworth created the famous "strange situation" experiment to test Bowlby's theory and identified two primary attachment categorizations: *secure and insecure.* Secure attachment, characterized by nurturing and consistent caregiving, promotes a safety net for the child to cope with difficult situations (Calkins & Hill, 2007; Kinniburgh et al., 2005; O'Connor & McCartney, 2007). Secure attachment is associated with a number of positive outcomes, including higher academic achievement, and is a predictor of child resilience (Calkins & Hill, 2007; O'Connor & McCartney, 2007). Insecure attachment is characterized by low levels of parental or caregiver sensitivity due to caregiver impairment, unpredictability, inconsistency, and possibly neglect and rejection. Children experiencing such negative patterns of care rely on more primitive and negative coping skills such as aggression, avoidance, and sometimes dissociation for self-regulation. Many negative outcomes, including psychopathology and poor academic performance, have been associated with early impaired attachment (Calkins & Hill, 2007; Kinniburgh et al., 2005).

Another very significant attachment relationship occurs in the school setting. Teacher–student relationships play a critical role in children's school achievement. Research indicates that children with higher-quality teacher–student relationships demonstrate higher levels of achievement and cognitive skills in elementary school than children with lower-quality teacher–student relationships (Immordino-Yang & Damasio, 2007; O'Connor & McCartney, 2007). For example, a study by Graziano, Reavis, Keane, and Calkins (2007) found that kindergarten students whose teachers were supportive performed significantly better on math and reading skills tests than children whose teachers were less supportive (as cited in Liew, 2012). Children who have strong relationships with teachers may be better able to concentrate, communicate with teachers when they have questions, respond to challenging situations, and use teachers "as secure bases from which to explore their surroundings" (O'Connor & McCartney, p. 345). Overall, children who report strong relationships with their teachers are more engaged in school and participate more in the classroom and school community.

In addition to the impact on academic achievement, the teacher–student relationship also has a significant impact on children's emotional development and self-regulation. As Diamond (2010) indicates, "teachers' expectations are part of the students' social world and have powerful effects and shape students' expectations for themselves" (p. 6). As students internalize these expectations, their emotional development is shaped by relationships built within the classroom. Therefore, teacher–student relationships may serve as the scaffolds on which a child can develop, practice, and internalize self-regulation skills (O'Connor & McCartney, 2007). This impact on emotional and regulatory development is so important that preliminary research indicates that positive teacher–student relationships may protect children even from negative family experiences (Liew, 2012; O'Connor & McCartney, 2007).

Teachers that are well attuned to children's emotional experience understand that the development of healthy self-regulation should follow an interactive process in the context of a safe relationship. The interactive process involves teaching and guiding the child, allowing her to try new skills, using mistakes as opportunities for growth, and giving frequent feedback and support. Development of self-regulation cannot occur in the context of a battle of wills or control, or in the context of simply telling the child what to do without an explanation as to why a proposed action is helpful. As a child matures, if her regulation relies solely on adult input, then she will learn regulation with anxiety. That is, if a child's ability to regulate is contingent on someone else, she may feel out of control or helpless when independently facing a novel or challenging situation. However, if in the context of a safe relationship, a child learns to understand her individual role in self-regulation, acquires new ways of managing her emotions, and has an opportunity to practice this regulation, then she will learn how to utilize internal tools to regulate her emotions and behavior. The next section highlights ways to promote self-regulation in students to maximize their emotional engagement and promote academic achievement.

Notice, Give, and Nurture

Because much of children's self-regulation involves processes at the biological and neurological levels, some may worry that this implies that self-regulation ability is somewhat fixed or predetermined. In actuality, there is an incredible amount of malleability associated with these processes. For example, those structures associated with higher-order cognitive functioning (e.g., prefrontal cortex) maintain plasticity in response to experience well into maturity (Zelazo & Carlson, 2012). For teachers, this poses an extraordinary opportunity for positive intervention through relationships and teaching. Addressing students' heart, mind, and spirit will positively impact their neural networks, attention, motivation, achievement, and overall resilience.

Do you recall the anterior cingulate cortex, or the ACC? The ACC supports the structures that identify and regulate emotional reactions, as well as structures that focus on controlling attention, decision making, and other cognitive processes (Dennis, 2010). Through the *notice*, *give*, and *nurture* approach, teachers can in some ways act as an external ACC and help students integrate both emotion and cognition into self-regulation, which in turns improves academic achievement.

Each chapter in this book will have a specific focus for the notice, give, and nurture approach, offering tools for teachers to promote student regulation. In this chapter, we will focus on how teachers can educate their students about the importance of emotions. The key message is: Emotions matter in everything you do, so becoming aware of how different emotions feel, what they mean, and how they impact yourself and others is essential for health, well-being, and success in school and life. When children are truly able to internalize this message, they become more resilient.

WHAT CAN I NOTICE?

Teachers are keen observers of their students—they can very quickly assess which students are struggling and need academic support. As discussed in this chapter, children's learning, emotions, and regulation are inextricably tied and cannot be considered separately. Therefore, when teachers are able to also notice what may be leading a child to struggle at the emotional level, they can construct meaningful interventions that will help children emotionally and academically.

So how can teachers better understand their students' emotional needs? This section offers six areas that teachers can specifically notice to assess how their students are functioning emotionally. When first meeting students, teachers may wish to conduct a baseline assessment that examines the areas below. An initial assessment can facilitate the creation of interventions that are individually tailored to students as well as serve as a means of tracking student progress.

1. Is the child demonstrating *age-appropriate emotional regulation skills*? In general, a child's ability to use emotional regulation skills develops with age, such that kindergarten students will need more assistance. By fifth grade, it is expected that students will be able to demonstrate some of these skills with more consistency and with less prompting. For example, 5- and 6-year-old children indicate that when you think of something pleasant, it makes you feel positive, while thinking of something unpleasant causes negative feelings (Stegge & Meerum Terwogt, 2007). This means that a primary way of coping for younger students is to avoid negative things or situations. However, 10-year-olds understand that one can take a different perspective on the same situation or event. This ability expands their coping repertoire significantly, and rather than relying on changing the actual conditions, the child tries to find the coping strategy that best fits the situation (Stegge & Terwogt, 2007). For example, a child may understand that if he has an argument with his best friend, it produces negative feelings initially, but staying in the same room with his friend and having a conversation to resolve the problem will bring about positive results.

2. Does the student demonstrate *self-awareness*? The Collaborative for Academic, Social, and Emotional Learning (CASEL) defines self-awareness as "the ability to accurately recognize one's emotions and thoughts and their influence on behavior" (Casel, n.d.). This ability increases over time. Students who have a higher level of self-awareness are better able to regulate their emotions. Components of self-awareness include:

   o *Noticing cues that the body is giving about the individual's current feeling state.* For example, if a child is nervous, body cues might include rapid heartbeat, sweating, restlessness, "butter-flies" in the stomach, aches and pains (in elementary school children, stomachaches and headaches are most commonly seen), tension, and perhaps fatigue. The child understands that the body is giving signals related to an emotion and does not immediately conclude that there is a physical ailment. As children's self-awareness increases, they come to understand that body cues may be signals for a particular emotion in a particular context. For example, a child may understand that his tummy starts hurting as he becomes nervous in anticipation of going to a new place with which he is not at all familiar.

o *Understanding how emotions influence thoughts.* As children develop self-awareness, they begin to recognize how their feelings impact their thoughts. For example, a child may learn that if she feels anxious when giving presentations, she may have thoughts like, "What if I forget the material? What if I do something embarrassing and everyone laughs? What if I stutter through the presentation?" With increased self-awareness, though she may still encounter these thoughts, she realizes that they are not based on actual past experiences, but rather on fear due to her anxiety about presenting before her class.

o *Understanding how emotions influence behavior.* Students will self-awareness will understand that how they feel may lead them to act in certain ways. The child in the example above, who is anxious when giving presentations, knows that because she feels anxious she is more likely to avoid eye contact with the teacher for fear of being called on first. She is also more likely to ask to go to the bathroom multiple times, or to fidget or shake her leg while sitting. Having this understanding is important, as it leads children to learn which behaviors to modify and how to choose appropriate coping skills for emotion management.

o *Understanding how one's words and emotions impact others.* Children with self-awareness are able to understand how their emotions impact not only themselves but others as well. They are able to modify their behaviors to positively influence how others feel. For example, Colin, a third-grader, is playing baseball outside with his friends during recess. Another classmate, Peter, asks if he can join the boys in their play. Colin tells Peter he cannot join in play because he can't catch a ball, and he'll make them lose if he joins their team. Later that day, Colin apologizes to Peter. Colin says that he realizes he was hurtful in what he said to Peter and that he feels bad about having embarrassed him like that in front of others. In so doing, Colin is demonstrating self-awareness by revealing his understanding of how his words, emotions, and behavior impacted Peter.

3. What is the child's functioning with respect to each component of self-regulation?

   o *Attention.* From an academic perspective, is the child able to maintain focused attention during a lesson? There are many distractions in a child's environment, including noises, others' conversations, and even minor interruptions like dropping a pencil. If the child is able to maintain attention, he may momentarily orient himself toward the noise, but he will very quickly return his attention to the teacher. From a social perspective, is the child able to focus on conversations with others? Is he able to direct his attention to the needs of peers? For example, while the student is speaking to his friend, is he able to wait until his friend has finished speaking before responding (i.e., good attention), or does he abruptly interrupt to talk about himself instead (i.e., poor attention)?

   o *Inhibition.* From an academic perspective, is the child able to refrain from engaging in another behavior when she is expected to focus on a specific task? For example, when working on an art project, is the child able to continue to work on the project without getting up and walking around the room instead? From a social perspective, is the child able to inhibit behaviors such as shouting at the teacher or at a peer when frustrated?

For attention and inhibition, there is a developmental progression that occurs, with kindergarten students needing additional cues and reminders to focus their attention and inhibit inappropriate behaviors. These skills increase progressively through the first and second grades, and by third grade students are able to focus their attention and inhibit inappropriate behaviors more consistently. By the fourth and fifth grades, these skills become a more consistent and automatic part of students' internalized repertoire.

- *Approach versus avoidance.* Does the child demonstrate a tendency to actively approach new things, people, or situations, or does the child avoid novelty and risk? A child with an active approach will likely enjoy taking on a challenging new project or trying a new task, even if it is unfamiliar or the outcome is uncertain. A child with an avoidant style will likely avoid novelty and be especially fearful if the outcome is not certain (Valiente, Swanson, & Eisenberg, 2012). For example, Jimmy worked with Mrs. Rogers for reading instruction. When Mrs. Rogers left on maternity leave, Jimmy had to work with Ms. Netti, the new reading teacher. Although he did not know her, Jimmy approached Ms. Netti easily and happily, quickly asking her many questions in order to get to know her. Sandy had also worked with Mrs. Rogers for reading instruction. The first day of Mrs. Rogers's leave, Sandy cried and refused to go to the reading room. Although she did not know Ms. Netti, Sandy told her teacher that Ms. Netti would be mean and that the work would be too hard, so she did not want to go to reading instruction. Jimmy's active approach facilitated a transition, whereas Sandy's avoidant style led to regulatory difficulties.
- *Negative versus positive emotionality.* The typical affect that a child demonstrates has a significant impact on both academic and social outcomes. Positive affect (e.g., joy, happiness, pride) is likely to enhance academic success through greater motivation, greater school engagement, and more active participation in learning (Valiente, Swanson, & Eisenberg, 2012). Positive affect also facilitates prosocial interactions and relationships with both peers and adults. Conversely, students with more

negative affect (e.g., anger, sadness, anxiety, withdrawal) may experience poor academic success due to their difficulties in participating in group assignments, fear of attempting new tasks, and inability to maintain attention and focus due to overwhelming emotions and reactions. From a social perspective, negative emotionality predicts low levels of social competence and more conflictual relationships with both teachers and peers (Valiente, Swanson, & Eisenberg, 2012).

It is important to note that students are not expected to show all positive or all negative emotions to the exclusion of other emotions. In fact, it is healthy and appropriate for students to demonstrate a range of emotions that are consistent with the particular situation and context. For example, Jill is a cheerful, outgoing girl. She has an infectious laugh and likes to hum while she draws. When her dog died, Jill was tearful and quieter than usual for a few days. Jill demonstrated an appropriate range of emotions that was consistent with a particular situation. It is when children's affect is more constricted in a negative way, absent from situations that would warrant such affect, that this becomes concerning. For example, Kyle is a bright student, yet he struggles to fit into the classroom. He becomes easily frustrated, consistently tries to get his peers' attention through behaviors such as singing loudly or throwing erasers at them, and yells out answers without waiting for the teacher to call on him. When redirected, he becomes angry and sometimes breaks his pencils or tears his papers in response.

4. Does the student demonstrate *resilience*? Resilience refers to the ability to bounce back from adversity. Resilience does not mean that a child will never experience a negative emotion or difficulty. Instead, it means that when a child experiences a negative emotion or difficulty, she is able to use coping skills to help her manage her feelings, learn from the situation, and resume functioning. Lilly, a first-grader with asthma, offers an example of a student with resilience. Lilly is frequently absent from school due to her illness, and it has been difficult for her to catch up with all her work. Her ability to engage in

physical activity is also limited, and therefore she has not had many opportunities to play outside with her friends during recess. Despite these difficulties, however, Lilly is generally in good spirits. She is able to tell the teacher when she needs to use her inhaler, she is able to talk to her friends about her asthma, and she has invited friends to stay inside to work on special projects when she is not able to go outside for recess. Lilly has days when she is frustrated by her illness, but in general, she bounces back from tough days and has found ways to stay integrated into her classroom as much as possible. She is excellent at asking for help from adults when she needs it, though she likes to "try it on my own," as she says, first.

5. Does the student demonstrate *flexibility*? I refer to flexibility as the ability to find alternative ways to examine a situation and/or develop different possible solutions. If Plan A does not work, does the student have a Plan B, or even a Plan C, or will he get stuck and fall apart if Plan A does not happen exactly as expected? Students who demonstrate greater flexibility are able to better regulate their emotions and to find appropriate coping skills for different situations. Jonathan, a fourth-grade student, offers an example of a student with limited flexibility. Jonathan was walking in line when a peer accidentally bumped into him. Jonathan was convinced that the peer had done it on purpose. Despite reassurance from the teacher and other peers who noticed what happened, Jonathan would not see the situation in a different light. Furthermore, he decided that the only way to resolve the situation was to wait for an opportunity to push the peer back. Jonathan demonstrates very little flexibility in analyzing a situation, considering possible explanations for it, and developing problem-solving strategies for managing what happened.

In contrast, Katie, a second-grade student, demonstrates significant flexibility. Katie loves manatees—they are her favorite animals and she has read many books containing manatee facts. She was waiting excitedly for the marine animal lesson in science class, keeping her fingers crossed that she could do her project on her favorite animal. The big day finally arrived, and during science class, the teacher gave out the assignments for the animal projects. Katie was assigned sea anemones. Though disappointed at first, Katie said, "That's OK; I know a lot about manatees, but I don't know too much about sea anemones, so I'll work on this and try to find out more about them." Plan A did not work out, but Katie was able to shift focus and develop a new strategy and positive outlook about Plan B.

6. Does the student demonstrate a *growth mindset* or a *fixed mindset*? Carol Dweck (2006) defines mindset as "the view that you adopt for yourself" (p. 6). She identifies two types of mindset: The *growth mindset* is the belief that your basic qualities can be cultivated through your efforts, while the *fixed mindset* is the belief that your qualities are carved in stone (p. 6). When a student approaches learning from a fixed mindset, she focuses on proving her intelligence or skills, is afraid of seeming incompetent, and does not take risks for fear of failing. In contrast, when a student approaches learning from a growth mindset, she is fueled by the challenge of something difficult and views it as an opportunity to achieve a goal. She is not afraid of mistakes, and sees how external circumstances may play a role in unexpected outcomes. A fixed mindset may lead a student to be more vulnerable to anxiety and helplessness, whereas a growth mindset may lead a student to be more flexible and hopeful.

Becky is a fifth-grade student. She worked very hard on her invention convention project and display board. She is generally viewed as a bright, capable student, and she wanted to prove that she had one of the best projects in her class. On the day of the convention, all students displayed their inventions and their boards, and students from kindergarten through fourth grade, as well as parents, were invited to see the projects. Becky became increasingly agitated as she saw that people were noticing the display boards next to hers more than they were noticing hers. She immediately started having thoughts like, "They like the other projects better than mine. I should have done the other project I was thinking about. I knew this one was dumb." When she received the final grading sheet for the project, Becky received a B+, as she had forgotten to include how much her invention would cost if someone wished to purchase it. Becky thought, "This is so unfair; the teacher doesn't like me."

The whole weekend after the invention convention, Becky was distressed, disappointed, and upset.

While this reaction is not too uncommon among students, why is it important not to dismiss it as simply "kids being kids"? If a student remains in a fixed mindset, she will interpret failures as personal faults, will tend to blame others for the outcome, will focus on the negative aspects of the situation rather than its learning potential, and will employ less effective and more passive ways of coping (e.g., staying in her room all day). In Chapters 2 and 3, we will discuss at more length how this mindset is associated with anxiety and depression in children.

Once you have assessed these six areas of your students' emotional functioning, what can you do? The next section offers suggestions for what you can give your students to foster the development of their regulatory and coping skills.

WHAT CAN I GIVE?

More learning occurs in a joyous, safe classroom where children feel accepted, secure, and cared for (Diamond, 2010). Teachers can contribute to this feeling of joy and safety in learning by giving their students the following things:

1. *A classroom that is visually inviting, bright, and cheerful.* As indicated earlier, especially for younger children, there will be a powerful association between pleasant things and a pleasant mood. When children are in a pleasant mood, they are more open to learning and retaining new information. This association carries strongly over time, and even students who are in high school report the powerful impact that an inviting, cheerful, and fun classroom has on their school engagement and learning.

2. *Direct and indirect messages that emotions matter and that emotional well-being is as important as academic success.* For example, are there posters that talk about how to be a good friend, or about taking care of your heart and mind? Do some of the classroom val-

ues and expectations include taking time to help yourself when you are distressed or help others who are distressed? Are direct connections made between how one feels and how one is able to problem-solve, remember things, or learn new information?

3. *Daily opportunities to develop an emotional vocabulary.* Sometimes students struggle to find the words to express how they are feeling, yet developing that emotional vocabulary is a critical skill. Therefore, teachers can give students the opportunity to use other means of describing their feelings—perhaps through colors or shapes. "I feel circle today" can be a child's way of expressing worry, or "I feel pink today" might be a way of expressing a state of calm and peacefulness. *How Do You Doodle? Drawing My Feelings and Emotions* by Elise Gravel (2013) is a book that can help children ages 6 through 10 express their feelings in different ways.

Emotional vocabulary can also be developed through stories. Circle time offers a natural opportunity to use books to encourage children to develop their emotion vocabulary as well as practice perspective taking, self-awareness, and flexibility. *Have You Filled a Bucket Today? A Guide to Daily Happiness for Kids* by Carol McCloud (2006) is a wonderful book that talks about how one's actions and words can impact others.

Another opportunity to develop an emotional vocabulary occurs when teachers try to learn more about what is causing students difficulty with a particular assignment or topic. For example, Frankie, a second-grade student, is struggling with math. When talking to Frankie, her teacher may ask what about the lesson is difficult, but she can also ask, "How are you feeling when doing your math problems?" This encourages Frankie to use emotion words and also helps her to make a connection between her emotions, thoughts, and behaviors.

Finally, specific activities can be focused on further developing students' understanding of emotion and related concepts, such as resilience. "Flight of the Bumblebee" is an example of an exercise that promotes critical thinking and problem solving, while making links to resilience and perseverance. Mary Kay Ash stated, "Aerodynamically the bumblebee shouldn't be able to fly, but the bumblebee doesn't know that so it goes on flying anyway." Teachers can engage in meaningful conversations with their students around this topic with questions such as, "Why does the bumblebee keep flying? How do you think it feels when it flies? What are some things you thought you couldn't do but you kept trying at and are now able to do? What worked best? What didn't go so well? What did you do then? Why did you keep trying?" By changing the words in the quote to make them more developmentally appropriate, this exercise can be used with students as young as 5 or 6 years old.

4. *Offer scaffolds to support students.* Even preschool children, with adequate scaffolds, are able to demonstrate good self-regulation. Visual cues, such as a picture of a "listening ear" that is held up when someone is speaking, can be very helpful to young students. For older students, prompts can be very helpful. For example, when talking to a fourth-grade girl about a misunderstanding she had with a friend, the teacher can offer prompts such as, "When you look back at the situation, does it seem different, or the same, as when you had the argument? How do you think your friend felt? Why? In what other ways might you think about what happened? What choices do you have, and which do you think would be best for you?" Offering open-ended questions rather than yes/no questions, as well as allowing spaces for silence in the conversation, can help students take more time to become more aware of their emotions, thoughts, and behaviors.

5. *Offer exercises that boost positive mood.* Much of children's learning develops through play. Give children opportunities to be playful in their learning. Role plays and skits can be fun to put together, but they can also provide a meaningful platform for students to observe, analyze, and respond to emotional situations in a safe manner. Give children the opportunity to perform acts of kindness—doing something nice for others boosts positive mood. A great exercise is to create "compliment cards." Each child has a blank card with his or her name written on it. All students are asked to write at least one thing they admire, like, or value about each person on his or her card. Such

mood-boosting activities have the very positive secondary effect of enhancing memory in class and overall connectedness to school.

6. *Educate students about what factors impact their mood.* You can help students develop self-awareness by giving them information about what factors impact their mood. For example, sleep is strongly associated with mood. With either too much or not enough sleep, students can experience disturbances in their mood. When students understand this connection, they feel empowered by having a concrete way to manage their mood. Exercise is another factor that positively impacts mood. This psychoeducation may be incorporated into class projects. For example, fifth-graders may be encouraged to prepare a "wellness fair" for their school, where they create materials that educate other students about the impact of sleep, exercise, and nutrition on emotions. Such an exercise presents an opportunity for students to learn about the mind–body connection, further develop self-regulation skills, and promote self-awareness.

7. *Set the stage for mindfulness.* Kabat-Zinn (1994) defines mindfulness as "paying attention in a particular way: on purpose, in the present moment, and nonjudgmentally" (p. 4). Mindfulness involves intentionally focusing attention on present-moment bodily sensations, feelings, thoughts, and images. This intentional focus engages important regulatory processes associated with executive functions and executive control. The nonjudgmental aspect helps to promote lower negative emotionality and increased emotional regulation. Researchers studying the benefits of teaching children mindfulness have found very promising results demonstrating positive effects on regulation (Roeser, Skinner, Beers, & Jennings, 2012). Teachers can give students the opportunity to practice mindfulness techniques by doing things such as:

   o *Teaching students deep-breathing exercises and encouraging students to scan their bodies.* What do they feel before the deep breathing? What about during and after? Where do they feel tension before the deep breathing? How did that change after the breathing exercise?

○ *Teaching students to visualize their thoughts as though they were watching a movie.* Encourage students to add images to thoughts and then watch those pictures go by as though they were on a movie screen.

In Chapters 4 and 5 of this book, specific activities that target all the components mentioned above are presented in detail.

WHAT CAN I NURTURE?

When one nurtures, one fosters, develops, and cultivates something. Through their roles, teachers nurture their students by fostering a love of learning, by cultivating their knowledge, and by developing their skills. However, to nurture also implies a relational aspect beyond the fostering of discreet skills. It involves using the power of the relationship to cultivate emotional wellness in a child to promote his or her general well-being. As will be discussed throughout the book, how children feel significantly impacts their sense of self, their engagement with school, and their overall emotional functioning. Teachers can use the power of their relationships with students to help create an environment that promotes emotional wellness. How can such emotional wellness be nurtured?

• *By establishing emotional safety.* Teachers can create a sense of safety in the classroom by sharing both direct and indirect messages that clearly state, "It is OK to talk about emotions, and I will listen and care." As Maya Angelou said, "I've learned that people will forget what you said, people will forget what you did, but people will never forget how you made them feel." When children feel safe to be themselves by freely expressing their thoughts and feelings, they are more receptive to learning. Even young children can feel the stigma related to a mental illness. They may worry about being teased, judged, or misunderstood. When teachers respond to students' emotional concerns in an empathic and nonjudgmental way, they foster a sense of emotional safety.

• *By broadening the concept of success.* When teachers give their students occasions to take risks and celebrate their failures as opportunities to learn, this promotes greater self-confidence and motivation. This broader conceptualization of success, that which includes making mistakes, allows for more independence, self-efficacy, and internal motivation—all factors directly related to resilience. Success should also be defined from a cooperative perspective. From a young age, students begin to feel the pressure of demonstrating individual success. When offered opportunities for cooperative learning activities that focus on teamwork and relationships rather than on competition, students benefit twofold: (a) they all learn more about other students and come to appreciate each person's unique talents and contributions, and (b) students who may be struggling with burgeoning mental illness are more cohesively integrated into the classroom and are able to focus on their skills and talent instead of on their symptoms.

• *By making a commitment to emotional health.* One of the most important aspects of nurturing derives from a commitment to spend time on addressing emotional needs. Unlike lessons that have designated time limits, fostering emotional development requires time, consistency, and attention. Teachers can nurture their students' emotional well-being by integrating emotional skills with academic skills. This is not to say that teaching emotional skills should interfere with or replace teaching academic skills. Instead, they can be combined so that one supports the other. For example, some children may be nervous prior to beginning a test. Others may need additional support during transitions. By incorporating simple emotional regulation skills such as deep breathing prior to a test or a transition, children can have an opportunity to regroup and self-regulate and feel empowered to begin the test or the new activity with more confidence. Nurturing comes from promoting these skills every day, thus helping children integrate the skills neurologically, emotionally, socially, and behaviorally.

The next four chapters of this book offer further suggestions and activities that may be incorporated into the classroom to continue to nurture emotional health in students.

CHAPTER TWO

Anxiety Disorders

Anxiety is when you think about bad stuff.
—Jonathan, third-grader

MENTAL HEALTH DISORDERS IN children are broadly classified as either externalizing or internalizing. *Externalizing disorders* are characterized by symptomatology that is more immediately notable and is behaviorally disruptive, such as impulsivity, hyperactivity, acting out, and lying. Anxiety and mood disorders are classified as *internalizing disorders*. Internalizing disorders involve symptoms that are directed inward and are less obvious in terms of immediately observable behaviors. These internal symptoms are intricately tied to difficulties in the understanding, processing, and regulating of emotions. Children who struggle with internalizing disorders experience symptoms across a variety of domains, including bodily sensations (e.g., increased heart rate and stomachaches), cognitive processes (e.g., difficulties with memory and attention), and behaviors (e.g., social withdrawal and isolation). Symptoms also significantly interfere with learning and social processes. Once established, internalizing symptoms tend to be stable over time, placing children at risk for various forms of adversity, including additional mental health disorders (Madigan, Atkinson, Laurin, & Benoit, 2013; Suárez, Bennett, Goldstein, & Barlow, 2008). Early identification of internalizing disorders is critical, as there is evidence that early intervention and the buffering effect of positive relationships can have a positive impact on outcomes for children with early symptoms (National Scientific Council on the Developing Child, 2012).

The next two chapters will review the development of childhood anxiety and depression, respectively, as well as information regarding symptoms, assessment, and treatment. Chapter 4 will focus on specific strategies teachers can use in the classroom to support the emotional and academic functioning of students struggling with these disorders.

Anxiety

Mrs. Garcia is very concerned about her fifth-grade student, Kelly. Kelly is an 11-year-old-girl with fears and worries that are increasingly interfering with her social development. Mrs. Garcia has known Kelly's family for some time, as she also taught Ava, Kelly's older sister. When Mrs. Garcia first met Kelly, she presented as a quiet and shy little girl who hid behind her older sister. Mrs. Garcia recalls seeing Ava prompting and reassuring Kelly once they arrived at school, walking Kelly to her class, and helping her during lunchtime and recess. When Kelly began the fifth grade, her mother spoke with Mrs. Garcia to share her concerns about her daughter's increasing anxiety. Kelly lives with a persistent worry that something will go wrong and that she will be unable to stop it from happening. Despite constant reassurance, Kelly seems unable to evade this sense of dread. Kelly also has specific fears, including that someone will break into her home, that her mom will develop a serious illness and die, and that a tornado may destroy their home. While she is not actively rejected by her peers, Kelly's shyness and consuming worries keep her from initiating friendships or engaging in school activities. Peers have simply learned to leave her alone, and she is often left with the desire, but no ability, to change this social situation.

In humans, fear and anxiety are present from infancy and serve a protective function related to avoiding danger (Beesdo-Baum & Knappe, 2012). Fear is an emotional response to a real or perceived threat, whereas anxiety relates to anticipation of future threat (American Psychiatric Association [APA], 2013). Infants begin to experience feelings of fear and are able to distinguish that fear as different from other emotions between 6 and 12 months of age (National Scientific Council on the Developing Child, 2010). As toddlers, children may be fearful of new situations and people. As children become more familiar with new settings and people during their transition into school, fears and worries may relate to real or imagined circumstances. These are common, and developmentally appropriate. For example, kindergarten students may be afraid of the dark, monsters, or some other imaginary creatures. Also at this age, some children may cry or become quite nervous during a thunderstorm, with its loud thunder and cracking lightning. Starting in first grade and continuing through fifth grade, children may develop specific fears (e.g., spiders, injections), may worry about natural disasters (e.g., earthquakes, hurricanes) or traumatic events (e.g., car accident, sudden loss or separation), or may begin to fear negative evaluation from others (Beesdo-Baum & Knappe, 2012; Davies, 2011). These fears are typically transient. As children develop a growing sense of predictability and control over their environment as well as develop more sophisticated ways to manage their emotions, the worries usually disappear, allowing successful adjustment to school and social routines (National Scientific Council on the Developing Child, 2010).

Some children, however, continue to experience an intense, persistent sense of anxiety. Their fears and worries are often diffuse, are not specific to a particular object or situation, and involve a general sense of threat (Beesdo-Baum & Knappe, 2012). If the fears are specific, attempts to avoid the feared stimulus are excessive and get in the way of normal functioning. Anxiety thus becomes maladaptive when it is persistent, involves extensive avoidance, causes distress and impairment, and impacts a child's emotional, social, and academic progress.

Anxiety disorders are among the most common forms of psychopathology in children and adolescents (A. A. Hughes, Lourea-Waddell, & Kendall, 2008; Silverman, Pina, & Viswesvaran, 2008). The following statistics highlight key information about the prevalence and onset of childhood anxiety.

- Estimates of prevalence rates for children ages 6 to 12 range from 7.1% to 28.2% (Merikangas et al., 2010).
- Average age of onset is 11, although anxiety may begin as young as preschool age; if untreated, levels of anxiety worsen over time (APA, 2013). Among adolescents diagnosed with anxiety disorders, approximately 50% report first onset at age 6 (Merikangas et al., 2010)
- Gender differences are small in early childhood but increase with age, becoming more frequent in girls than boys at a ratio of approxi-

mately 2:1 to 3:1. Age differences begin to appear around age 9, then more consistently around 13 to 15 years (APA, 2013; Beesdo-Baum & Knappe, 2012).

- About 50% of children with a primary anxiety disorder also have a second anxiety disorder or other behavioral disorder (Beesdo-Baum & Knappe, 2012).

WHAT CONTRIBUTES TO THE DEVELOPMENT OF ANXIETY DISORDERS?

When children struggle with anxiety disorders, it is often challenging to identify a primary reason leading to the diagnosis. Anxiety disorders, like other psychiatric disorders, likely have their origins in the interaction between biology and early life experiences (March, 2011). There are a number of factors that contribute to a child's presentation of anxiety, including those from the biological, neurological, psychological, and social realms (see Figure 2.1). This broader exploration allows not only for a deeper understanding of the child's presentation, but also

Factors Influencing the Development of Anxiety Disorders in Children	
Biology	• Genetic heritability of approximately 30%–45% • Creates vulnerability
Neurobiology	• Amygdala and hippocampus response • Stress response system • Increased levels of cortisol • Negative impact on prefrontal cortex
Temperament	• Behaviorally inhibited • Negative attention and memory bias
Psychological Factors	• Low self-esteem • Low sense of control • Use of avoidance and suppression
Social Factors	• Attachment • Parental psychopathology • Early learning experiences • Exposure to trauma

FIGURE 2.1. Factors influencing the development of anxiety disorders in children.

for more careful treatment planning that targets multiple areas contributing to symptomatology.

Biology

From a genetic perspective, anxiety runs in families. That is, children of parents with an anxiety disorder have an increased risk of also developing an anxiety disorder, with genetic heritability of approximately 30% to 45% (Beesdo-Baum & Knappe, 2012; Dozois, Seeds, & Collins, 2009). Some heritability estimates are higher, with a reported 73% found in children with separation anxiety disorder (APA, 2013). Other parental psychopathology, including depression, may also contribute to children's development of anxiety disorders (Beesdo-Baum & Knappe, 2012). It is important to note, however, that genetic vulnerability does not singly and absolutely determine whether a child will develop an anxiety disorder. The interaction between biology and environmental factors better explains the onset of any childhood disorder.

Neurobiology

Two brain structures are notably involved in the conditioning of fear in animals and humans: the amygdala and the hippocampus (Garber & Weersing, 2010; National Scientific Council on the Developing Child, 2010). The amygdala identifies whether an object, situation, or person is threatening. The hippocampus then links the fear response to the context in which the threatening object, situation, or person was found. Once the threat is perceived, the body responds by producing elevated stress hormones, including cortisol. This stress response system is a natural response to threat, and once the threat subsides, stress hormone levels go down and the body's nervous system resumes typical functioning. However, children with internalizing disorders have a more reactive stress response system than children without internalizing disorders. Whether due to prolonged exposure to stressors (e.g., trauma, violence) or to inaccurate perception of threat, these children have a biochemical overactivity that translates into symptoms of significant anxiety. Furthermore, this persistent activation of the stress response system "adversely affects brain architecture" in the critical regions of the amygdala, hippocampus, and the prefrontal cortex by "overproducing neural connections in those regions, while [the] regions dedicated to reasoning, planning, and behavioral control may produce fewer neural connections" (National Scientific Council on the Developing Child, 2005/2014, p. 2). Recall that the prefrontal cortex is paramount for the emergence of executive functions. The abilities associated with the executive functions include decision making, planning, problem solving, inhibiting impulsivity, and focusing attention. These skills are critical for children's social and academic progress.

Temperament

Temperament refers to aspects of a child's personality that are innate and that have an impact on how he or she responds to change or novelty, how intense his or her reaction to change may be, how persistent he or she may be with a new task, and how much attention he or she devotes to a person, thing, or activity. According to Kagan's (1989) classification, children who are shy, resistant to change or new situations, and who tend to withdraw under stress fall under the temperamental category of behaviorally inhibited (as cited in Davies, 2011). Children with this type of temperament have distinct physiological responses, such as increased heart rate and cortisol levels (Davies, 2011; Dozois et al., 2009). They may present as irritable and difficult to soothe in infancy, as fearful in toddlerhood, as shy and weary in childhood, and as hypervigilant and withdrawn in adolescence and adulthood (Davies, 2011; Dozois et al., 2009; Essex, Klein, Slattery, & Hill, 2010). Behaviorally inhibited children may be unable to relax and be spontaneous in all but very familiar settings (Eisenberg, Hofer, & Vaughan, 2007). Not only are these children likely to withdraw socially during elementary and middle school, but they also have the greatest risk for anxiety disorders (Davies, 2011; Essex et al., 2010).

A behaviorally inhibited temperamental type, however, is not a sufficient cause for anxiety disorders. Numerous studies indicate that not all children with a behaviorally inhibited temperament develop clinically significant anxiety disorders (Biederman et al., 2001). It is likely that the link between this temperamental style and anxiety disorders is additionally influenced by environmental characteristics or other temperamental traits (Muris, vanBrakel, Arntz, & Schouten, 2011; Vervoot et al., 2011). For example, behavioral inhibition is related to negative emotionality, that is, the propensity to experience negative emotions, increased wariness, vigilance, physiological arousal, and emotional distress (Essex et al., 2010). As Muris and colleagues (2011) indicate, behaviorally inhibited children experience more social rejection, interpret ambiguous social encounters as rejecting, avoid social stressors, and respond to social rejection with explanations of personal incompetence and avoidance. The combination of temperament, negative emotionality, and social responses across early and middle childhood may set the stage for the development of anxiety disorders, especially early social anxiety (Fox & Pine, 2012; Muris et al., 2011).

Attentional control is a specific component of the overarching temperament trait of effortful control, and it represents the ability to focus and switch attention (Sportel, Nauta, deHullu, deJong, & Hartman, 2011). When children have high levels of attentional control, they are able to focus their attention away from perceived threat and away from high negative emotionality. Conversely, children with low attentional control are not able to disengage attentional focus from perceived threats. In addition to heightened attention to negative situations, children with low attentional control have information-processing biases toward threat and interpretation of ambiguous situations as negative or threatening (Garber & Weersing, 2010). In addition to increased attention to the negative, children who struggle with anxiety also have a negative memory bias. That is, they interpret ambiguous situations as negative, and they also remember more of the negative associations of that situation. For example, the more salient memories for them may involve their perceptions of others' negative expressions (e.g., furrowed brows) and anger (e.g., strong tone of voice) and their own feelings (e.g., scared, worried). Therefore, from a temperamental perspective, the combination of high behavioral inhibition and negatively biased attention and memory may place children at the highest levels of risk for the development of anxiety disorders (Dozois et al., 2009; Essex et al., 2010; Garber & Weersing, 2010; Sportel et al., 2011).

Psychological Factors

Children struggling with anxiety disorders have specific psychological vulnerabilities that impact their emotional processing and functioning. A global vulnerability is related to low self-esteem and a low sense of control (Suárez et al., 2008). Anxious children perceive themselves as socially and academically incompetent, as less worthy of support than other children, and as much less able to actively do anything to change their situations. For these children, "failures or perceived deficiencies are indications of a chronic inability to cope with unpredictable and uncontrollable negative events, and this sense of uncontrollability" is associated with high negative emotions and the inability to down-regulate these emotions (Suárez et al., 2008, p. 9).

Children struggling with anxiety disorders also develop specific psychological vulnerabilities, which are in turn related to the specific disorder developed. For example, a child may develop a specific phobia to cats after being scratched and hurt by one. In this case, the child is exposed to a true threat or danger and subsequently generalizes that fear to all cats. A child may also develop a specific fear after experiencing a false alarm in his stress response system that leads him to perceive a situation as threatening. For example, if a child experiences symptoms of a panic attack (e.g., sweaty palms, increased heart rate, feeling numb, feeling short of breath) while giving a presentation in class, he may generalize his fear to all situations where he has to speak before a group of people. In this example, the child experiences giving presentations as threatening and as situations where he lacks control, and this may be associated with social anxiety. Finally, a child may develop a specific vulnerability through observation or suggestion. Sean, a fifth-grade student, witnessed his friend faint while in science class. After this event, Sean started to feel dizzy, anxious, and afraid during science class.

The feelings of helplessness and incompetence prompted by anxiety influence which coping skills children will use in an attempt to relieve their distress. There are two general categories of coping skills children may use when distressed: reappraisal and suppression. *Reappraisal* involves changing the way one thinks about a situation in order to change its emotional impact (E. K. Hughes, Gullone, Dudley, & Tonge, 2010). For example, prior to starting a spelling test, a third-grader may worry that she will not do well. If she uses reappraisal, she may think, "Sometimes I worry about how I will do with spelling, but I know that I studied and practiced my words all week, so I will know the words and will get a good grade on the test." By identifying her fear and changing the way she thinks about the situation, this student is able to change her emotions to more positive and calmer ones, thereby allowing herself to focus her attention on the test.

In contrast to this example, children who struggle with anxiety often use suppression as a coping strategy. Suppression is based on avoidance and involves hiding one's emotional response from others (Campbell-Sills & Barlow, 2007; Hughes et al., 2010). For example, suppose another third-grade student in the same class struggles with anxiety. She is also very nervous about the spelling test and worries that she will not do well. She pretends she is fine and does not tell the teacher about her fear of failing. She tries to just not think about the fear. While this student's attempt to put the worry out of her mind constitutes effort to decrease her experiencing of negative emotions, this approach actually increases symptoms of anxiety and distress (Amstadter, 2008). The key distinction here is that the anxious child is not actively employing an action-based coping skill to manage her anxiety (e.g., identifying the fear and challenging negative thoughts) but is instead trying to avoid the emotion altogether. This more passive style of coping does not effectively get rid of the anxiety, as despite efforts to ignore it, the worries persist and children are unable to shift their attention away from the fear and threat.

Social Factors
Attachment

As Davies (2011) indicates, "attachment has four main functions: providing a sense of security, regulating affect and arousal, promoting the expression of feelings and communication, and serving as a base for exploration" (p. 8). When children and their caregivers have secure attachments, children can consistently count on their caregivers to provide safety, predictability, and comfort. Children can also rely on caregivers to provide help with regulation when the children are emotionally distressed. For example, a baby may become upset and communicate this to his mother by crying, fussing, and looking anxious. His mother responds by pulling him close, giving him hugs and kisses, and murmuring words of comfort. The baby's emotional distress decreases, as does his physiological arousal associated with a stress response. Through this experience of being soothed, the baby can learn and internalize ways to soothe himself. As the child grows, this sense of consistency and self-regulation helps him feel competent in controlling his distress and negative emotions (Davies, 2011).

When attachment relationships are insecure or disorganized; however, the child's sense of safety, control, and emotional regulation are significantly impaired. When children's attachment relationships are disrupted by inconsistent parenting, children may develop anxiety and overdependence. The children are so worried about maintaining the caregiver's attention and availability that it interrupts their developmental tasks of independence and exploration. Over time, children develop anxiety related to whether their needs can be met, may feel a sense of helplessness or control over others' behaviors, and may develop a sense of overall uncertainty and perception of threat or danger. In fact, research demonstrates that children with insecure attachments are twice as likely as children with secure attachments to develop internalizing disorders (Madigan et al., 2013). Temperament can further pose vulnerability for children with disrupted attachments, with children who combine a behaviorally inhibited temperament with an insecure attachment status displaying the highest levels of anxiety disorders symptoms (Muris et al., 2011).

Parenting

In addition to the attachment relationship, other parent–child relationship factors may act as either protective or risk factors in the development of childhood anxiety disorders. When parents are warm and consistent and encourage children to have a level of independence and exploration that is appropriate for their age, children in turn are able to gain a sense of mastery of their environment and of their ability to successfully control it. This early experience of success, coupled with the reassurance that parents will be there if the child needs assistance, builds confidence and a repertoire of new skills and contributes to self-regulation. For example, suppose a preschooler is playing on the playground and wants to go on the slide for the first time. If parents encourage this exploration by telling her, "Go ahead! Try out the slide and see how fun it is! Sit down with your legs out and go!" they are fostering independence as well as sharing skills for mastery. This type of approach offers protection, or buffering, against any potential biological or psychological vulnerability.

Alternatively, when parents inhibit normative exploration and independence through overprotection or anxious responses to the child's behavior, they foster a general sense of apprehension in the child. The child may learn to perceive his or her environment as unpredictable and threatening, thus contributing to an overall sense of uncontrollability and helplessness. In our example above where the preschooler is on the playground, if her parents respond with, "Don't go on the slide; it's dangerous and you can get hurt," or "Don't touch the trees; you might be allergic or get bugs on you," the child will learn to fear new experiences. Further, this promotes a sense of uncontrollability as well as avoidance behaviors. Research indicates that this type of parenting acts as a risk factor in the development of anxiety disorders (Beesdo-Baum & Knappe, 2012; Creveling, Varela, Weems, & Corey, 2010; Dozois et al., 2009; Hiebert-Murphy et al., 2011; Muris et al., 2011).

Another risk factor for the development of childhood anxiety disorders is critical parent evaluation of the child's emotional behavior. For example, if parents respond to children's upset by saying things such as, "Stop crying; it's not that big a deal," or "I just don't get what you're so upset about," they do not acknowledge or validate the child's experience. The child may learn to suppress his or her emotions, may not develop more adaptive forms of emotional expression, and may feel additionally stressed or anxious (Festa & Ginsburg, 2011; Stegge & Meerum Terwogt, 2007).

At times, parents' difficulty with allowing independence or exploration in children is related to their own struggles with mental health disorders (APA, 2013; Beesdo-Baum & Knappe, 2012). Parents suffering from untreated internalizing disorders may be less attuned to their children, may have a more difficult time responding consistently to children's emotional needs, may be more critical of children's emotions or behavior, and may model more anxious responses and avoidant behaviors (Dozois et al., 2009). These parent–child dynamics, in turn, create an interaction with biological and psychological vulnerability that leads to the development of childhood anxiety disorders.

Adverse Life Events

Adverse life events in childhood can have a significant and long-lasting negative impact on children's emotional health. As researchers from Harvard University's Center on the Developing Child indicate, early adversity may act as the "signature that releases a child's genetic predisposition for anxiety, building a brain architecture that responds to lower levels of stress with excessive fear and anxiety, leading to lifelong consequences for mental health" (National Scientific Council on the Developing Child, 2010, p. 3). Indeed, numerous studies have found a strong association between adverse life events (e.g., loss of a parent, humiliation, bullying, sexual abuse, physical abuse, neglect, extreme poverty, neighborhood violence, domestic violence) and almost all mental disorders, including childhood anxiety disorders (APA, 2013; Beesdo-Baum & Knappe, 2012; National Scientific Council on the Developing Child, 2012).

Children's long-term outcomes are particularly in peril when they are exposed to prolonged, threatening circumstances such as any type of abuse, significant family conflict or domestic violence, or persistent threats of community violence (National Scientific Council on the Developing Child, 2010). When children are constantly exposed to these stressors, they remain in a perpetual state of fear and anxiety. As attunement to threat and avoidance behaviors may actually be helpful in the context of dangerous situations, children learn these responses quickly. However, they do not unlearn these patterns or recover easily, thus leading to long-term outcomes that impact their social, emotional, academic, and even physical functioning (Muris et al., 2011; National Scientific Council on the Developing Child, 2010).

Children may experience another form of adversity in the context of their peer relationships. Children with anxiety disorders tend to be perceived by their peers as shyer, more withdrawn, and less likable (Mychailyszyn, Beidas, Benjamin, Edmunds, Podell, Cohen, & Kendall, 2011). Whether by their own withdrawal or through active rejection by peers, children struggling with anxiety often find themselves alone and find it difficult to establish and maintain friendships. Children who are neglected or actively rejected by their peers report higher levels of anxiety and depression during childhood and into adolescence (Festa &

Ginsburg, 2011). Without a supportive peer network, children may feel socially incompetent, helpless, and isolated. This diminished sense of self-esteem and efficacy contributes to feelings of anxiety and further isolation through avoidant behaviors. Therefore, children with poor peer relationships, through the combination of low self-esteem, anxiety due to rejection, active avoidance, and lack of social support, are at high risk for the development of anxiety and mood disorders (Festa & Ginsburg, 2011; Suárez et al., 2008).

HOW DOES ANXIETY MANIFEST IN ELEMENTARY SCHOOL CHILDREN?

Research from the Mental Health Foundation indicates that emotional problems such as anxiety and depression are commonly neglected or missed (Loades & Mastroyannopoulou, 2010). While anxiety disorders are among the most common psychiatric disorders in childhood, they often go unnoticed by parents and teachers, as anxious children are generally compliant, follow rules, and do not draw attention through negative or defiant behaviors (Beesdo-Baum & Knappe, 2012; Herzig-Anderson, Colognori, Fox, Stewart, & Warner, 2012; Silverman et al., 2008). Indeed, research confirms that teachers are more likely to seek additional support for children with externalizing (i.e., behavioral) disorders than children with internalizing disorders. This section describes the manifestation of anxiety symptoms in elementary school children.

Anxiety manifests in children across several areas, including their emotional experience, how they think about and interpret situations, and how they behave in response to these interpretations. These emotions, thoughts, and behaviors, in turn, have a direct impact on their relationships (Dozois et al. 2009). (See Figure 2.2.) While the constellation of symptoms related to emotions, thoughts, and behaviors are difficult to tease apart, each of these domains is addressed separately to facilitate an understanding of what symptoms might look like in the school setting. It is important to note that the presence of individual symptoms is not sufficient to warrant a diagnosis. It is only when children exhibit numerous symptoms, over a prolonged period of time (e.g., one month or longer), and those symptoms impact social and/or academic functioning, that the presence of an anxiety disorder should be considered.

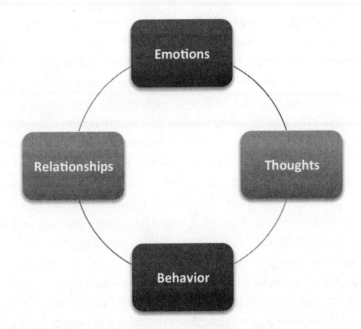

FIGURE 2.2. Anxiety has a direct impact on children's emotions, thoughts, behaviors, and relationships.

Emotions

According to Dr. David Barlow, a preeminent anxiety researcher, anxiety disorders are "essentially ailments of emotion" (Amstadter, 2008, p. 213). In comparison to children without anxiety disorders, those struggling with anxiety experience their emotions more intensely, have more negative affect (e.g., sadness, shame, and fear), perceive themselves as less able to manage their emotions, and have deficits in understanding their own and others' emotions. Importantly, the timing and the intensity of the negative emotions is problematic (Amstadter, 2008). Children with anxiety disorders demonstrate a heightened fear response and subsequent negative affect even when an actual threat or danger is not present (Amstadter, 2008; National Scientific Council on the Developing Child, 2010).

While the experience of negative emotions is heightened in children with anxiety, their ability to tolerate these intense, negative feelings is diminished. During normative development, starting at around age 9 or

10, children begin to weigh the short-and long-term consequences of different emotional regulation strategies. Younger children typically try to avoid negative situations to avoid negative feelings. Older children, however, consider the possibility that, while facing a negative situation may initially cause intense emotions, engaging in that situation will lead to problem solving and therefore relief and positive emotion. The long-term positive consequences are viewed as important enough to tolerate the emotional distress in the short-term (Stegge & Meerum Terwogt, 2007). For example, suppose that Lisa, a fifth-grader, found out that her best friend Becky was mad at her while talking to mutual friends. Lisa felt sad, confused, and worried about what might have upset Becky. Lisa decided that although it might feel uncomfortable, she would approach Becky and ask her directly what happened. Lisa understood that while the initial confrontation might be anxiety provoking, she would likely find a reason for Becky's upset and therefore find an opportunity to restore the friendship. Children with anxiety disorders are avoidant of negative and intense feelings or may not be able to tolerate them sufficiently in the short term to wait for the long-term resolution. In Lisa's example, if Lisa had struggled with an anxiety disorder, she would likely have experienced very significant distress upon hearing about Becky's upset. Lisa's response would have been to blame herself for whatever happened, feel ashamed of being a bad friend, and avoid future contact with Becky.

Emotions that children with anxiety disorders may exhibit include:

- Sadness
- Fear
- Worry
- Helplessness
- Hopelessness
- Frustration
- Irritability
- Shame
- Embarrassment

Emotions include a person's affective state as well as distinct physiological responses (Amstadter, 2008; Peterson & Park, 2007). Children with anxiety disorders exhibit heightened physiological responses and more somatic complaints compared to normal control children (Warner et al., 2011). In fact, approximately 50% to 80% of children with chronic abdominal pain also meet criteria for one or more anxiety disorders (Warner et al., 2011). Children with anxiety disorders are also hyperaware of their bodily symptoms and changes, often misinterpreting physical sensations as threatening or dangerous (Muris, Mayer, Kramer Freher, Duncan, & van den Hout, 2010). For example, Brian, a third-grader, went to the playground right after lunch. He ran around, climbed the monkey bars, and spun around. When he returned to the classroom, he felt a slight stomachache. Instead of realizing he must have run or spun too much right after lunch and reassuring himself that the stomach upset would go away soon, he became very anxious, worrying that there was something seriously wrong with him. He asked to go to the nurse's office immediately and was not able to return to class for the rest of the day. Children with anxiety disorders are often "frequent flyers" at the nurse's office and may complain of various and diffuse somatic symptoms for which there appears to be no clear cause.

Somatic complaints that children with anxiety disorders may exhibit include:

- Headaches
- Stomachaches
- Muscle tension
- Nausea
- Shortness of breath
- Restlessness
- Fatigue
- Cold or sweaty hands
- Rapid heart rate
- Dizziness

Thoughts

Children suffering from anxiety disorders perceive the world as a dangerous place. They experience constant apprehension and worry (Kendall, Furr, & Podell, 2010). Worry takes the form of repetitive, negative thoughts that focus on potential future threats (Dozois et al., 2009). For example, Allie, a second-grader struggling with separation anxiety, may repetitively ask her mom questions such as, "If you run out of gas, who will pick me up at school?" or "What if you don't remember that today is early dismissal and I'm left alone at school?"

It is not uncommon for children without emotional disorders to ask such questions. Once they receive the responses to the questions, they interpret that information as true, reliable, and under their control. In contrast, children with anxiety disorders continue to worry and focus on potential threats (e.g., being left alone at school). Importantly, this constant worry is fueled by thoughts of lack of control (e.g., "There is nothing I can do to keep Mom from forgetting") and lack of capacity to deal with difficulty (e.g., "I won't know what to do if she's not there at pickup time"). This leads to further physiological arousal, negative affect, agitation, and helplessness (Dozois et al., 2009; Suárez et al., 2008).

A person's general outlook, or attributional style, has a significant impact on his or her interpretation of events and situations. Children with anxiety disorders tend to have a pessimistic outlook that reflects a sense of uncontrollability (Garber & Weersing, 2010). This helplessness derives from internal, global, and stable attributions that children make regarding negative events. For example, Connor, a fourth-grade student, was hoping that he would be named citizen of the month in school. When he heard over the announcements that another student had been chosen, Connor's interpretation of the situation was based on internal ("I must not be good enough to be citizen of the month"), global ("I'm not going to be chosen for any special recognition") and stable ("Things will never change") attributions. The nature of the worry and specific thoughts related to that worry vary by the type of anxiety disorder. However, despite the type of anxiety disorder, all children with anxiety share a common sense of vulnerability, helplessness, and uncontrollability.

Thoughts that children with anxiety disorders may exhibit include:

• "I don't want to work on that group project. Everyone will see that I don't know what I'm doing."

- "If I get up in front of the class to share my science report, I will trip and fall and everyone will laugh at me."
- "The teacher will call on me and I won't know what to say."
- "I have butterflies in my stomach and I'm sweaty—I don't know what's happening and I must be going crazy."
- "Our team didn't win. It must have been my fault."
- "I'm not even going to try; things are going to go wrong anyway."

Behaviors

The constellation of negative thoughts and affect, low tolerance for distress, and perceived inability to manage mood or alter situations leads children to have behavioral responses in which the immediate goal is to escape anxiety. Behavioral avoidance of fearful events and stimuli, therefore, is a hallmark symptom of anxiety disorders. A majority of the time, the avoidance behavior is associated with more internalizing symptoms, including withdrawing, crying, or asking for help. Sometimes, however, children may exhibit more oppositional behavior, including tantrums or overt refusal to complete tasks, as they are attempting to escape from a situation, feel they are unable to do so, become distressed, and have difficulty maintaining behavioral control.

For example, children with social anxiety disorder may refuse to go to school, as they worry that peers will negatively judge them or that they will somehow be humiliated. By avoiding school altogether, they are able to escape the perceived threat and anxiety that social situations entail. Similarly, when children struggle with specific phobias, they avoid any situation or context in which they may encounter the feared stimulus. If a child is afraid of blood, he will resist going to the doctor's office and any situation where injury may occur.

For children whose anxiety is related to many different stimuli or contexts, such as in generalized anxiety disorder, behavioral avoidance may not be a feasible option. In such cases, children may develop other maladaptive coping strategies to avoid anxiety, including avoiding eye contact, engaging in rituals or other superstitious behaviors, or attachment to objects or people who are associated with a sense of safety (Suárez et al., 2008). These strategies are used for emotional avoidance and represent children's efforts to prevent themselves from experiencing negative affect (Dozois et al., 2009). Carmen is a third-grader who struggles with separation anxiety. She declines invitations to birthday parties and play dates for fear of separation from her mother. When in school, she carries a small scarf that her mom knitted for her. Carmen touches the scarf before she starts any new class or activity as a way of preventing any harm from coming to her mother.

Behaviors that children with anxiety disorders may exhibit include:

- Asking to go to the nurse's office
- Asking to call parents
- Pacing
- Hand-wringing
- Clinging to parents or caregivers
- Crying when asked to speak in front of the class
- Hiding under desks when significantly distressed
- Argumentativeness—not for the sake of arguing or being disruptive, but as an attempt to gain control ;w
- Asking questions multiple times
- Seeking frequent reassurance or assistance
- Staying alone during free time (e.g., recess, lunch)
- Complaining of being tired and asking for breaks to rest (children with anxiety may have difficulty sleeping due to nighttime fears or nightmares)
- Idiosyncratic ritualistic or repetitive behaviors
- Difficulty concentrating
- Complaining of not being able to remember or understand new information
- Refusing to transition
- Tantrums (particularly in younger children)
- Oppositional behaviors such as refusing to go to another class or to complete an assignment (related to behavioral avoidance of feared situation/person/context)

Relationships

The persistent feelings of worry and uncontrollability associated with anxiety take a significant toll on children's individual functioning. Anxiety can also drastically impact children's relationships. As mentioned earlier, children with anxiety disorders are more withdrawn, have difficulty establishing and maintaining friendships, and may be actively neglected or rejected by their peers. Peer relationships are pivotal for development during middle childhood, and a lack of peer engagement can have devastating emotional effects.

Family relationships also feel the strain of the daily struggles associated with anxiety. Hiebert-Murphy and colleagues (2011) conducted a focus group with parents of kindergarten children struggling with anxiety. Parents reported that dealing with their children's anxiety was stressful and challenging on several levels. First, parents explained that they felt emotionally trapped and experienced a range of emotions including frustration, impatience, embarrassment, and sadness. Second, the additional time and energy required to meet the child's needs had a subsequent negative impact. For example, when their children struggled with separation anxiety, parents reported having to stay at the school more frequently or for a longer period, thus interrupting their work schedules or availability for other siblings (Hiebert-Murphy et al., 2011). Finally, parents often experienced their own worries and fears related to their child's behavior and future functioning. Thoughts including "Was this my fault?" or "Will he ever be more flexible?" or "Will she be able to have friends and be happy?" all lead to parents' own struggles with sadness and anxiety.

A less explored yet equally important family relationship is that of the child with his or her siblings. In some families, siblings may adopt the role of protector, shielding the child with anxiety from potentially negative situations. While the intent in this is positive and caring, the negative unintended effect is further reinforcement of the child's avoidant behaviors. In some families, siblings may be required to participate in additional activities to help the child struggling with anxiety. Recall Kelly and her sister Ava? Ava was charged with walking her sister into school and the classroom, making sure she was not alone during recess, and staying with her upon dismissal. Siblings may respond in different ways to this additional responsibility, including with acceptance, with resentment, or potentially with overt anger and rejection of the child with anxiety.

Finally, the teacher–student relationship may also be impacted when children struggle with significant anxiety. The time before a child is diagnosed may be particularly challenging, as there may be a pattern of inconsistent behavior and academic performance that seems confusing within the classroom setting.

Liam was in Mrs. Marinelli's fifth-grade classroom. Some days, when he was able to stay in the classroom, he completed his work and was able to achieve at grade-level expectations or even surpass them. Some days, however, were very difficult and he could scarcely remain in the classroom. During these hard days, he refused to comply with Mrs. Marinelli's requests to complete his work, saying he had a stomachache and needed to go to the nurse's office. Mrs. Marinelli felt confused and frustrated, as she maintained a consistent routine in her classroom and thus could not understand what was triggering Liam's behavioral changes. She confided in the school psychologist, saying that she felt exhausted in having to deal with Liam and that at times she felt as if the fact that he could do the work yet refused to do it was an insult to her.

When children's anxiety symptoms are disruptive across multiple settings, relationships that are mutually supportive and involve close communication are critical. Strong student–teacher and parent–teacher relationships, for example, are important parts of a child's overall treatment plan and daily support. Strategies for assisting children in the classroom are presented in Chapters 4 and 5.

HOW DOES CULTURE PLAY A ROLE IN THE MANIFESTATION OF CHILDREN'S ANXIETY SYMPTOMS?

The symptom expression presented thus far follows a mental health disorder conceptualization largely guided by Western views and philosophies. Given the rich diversity of our population, however, one must also consider cultural differences in perceptions and approaches to mental illness that may influence how symptoms are expressed and interpreted (Varela & Hensley-Maloney, 2009). For example, in Asian and Latino cultures, social mental illness carries a heavy stigma for the individual and the family (Ang, Lowe, & Yusof, 2011; Varela & Hensley-Maloney, 2009), and therefore symptoms may not be expressed as psychologically based but as more physiologically based. A culture's orientation (e.g., individualistic vs. collectivistic) and values (e.g., respect for elders) also impact how children are taught to express their experiences of fear, anger, worry, and separation (Ang et al., 2011; Juang, Syeng, & Cookston, 2012; Martinez, Polo, & Smith Carter, 2012; Pina, Little, Wynne, & Beidel, 2013; Varela & Hensley-Maloney, 2009).

Research highlights different levels of prevalence and expression of specific anxiety symptomatology and disorders based on cultural and racial differences. For example, African American youth generally have significantly lower (or similar) social anxiety levels than their White counterparts, and among African American children, anxiety seems to manifest itself largely in terms of physical symptoms (Pina et al., 2013). Somatization, harm avoidance, and separation anxiety may be higher among Latino youth than African American and European American youth (Martinez et al., 2012). The finding that Latino children worry more than children of other ethnicities is perhaps the most corroborated in the research literature (Varela & Hensley-Maloney, 2009).

Two examples of culture-based expression of anxiety are *ataque de nervios* and *khyâl*. These cultural syndromes are associated with panic attacks and panic disorder (APA, 2013). In the Latino culture, *nervios* (literally translated "nerves") is a term used to describe a wide range of negative emotional conditions, including anxiety, troubling states, and somatic distress (Varela & Hensley-Maloney, 2009). *Ataque de nervios* (literally translated "attack of nerves") involves trembling, uncontrollable crying or screaming, depersonalization, and at times even aggressive or suicidal behavior. *Khyâl*, or soul loss attacks, occur among Cambodians, and are associated with different types of exertion. They involve the physiological symptoms of panic attacks, including palpitations, trembling, sweating, sensations of shortness of breath, and unsteadiness or light-headedness (APA, 2013).

Another significant factor influencing differences in symptom experience, manifestation, and interpretation is acculturation. Acculturation "refers to the process of psychological, behavioral, and social adaptation in response to sustained intercultural contact, such as during immigration" (Juang et al., 2012, p. 917). Often, children may acculturate faster than their parents, leading to intergenerational conflict. For example, children may speak English when their parents do not, or children may receive conflicting messages about the level of autonomy or independence they should have based on their observations of peers versus their experience at home. This discrepancy within the family often leads to strained communication and interactions, resulting in negative psychological sequelae (Szapocznik & Williams, 2000). Supporting this notion, Juang and colleagues (2012) report that greater levels of acculturation-based conflict are associated with higher levels of anxiety, somatization, loneliness, depressive symptoms, and lower self-esteem among Asian-heritage families.

Finally, one must consider different social factors impacting minority populations that have a direct influence on their psychological functioning. Immigration-related factors include traumatic events (e.g., loss, separation, abuse) endured during travel into the United States, undocumented status, and poverty. These factors have been linked to significant anxiety and depression in children and adolescents (Stein, Gonzalez, & Huq, 2012). Perceived discrimination and racism are further associated with anxiety and depression symptoms (Martinez et al., 2012; Telzer & Vasquez Garcia, 2009). Finally, current assessment, diagnostic, and treatment methods may not adequately capture culture- or race-specific manifestations. This likely impacts information about prevalence rates, the adaptation of treatment approaches to account for cultural variations, and treatment implementation (Pina et al., 2013).

WHAT ARE THE DIFFERENT KINDS OF ANXIETY DISORDERS DIAGNOSED IN CHILDHOOD?

The American Psychiatric Association's *Diagnostic and Statistical Manual of Mental Disorders* (DSM) is the standard classification of mental disorders that mental health clinicians rely on for diagnosis. The most recent edition of the DSM is the DSM-5, and it is the anxiety disorders listed in this edition that are identified below (APA, 2013). Anxiety disorders are closely related to one another and share many features, including emotional distress, avoidance, and disruption of daily functioning. However, disorders "differ from one another in the types of objects or situations that induce fear, anxiety, or avoidance behavior, and the associated cognitive ideation" (APA, 2013, p. 189).

• *Separation anxiety disorder.* This is the most prevalent anxiety disorder in children under 12 years of age. Children with separation anxiety disorder are fearful of separation from primary caretakers or attachment figures in a way that is developmentally inappropriate and interferes with daily functioning. Children may report persistent worries about harm coming to the attachment figures, or about situations that will lead to separation from attachment figures. Children experience intense distress when separated from attachment figures or when imagining a situation that would lead to separation from them (e.g., being kidnapped, getting lost). Children suffering from separation anxiety disorder are very reluctant to leave home, are afraid of being alone, and may not even be able to sleep alone due to the fear of separation. Reports of physical symptoms such as headaches, stomachaches, and nausea are common, and are especially frequent in the context of anticipating separation (APA, 2013).

  Possible manifestations in the classroom:

  o Reluctance to attend school
  o After arrival at school, difficulty staying in the classroom
  o Asking parents to stay outside the classroom
  o Asking to call parents
  o Refusing to go on field trips
  o Extreme nervousness upon any change in school setting (e.g., going to a different classroom) or classroom routine
  o Difficulty concentrating on work due to distress over separation
  o Declining invitations to peers' sleepovers or birthday parties

• *Selective mutism.* The core feature of this diagnosis is a consistent failure to speak in social situations where children are expected to speak (e.g., in class, with peers). Children struggling with selective mutism do not respond when spoken to and do not initiate conversation, and this occurs in interactions with children and/or adults. Children may experience strong social anxiety, and their symptoms may be so severe that they speak only with parents or siblings but not with others outside the immediate home. This lack of communication is not due to a lack of knowledge of the language (as may be the case for children for whom English is not their first language) or to a communication disorder. Selective mutism is a relative rare disorder and is more typically seen in younger children (APA, 2013).

Possible manifestations in the classroom:

  o Refusal to respond to teacher- or peer-initiated questions/ interactions in the classroom
  o Lack of participation in any activity that requires verbal participation (e.g., reading out loud, group activity, participating in a class play)

- *Specific phobia.* The core feature of this diagnosis is anxiety or fear related to a specific object or situation. Children with a specific phobia experience extreme distress related to the feared object or situation, and their responses are out of proportion to the actual danger the situation or object may pose. They will also demonstrate extreme avoidance of the object or situation. For example, a child with a needle phobia will demonstrate significant distress even when just looking at a picture of a needle. A more significant perceived threat, such as going to the doctor for vaccinations, may result in crying, tantrums, freezing, or even panic attacks. These responses are related only to the specific feared object or situation and are not generalized to other settings, objects, or situations. It is not uncommon for children to have more than one specific phobia, and these fears may begin as early as age 7 (APA, 2013).

Possible manifestations in the classroom:

  o *Without* exposure to the feared object or situation, children with a specific phobia are typically able to functional normally in the classroom.
  o *With* exposure to the specific feared object or situation, children with a specific phobia may complain of physical symptoms such as sweaty hands, racing heartbeat, nausea, or

near-fainting responses. Children may also appear clingy to parents, or they may cry or have a tantrum. For example, a child with a specific phobia of spiders may become very distressed and clingy and refuse to enter the classroom on the day of an in-house field trip where animal sanctuary workers will bring animals into the classroom.

• *Social anxiety disorder (previously called social phobia).* The core feature of this diagnosis is a "marked, or intense, fear or anxiety of social situations in which the individual may be scrutinized by others" (APA, 2013, p. 203). In children, this fear must occur in interactions with peers, not just in interactions with adults. Children who struggle with social anxiety disorder worry that others will think they are stupid, boring, crazy, unlikable, awkward, weird, and so forth. They also worry that they will do something to show their anxious feelings, such as blush, trip, stumble over their words, stammer, or sweat, and that others will evaluate them negatively or openly reject them as a result. Children with social anxiety disorder will either avoid social situations altogether or else endure them with extreme distress. As with other anxiety disorders, the actual threat or negative response is much less than that perceived by the child (APA, 2013). in with social anxiety disorder, as they

Possible manifestations in the classroom:

o Extreme anxiety over situations that frequently occur in the classroom, including interacting with peers, being observed, and performing in front of others
o Avoidance of eye contact
o Avoidance of raising hand in class
o Eating alone rather than in a crowded cafeteria
o Avoidance of making presentations in front of the class
o Frequent absences to avoid evaluative situations
o Frequent requests to go to the nurse's office due to somatic complaints
o In severe cases, school refusal

• *Panic disorder.* The core feature of this disorder is the recurrence of unexpected panic attacks. A panic attack is the basic emotion of fear occurring at an inappropriate time (Suárez et al., 2008). It is characterized by "an abrupt surge of intense fear or intense discomfort that reaches a peak within minutes" (APA, 2013, p. 209). When having a panic attack, a child experiences several cognitive and physical symptoms, including rapid heartbeat, shaking, sweating, feeling dizzy, nausea, sensations of shortness of breath, numbness, tingling, fear of dying, and fear of going crazy (APA, 2013). Research indicates that not everyone who experiences a panic attack will develop panic disorder. Suárez and colleagues (2008) suggest that how a person reacts to a panic attack differentiates "nonclinical panickers" from those with clinical panic disorder. In children with clinical panic disorder, in addition to the actual experiencing of panic attacks, the child also worries about having more panic attacks, in turn leading to avoidance behaviors (e.g., not leaving the house for fear of having a panic attack). Panic attacks may occur in childhood but more typically occur during adolescence (APA, 2013).

Possible manifestations in the classroom:

o Intense fear or discomfort that seems to appear "out of the blue"
o Physical symptoms such as those listed above, and the feeling that something is physically very wrong

• *Agoraphobia.* The core feature of this disorder is an intense fear of real or anticipated exposure to "a wide range of situations" (APA, 2013, p. 218). These situations include using public transportation, open spaces (e.g., bridges, open parking lots), enclosed places (e.g., elevators, restaurants, shops), standing in line or being in a crowd, and being alone outside the home. While these are the most typical feared situations, fear related to other situations is also possible (APA, 2013). Youth with agoraphobia may be afraid of these situations, as they worry that if they experience a panic attack or other embarrassing or incapacitating symptoms, escape or seeking help will be very difficult. Therefore, youth either insist on having company when in a particularly feared situation or avoid such situations altogether. Agoraphobia may occur in childhood, but it is rare. Agoraphobia more typically begins in late adolescence and early adulthood. If untreated, the most severe presentation of agoraphobia can result in a person's becoming completely homebound.

Possible manifestation in the classroom:

- o If agoraphobia occurs in childhood, the most significant worry is of being outside the home alone. Therefore, school refusal is extremely likely.
- o If children with agoraphobia leave the home setting, they may report cognitive and physical symptoms associated with panic attacks. They may also report fears of vomiting, feeling disoriented, or worries about getting lost.

• *Generalized anxiety disorder.* The core feature of this disorder is excessive anxiety and worry, for most of the time, about a number of events or activities. For example, children may worry about their competence or the quality of their performance, either at home or at school. Children struggling with generalized anxiety disorder have great difficulty controlling this worry and have intrusive thoughts that frequently interfere with their daily functioning. In addition to the worry, children may also feel "on edge" or have restlessness, fatigue, difficulty concentrating, irritability, muscle tension or soreness, headaches, gastrointestinal distress, a feeling that their mind is "going blank," or sleep disturbances (APA, 2013). Generalized anxiety disorder typically begins in adolescence, though symptoms may be seen during middle childhood. Earlier development of symptoms is associated with comorbidity (i.e., development of other disorders) and higher levels of impairment (APA, 2013). Children struggling with generalized anxiety disorder experience significant emotional and physical distress. The consistency of these feelings takes a toll on the children, and the disorder leads to significant disability. Youth with generalized anxiety disorder are more likely to report suicidal ideation or to attempt suicide than youth without disorders, and are also more likely to report or attempt suicide than those with depression alone (Strawn, Wehry, DelBello, Rynn, & Strakowski, 2012).

Possible manifestations in the classroom:

- o Appearing distressed and fatigued
- o Preoccupation with excessive worries, leading to disturbances in attention and processing, taking excessive time to complete work, and inability to devise ways to efficiently problem-solve, approach new situations, or complete assignments
- o Avoidance of social situations
- o Sadness or withdrawal
- o Feeling of paralysis when confronted with unexpected situations (e.g., pop quiz, being asked to respond to a question without having raised a hand)

There are additional diagnoses within the current DSM-5 category of anxiety disorders. These include "Substance/Medication-Induced Anxiety Disorder," "Anxiety Disorder Due to Another Medical Condition," "Other Specified Anxiety Disorder," and "Unspecified Anxiety Disorder" (APA, 2013). These disorders either are associated primarily with medical conditions or constitute a constellation of symptoms that do not meet full criteria for other disorders. These are very rarely used with children and are beyond the scope of this discussion.

Upon reviewing the list of anxiety disorders described above, readers may wonder why obsessive-compulsive disorder and posttraumatic stress disorder (PTSD) are not included. Obsessive-compulsive disorder is characterized by the presence of obsessions and/or compulsions.

Obsessions are recurrent and persistent thoughts, urges, or images that are experienced as intrusive and unwanted, whereas *compulsions* are repetitive behaviors or mental acts that an individual feels driven to perform in response to an obsession or according to rules that must be applied rigidly. (APA, 2013, p. 235)

While there are close relationships between the anxiety disorders and the obsessive-compulsive and related disorders, the latter are considered a distinct set of disorders within the new DSM-5 classification (APA, 2013).

PTSD is now included within the category of trauma- and stressor-related disorders. As the DSM-5 indicates, in some cases, symptoms of psychological distress following a traumatic event can be understood within an anxiety- or fear-based context (APA, 2013). However, there are numerous other manifestations, including sadness, anhedonia (lack of interest in activities previously seen as pleasurable), aggression, anger, and dissociation. Due to the variable presentation of the disorder, PTSD and other trauma-related disorders are now grouped under a separate category (APA, 2013).

COMORBIDITY AND ANXIETY DISORDERS

Comorbidity is the co-occurrence of mental health disorders. Studies reveal strong associations between anxiety disorders and depressive disorders, with rates of comorbidity ranging from 30% to 75% (Dozois et al., 2009; Garber & Weersing, 2010; E. K. Hughes et al., 2010). Stated differently, children with an anxiety disorder have up to 29 times the risk of developing depression (Essau, Conradt, Sasagawa, & Ollendick, 2012). Certain presentations of anxiety disorders, including more severe impairment and occurrence of panic attacks, are associated with increased risk for depression (Beesdo-Baum & Knappe, 2012). Anxiety disorders typically precede mood disorders, and children with comorbid anxiety and depression tend to develop depressive symptomatology earlier than children with a diagnosis of depression without comorbid anxiety (Strawn et al., 2012). Additionally, children with both diagnoses tend to experience more acute symptoms and are more distressed than children with only one diagnosis (Essau et al., 2012).

Special Topic: School Refusal

Tyler is a fourth-grade student whose academic testing has revealed vocabulary, reading, and mathematics skills at or beyond grade level. Tyler's current functioning, however, is significantly impaired by his inability to consistently remain in the classroom. Mornings are extremely difficult for Tyler and his parents. He complains of feeling nauseated and sick, pleads with his parents to allow him to stay home, and refuses to go into the classroom when his parents finally manage to get him to school. At night, Tyler barely sleeps and says he feels trapped and out of breath, and he insists on going outside for a walk, even in the middle of the night. He makes frequent visits to the nurse's office due to "sharp, stabbing pains in his stomach." When Tyler is able to stay in the classroom, his teacher reports that he "seems fine" and is able to do his work. However, Tyler's requests to leave the classroom are becoming more frequent, and his grades are suffering as a result.

School refusal behavior refers to either refusal to go to school or difficulty remaining in class for an entire day (Maeda, Hatada, Sonoda, & Takayama, 2012). Disrupted patterns of school attendance include (a) being completely absent for periods of time, (b) attending school but then leaving early or skipping certain classes, and (c) consistently arriving late to school (Beidel et al., 2010; Kearney & Albano, 2007). Therefore, both children who miss school for prolonged periods of time and those who attend school but experience significant distress related to staying in school display school refusal behaviors (Kearney & Albano, 2007). This pattern of behavior is different from truancy. Children with truant behavior actively attempt "to conceal nonattendance and often [have] a pattern of behavior problems" (E. K. Hughes et al., 2010, p. 692).

School refusal is not a formal diagnosis, yet it often presents in children who struggle with anxiety and depression. It is important to note that while internalizing symptoms often lead to school refusal behaviors, approximately 20% to 30% of children with school refusal do not meet criteria for any psychiatric diagnosis (Hella & Bernstein, 2012). School refusal is seen equally in boys and girls, and the average age of children with school refusal behavior is 10 to 13 years old. However, school refusal may also occur during transitional periods, such as entry into kindergarten and into high school (Grills-Taquechel, Fletcher, Vaughn, Denton, & Taylor, 2013; E. K. Hughes et al., 2010; Kearney & Albano, 2007). In childhood, school refusal is associated with negative outcomes, including disruption of social, family, and educational development. Without treatment and with symptom progression, long-term outcomes include problems related to education, employment, and social and mental health in adolescence and adulthood (Grills-Taquechel et al., 2013).

Some instances of school refusal are normative, especially when children are transitioning into a new school setting. For example, kindergarten students may be hesitant to leave parents in the morning, or may ask to stay home from school. This behavior usually remits once the child becomes adjusted to his or her new settings and school personnel. In contrast, substantial school refusal behavior lasts at least two weeks, and acute school refusal lasts more than one calendar year (Kearney & Albano, 2007). Kearney and Albano (2007) propose four main reasons, or functions, for school refusal behavior:

1. To avoid negative affectivity (depressive or anxious symptoms, somatic complaints) triggered by school-related stimuli
2. To escape school-related aversive social or evaluative situations
3. To seek or receive attention from family or other significant people in one's life
4. To seek or obtain rewards outside school, such as staying home and playing video games or watching TV

Children with school refusal behavior may fall under one of the categories listed above, yet as many as one third may fall under two or more categories (Kearney & Albano, 2007). Therefore, it is critical to conduct a careful analysis of the function served by the school refusal. Treatment approaches vary based on the functionality and duration of the behavior. Recommendations for teachers for managing school refusal behaviors are included in Chapter 4.

The Impact of Anxiety on Learning

One of the most significant negative outcomes of childhood anxiety is poor academic functioning and high risk for dropout (A. A. Hughes et al., 2008). Anxiety has a profound influence on children's learning, achievement, and school functioning in a number of ways. For many children, school-related stimuli may be particularly salient triggers for fear and anxiety. As a result, children may exhibit behavioral avoidance and an inconsistent attendance pattern that impairs their academic and social progress (Grills-Taquechel et al., 2013). Negative emotional responses, cognitions, and physical symptoms further interfere with children's ability to focus on learning. Importantly, brain structures associated with learning are adversely impacted by a chronically aroused stress response system (National Scientific Council on the Developing Child, 2010). Whether the prolonged activation of the stress response system is triggered by actual threat, such as abuse or trauma, or by perceived threat, there is significant and long-lasting impact on a child's biological readiness for learning. For example, stress-induced damage to brain cells in areas that support learning may lead to increased impairment in subsequent memory formation (National Scientific Council on the Developing Child, 2010). Numerous studies have quantified this impact, and report specific patterns of underachievement on school-based measures (A. A. Hughes et al., 2008; Ialongo, Edelsohn, Werthamer-Larsson, Crockett, & Kellam, 1995).

For children with anxiety disorders, one of the biggest obstacles in the classroom entails shifting their attention away from anxious thoughts and toward the teacher and academic material. Children with high levels of anxiety are more susceptible to distraction than children with low levels of anxiety (Eysenck & Derakshan, 2011). As they struggle to maintain focus, the intrusion of worries will likely make children miss certain parts of the teacher's instructions or of test questions, for example. Children feel temporarily lost or confused, and this increases their anxiety, thereby creating a cycle that further impedes their ability to maintain focus. Some studies suggest that the propensity to become distracted increases when the distracting context involves perceived negative emotion, such as an angry tone of voice or a mad face (Eysenck & Derakshan, 2011). Therefore, children's inability to shift away from anxious or worried thoughts may be particularly salient when they perceive either peers or teachers as being upset, angry, or disappointed.

For teachers, a particularly challenging aspect of their anxious students' functioning may be associated with the variability of their performance. Sarah's second-grade teacher said of her student, "I don't get it. If I sit with her and do the work, she is able to complete things properly, but when she's on her own, she doesn't do it. I know she has the ability and can do it, but why won't she?" According to Ansari and Der-akshan (2011), children with anxiety struggle with processing efficiency (i.e., the amount of resources they need to achieve the correct outcome), but not necessarily with performance effectiveness (i.e., the ability to do the task). Therefore, with additional external resources, as when Sarah's teacher sits with her and helps her maintain focus, children are able to complete work more consistently. When alone, however, they may have too few resources to mobilize, thus leading to inconsistent academic performance.

Environmental stressors such as abuse and exposure to violence can lead to chronic anxiety and fear in children, in turn triggering prolonged activation of the stress response system. This type of activation inter-feres with the chemistry of the brain circuitry associated with learn-ing and self-regulation, especially when the disruption occurs during sensitive times of childhood development (National Scientific Coun-cil on the Developing Child, 2010). For example, executive functions (include working memory, inhibitory control, and cognitive flexibility) begin to emerge around age 5. These functions are the building blocks for children's academic and social learning (Center on the Developing Child at Harvard University, 2011). By age 7, however, some of the brain circuits underlying executive functions may be similar to those found in adults. When children are exposed to highly stressful situations or environments, they have great difficulty engaging their executive func-tions, even in places like school, where they may be safe (Center on the Developing Child at Harvard University, 2011).

With respect to the relation between anxiety and specific measure-ments of school achievement, studies report decreased performance across several domains. Ialongo and colleagues followed first-grade children for four and a half years. Based on self-reports of anxiety symptoms, children in the top third in terms of number of symptoms were 10 times more likely to be in the bottom third of achievement in the fifth grade (Ialongo et al., 1995; Valiente, Swanson, & Eisenberg, 2012). In a study by Grills-Taquechel and colleagues (2013), students who reported more symptoms of separation anxiety at the end of first grade also tended to have lower reading achievement scores. This is con-sistent with another of the researchers' findings, namely, that children in the top quartile of anxiety in the fall of first grade were nearly eight times more likely to be in the lowest quartile of reading achievement and twice as likely to be in the lowest quartile in math achievement in the spring of first grade. Importantly, anxious symptoms as measured in first grade significantly predicted anxious symptoms in fifth grade (Grills-Taquechel et al., 2013). Other studies have found even longer predictability of poor performance, with anxiety symptoms predicting lower reading and math achievement scores over an eight-year period (Grills-Taquechel et al., 2013).

Diagnosis, Treatment, and Referral

DIAGNOSIS

In general, the most reliable diagnoses are those based on various sources of data. Given that children's presentation fluctuates across settings, gathering qualitative observations and quantifiable measurements of symptoms from multiple reporters (e.g., the child, parents, teachers, and other caretakers) is important in gaining as comprehensive an understanding of the child's distress as possible. This broad-based perspective is important in determining level of functional impairment and designing treatment goals accordingly. It is further important, given the high comorbidity of anxiety disorders with other mental health disorders, that different treatments be selected based on the primary presentation. For example, anxiety and depression are highly comorbid in late childhood and early adolescence. When the symptoms of depression are more prominent and more severe than those of anxiety, treatment for depression would be recommended as the initial treatment approach (Kendall et al., 2010).

TREATMENT

Childhood anxiety disorders have a chronic course and do not resolve without treatment (Lau, Pettit, & Creswell, 2013; Mychailyszyn et al., 2011). Therefore, developmentally appropriate treatment approaches are critical in addressing childhood disorders. Cognitive behavioral therapy (CBT) is a treatment modality that has been widely used and studied in treating anxiety disorders in children, with strong research support for both its feasibility and effectiveness (Cartwright-Hatton, Roberts, Chitsabesan, Fothergill, & Harrington, 2004; Elkins, McHugh, Santucci, & Barlow, 2011; Silk et al., 2013; Silverman, Kurtines, Ginsburg, Weems, Lumpkin, & Carmichael, 1999). CBT may be conducted individually, in groups, or with a combination of individual and group treatment. CBT includes several main treatment elements: psychoeducation, somatic management skills, cognitive restructuring, gradual exposure to feared situations, and relapse prevention plans (Kendall et al., 2010). While these skills follow a certain format in the clinical, office-based session, these principles can also be applied in the school setting. Classroom-based strategies based on these principles are found in Chapter 4 of this book.

Additional treatment strategies include use of medication, especially the category of medicines called selective serotonin reuptake inhibitors (SSRIs). Medication is most commonly used in combination with CBT, and this combination has been shown to yield the highest remission rates (Ginsburg et al., 2011; Maslowsky et al., 2010). However, between 30% and 50% of children who receive CBT and medication will still demonstrate some symptomatology, even if the initial intensity has been markedly reduced (Ginsburg et al., 2011). This highlights a need to provide additional support to children outside the immediate treatment hour. For example, inclusion of a family treatment or parent-training component to complement individual therapy has been found to be helpful in treating childhood anxiety (Lau et al., 2013). School-based approaches that focus on social skills development or enhancement of emotional management skills have also been successful in reducing anxiety symptoms among children and adolescents (L. D. Miller et al., 2011). Such a multifaceted approach is critical, as when children are able to use what they learn in individual treatment across multiple settings and with different people, they are better able to generalize their emotion and behavior management skills.

A growing area of interest in the treatment of childhood anxiety disorders is the use of mindfulness practice to enhance emotional regulation skills. The concept of mindfulness in psychology is adopted from Buddhist principles of mindful meditation. Mindfulness means "paying attention in a particular way, on purpose, in the present moment, and non-judgmentally" (Shapiro, Carlson, Astin, & Freedman, 2006). The goals of mindfulness practice are to increase conscious control over attentional processes, to integrate emotional and rational thinking, and to experience a sense of acceptance with oneself (Lynch, Chapman, Rosenthal, Kuo, & Linehan, 2006). Mindfulness has been widely used in the treatment of adult anxiety, and a number of studies have investigated its effectiveness in treating childhood anxiety. Positive preliminary results have led to a number of school-based mindfulness curricula targeting the prevention of anxiety symptoms (Lee, Semple, Rosa, & Miller, 2008; Semple, Reid, & Miller, 2005).

REFERRAL

With respect to initiating a referral, the key message is, "The earlier, the better." As Beesdo-Baum and Knappe (2012) indicate, the best prognostic indicators for the course of an anxiety disorder are symptom severity and duration of illness. Therefore, if symptoms are identified early, when their severity is not at its most acute, there is a higher likelihood of successful treatment and relapse prevention. In general, when children struggle with anxiety in a manner that impedes their social or academic functioning for one month or longer, a referral is warranted. Recommendations for initiating a referral include:

- If you are concerned about a student, keep a record that documents:

  o A description of the behaviors of concern
  o How long the behaviors have been present
  o When the behaviors tend to occur
  o Which people, situations, or settings seem to trigger the behaviors
  o The child's description of his or her emotional state
  o How the behaviors are impacting the child's social and academic functioning

- Talk to other teachers or school personnel who interact with the child to determine how pervasive the change in the child's behavior may be.

- Reach out to parents as early as possible to communicate your observations. Ask whether they have observed similar behaviors at home. When communicating with parents, it is often more useful to indicate how specific behaviors are impacting the child socially and academically rather than attempting to identify the reason for the behavior or to diagnose the child's condition.
- Contact school administrators to determine your school's referral protocol. Whereas some schools have mental health practitioners on campus, other schools do not and different personnel are responsible for receiving and following up on referrals (e.g., guidance counselors).

This careful observation, inquiry, and communication are invaluable for successful referrals. Treatment providers may use this information for diagnostic purposes as well as for the development of treatment goals. Furthermore, this process can facilitate a treatment plan where the teacher supports use and generalization of coping skills in the classroom.

Notice, Give, Nurture

The CBT model indicates that a child's symptom presentation is the result of an interactional process between emotions, thoughts, and behaviors. This interaction is not linear or hierarchical; instead, each component impacts the others with different intensity and at different times based on a particular context. This interrelationship of the child's internal factors in turn impacts his or her external relationships. In the school setting, these relationships focus on the teacher and peers. Developing an awareness of the factors or situations that trigger a student's anxiety is critical in developing helpful classroom strategies for student support. Therefore, the notice, give, and nurture section of this chapter focuses on strategies for understanding a child with anxiety symptoms as well as on creating a classroom atmosphere that fosters safety.

WHAT CAN I NOTICE?

Noticing and assessing children's affect and behavior in the classroom should occur with intentionality. Intentionality refers to utiliz-

Major Developmental Tasks of Middle Childhood	
Task	Process
Development of the prefrontal cortex	• Occurs between 5 and 8 years • Leads to emergence of executive functions, including working memory, cognitive flexibility, selective attention, and inhibitory control
Attachment	• Children learn that secure attachment figures and relationships are readily available when needed • School-age children with secure attachments are more able to independently cope with novelty, separations, and mild circumstances of threat • Children develop growing attachment relationships with peers
Self-regulation	• Beginning around age 8, children begin to recognize the needs of others and manage their behavior accordingly • Beginning around age 10, children develop increasing ability to express and share complex emotional states and concerns • Moral reasoning emerges based on values learned earlier • The ability to distinguish fantasy from reality and to think logically reduces school-age children's anxiety • Children increasingly develop coping skills based on the different contexts they find themselves in • Increased executive function skills promote stronger self-control • Children develop the ability to compare themselves to others and inhibit behavior that may make them seem different from peers • Children develop increased ability to tolerate negative or conflicting feelings
Self-control	• Strong emphasis on feeling and acting in a controlled manner based on internal standards • Guided by increasing ability for self-observation
Social perspective taking	• Beginning around age 6, children become more able to understand others' perspectives, including those that may differ from their own • Beginning around age 8 to 9, children become more able to infer other people's intentions • Beginning around age 10 to 12, children become more able to hold different points of view in mind at the same time (e.g., understand that a peer can have good and bad qualities as a friend)

(continued)

FIGURE 2.3. Major developmental tasks of middle childhood
Source: Based on Davies (2011).

Task	Process
Prosocial skills	• School-age children are better able to analyze and interpret the feelings of others, as well as to notice when a peer may need help and provide it
Play	• Increasingly characterized by organized games (e.g., sports) • Continues to offer a respite from daily structured demands • Hobbies become more prominent • Internal fantasy increases, allowing rehearsal of plans, exploration of oneself in other roles, and understanding of others' perspectives; contributes to creative thinking and development of positive coping skills

FIGURE 2.3 *continued*

ing a knowledge base (e.g., of child development, of factors impacting development, or of how anxiety manifests in childhood) as a guiding principle for observation.

Elementary school children fall under the developmental category of middle childhood—from age 6 to 12. During this period, as Davies (2011) indicates,

> good self-regulation is essential to the developmental tasks of school age, which involve the child's developing a sense of her capacity to work, to learn skills through practice, and to develop feelings of competence and self-esteem based on how she compares with peers. (p. 328)

Some of the major developmental changes of middle childhood are found in Figure 2.3.

As noted elsewhere in the chapter, anxiety disorders have a profound negative impact on each of the developmental processes described above. Childhood anxiety disorders, therefore, affect not only affective functioning, but also overall self-regulation and development.

Noticing children's relative difficulties within these domains is critical, as this assists in the early recognition of emotional disorders. From a developmental perspective, typically developing children generally do not view themselves as globally successful or unsuccessful (Davies, 2011). While some may have a healthy sense of self-esteem (e.g., "I'm so awesome!") that seems to generalize to all aspects of their lives, when asked more specifically, children are able to identify areas of relative strengths and weaknesses. For example, David may indicate that he is an excellent football player, but he's not so great at hockey. Similarly, he may say that he does well in math, but needs to study a bit more for geography.

Children who struggle with emotional disorders tend to make more internal, global, and stable attributions regarding their relative weaknesses and have a more difficult time identifying areas of relative strengths. They tend to use words like *always* and *never* in their evaluation of their capacity to exert control and change. For example, a child struggling with anxiety may say, "I'm not going to bother trying—I'm always going to be the worst student in the class." When children see themselves as more globally inefficient, they demonstrate lower motivation and increased avoidance. This, in turn, reinforces their negative beliefs about failure and lack of control, thereby leading to social and academic disengagement and failure.

Noticing as intentional observation and assessment is also important in the determination of what the feared stimuli might be for children with anxiety disorders. An understanding of childhood anxiety disorders serves as the guiding knowledge base for this intentionality. With respect to feared stimuli, some children may exhibit specific fears, such as those involved in phobias. Their reactions will be predictable based on the exposure to the particular feared situation or thing. For example, for a child who has a blood phobia, getting hurt on the playground and having to go to the nurse's office will elicit significant distress. The distress is circumscribed to the particular situation and is not exhibited in other contexts. In contrast, for children who may have developed anxiety as a result of abuse and trauma, feared stimuli may be more difficult to detect, as they may be idiosyncratic to the child's particular experience. For example, if a child has been the victim of sexual abuse, her anxiety triggers may include having to close her eyes, or the turning on and off of lights. Classroom routines often include asking children to engage in these behaviors (e.g., saying, "Close your eyes and picture in your mind what the character in this book may look like"; turning lights on and off to signal cleanup or transition times). Of critical importance to early identification is noticing changes from the child's normative functioning, the frequency of distress, and the overall impact of this distress on the child's functioning.

Noticing of child-specific factors is paramount, but perhaps equally important is noticing the emotional climate of the classroom and its ability (or lack thereof) to support students struggling with anxiety disorders. Below are some components that contribute to a classroom's emotional climate:

- What are the explicit and implicit messages children receive about the importance of emotions?
- How empathic or tolerant are students of peers' emotional struggles?
- What supports exist to accommodate the emotional and academic needs of students with anxiety?
- What arrangements in the physical space and layout of the classroom provide opportunities for emotional regulation?

Specific suggestions addressing these questions are offered in Chapter 5.

WHAT CAN I GIVE?

One of the important things to give students struggling with anxiety is a sense of safety. Safety as an organizing construct includes attunement to the child's needs, empathy and warmth in teacher–student relationships, consistency through a predictable environment with stable yet flexible (i.e., not rigid) routines, and encouragement of autonomy without consequences for failure (Suárez et al., 2008; Thompson & Meyer, 2007).

The structure of some classrooms may meet all these factors, and others may not be as able to offer all factors consistently. This is indicative not of a bad versus a good teacher, or of a correct versus incorrect environment, but rather of the goodness of fit between the student, teacher, and classroom environment. How can goodness of fit to maximize students' emotional and academic functioning be promoted?

- *By increasing teacher awareness of the development and course of anxiety symptomatology.* For example, research indicates that fear learning can occur quickly and early in life, but fear unlearning is more difficult and achieved later in life. Therefore, early fear learning (like that associated with anxiety disorders) can have long-term effects on children that may take years to remediate (National Scientific Council on the Developing Child, 2010). If classroom routines and structures are set with expectations for prompt assimilation to change, such a setting may not offer the best goodness of fit for children with anxiety. In contrast, a classroom environment that is flexible to accommodate different learning and transition paces may offer better goodness of fit.

- *By using this knowledge of childhood anxiety in general and of individual students' particular presentations to plan for children's subsequent class settings.* For example, Ethan, a child struggling with social anxiety, had a good year while in Mr. Lee's third-grade class. At the end of the academic year, Mr. Lee met with the principal, Ethan's parents, and the fourth-grade teachers to determine which fourth-grade classroom would offer a set of supports and relationships similar to those developed in the third grade to foster Ethan's continued success.

Teachers can also give students the power of language to promote positive self-image and to decrease shame and stigma associated with childhood anxiety. Language can be incredibly powerful in terms of the explicit and implicit messages it conveys, its potential to act as an anxiety trigger, and its potential to positively impact affect and self-image. Below are suggestions for giving students the power of language.

- When children develop emotional disorders, they often worry that others will judge or characterize them solely by the presence of the disorder rather than by other qualities, personality traits, or talents. How one refers to students with emotional disorders can reinforce this type of overgeneralization, or stereotyping. For example, referring to a student as "the anxious child" implies that anxiety is the overarching, defining feature of the child. More appropriate language to use is "the child struggling with anxiety" or "the child with an anxiety disorder." While on first look, the differences may seem subtle, the impact of the language is significant. The latter phrasing indicates that there is a whole child with other interests, talents, and unique qualities who also happens to have anxiety.

- As Thompson and Meyer (2007) indicate, "emotion regulation can be facilitated or impaired by how others evaluate one's feelings" (p. 255). Empathic, genuine, constructive responses convey to children that their feelings are valid and justified. Furthermore, this type of response offers social support and modeling for appropriate emotional communication. For example, in response to a child's anxiety over transitioning to a new activity, a teacher may respond by saying, "It sounds like changing to a new activity is making you nervous. Sometimes change can be hard, but why don't we talk together about what the new activity will be like, so we can figure out what would make the transition a little easier." Conversely, critical, harsh, dismissive responses laden with judgment evoke further anxiety in a child. Such a respond may sound like, "I don't understand what you are so nervous or worried about. We change to new activities all the time." Instead of hearing a possible explanation and solution for his current situation, he will hear confirmation of his perceived failures (Thompson & Meyer, 2007).

WHAT CAN I NURTURE?

The management of anxiety symptoms is not an easy or quick process. It involves consistency, sustained efforts to support children in their use of coping skills, and continued evolution of supports to meet children's developmental changes and transitions. Teachers can nurture efforts to offer continued supports to their students, both in the short term and in the long term. What kinds of supports should be nurtured over time?

- *Opportunities for conversations about emotions.* The message that emotional well-being is as important as academic well-being is an important one to nurture. Students should understand that in the same way we learn math, reading, and science, we also need to learn ways to positively cope with emotions. During a developmental phase when children compare themselves to each other and establish performance-based status hierarchies, it is important to provide different ways for children to find success, including opportunities for positive emotional self-management and support of others (Davies, 2011).

- *Encouragement of bravery.* Silk and colleagues (2013) conducted a study investigating the effects of parental encouragement of bravery in their children (ages 9–13) struggling with anxiety. *Bravery* was defined as encouragement of approach behavior in the context of potential threat. Results of the study indicated that children whose parents were more encouraging of bravery did better in treatment than children whose parents were less encouraging (Silk et al., 2013). This finding was particularly important, as it identified a way in which parents could facilitate exposure and use of coping skills outside the office or clinic setting. Generalization of coping skills is associated with better post-treatment functioning (Silk et al., 2013). Given the success of parental encouragement of bravery, teachers should also encourage and nurture bravery in the classroom, thus allowing yet another opportunity for children to practice their coping skills and generalize them to another setting.
- *Establishment of supportive relationships.*

  o *Teacher–student relationships.* A nurturing relationship with a teacher can have a profound and long-lasting effect on a child's sense of self and emotional well-being. Think back about your own elementary school experience. There is always at least one teacher who stands out as a favorite for many reasons, including his or her nurturing and empathic demeanor, playfulness, or genuine interest in you. When children struggle with anxiety, they often feel out of control, helpless, and powerless over their situations. A supportive relationship with a teacher can offer a comforting sense of safety, models for coping, and assistance with self-regulation until the child is able to better use internal self-regulation skills.

  o *Peer relationships.* Specific friendship qualities such as validation, tolerance, and opportunities for positive interactions are associated with lower levels of general anxiety in children, and specifically with lower levels of social anxiety (Festa & Ginsburg, 2011; LaGreca & Harrison, 2005). Teachers can nurture the development of such qualities by offering opportunities for children to practice them in the classroom. Role plays around active listening, responding to friends in need, and prosocial interactions can be very helpful in allowing children to practice these skills outside the context and pressure of an actual relationship.

o *Teacher–parent relationships.* When supporting children with anxiety disorders, open and frequent communication with parents is important. Parents' reports of their children's distress can assist teachers in their understanding and management of student behaviors. Similarly, teachers may share helpful strategies used in the classroom that parents may use at home to promote consistent practice of coping skills. Jackson is an 8-year-old boy with mild symptoms of anxiety. When nervous or worried, he often complains of stomach pain. At times, he is hesitant to leave his home due to fears that he will develop a stomachache and have to use the bathroom. During a parent-teacher conference, Jackson's mom spoke to his teacher and shared her strategies for managing Jackson's anxiety. Specifically, she said that Jackson worries that others will find out about his stomachaches, so he has developed a special signal to use with is mom when he is feeling nervous or worried. When she sees the signal, they use deep breathing and relaxation and challenge his negative thoughts. Jackson's teacher used this information and, together with Jackson, created a special signal to use at school. Jackson's teacher now uses the same kind of deep breathing and relaxation skills his mom does when he reports stomach upset but also when encouraging him to try new and potentially anxiety-provoking things, such as changing to a new learning center with different peers.

This chapter has offered a review of the development of childhood anxiety, as well as information regarding the manifestation of symptoms in the classroom, diagnosis, treatment, and referral. This notice, give, and nurture section has focused on factors that serve as scaffolds for additional classroom supports for children struggling with anxiety disorders. Specific recommendations for accommodations and interventions are provided in Chapter 4.

CHAPTER THREE

Depressive Disorders

Depression is isolating yourself from the world with constant sadness.

—Terry, fifth-grader

THE PREVIOUS CHAPTER EXAMINED anxiety disorders in childhood. This chapter examines another set of internalizing disorders diagnosed in childhood, the *depressive disorders*. The hallmark of depressive disorders is a core inability to emotionally self-regulate and a persistent presence of sad, empty, or irritable mood (American Psychiatric Association [APA], 2013; Goldman, 2012). As with anxiety, however, there is a different presentation of symptoms in children as compared to adults. Children may have "mood lability, irritability, low frustration tolerance, temper tantrums, somatic complaints, and/or social withdrawal instead of verbalizing feelings of depression" (Birmaher & Brent, 2007, p. 1504). Children who struggle with depressive disorders experience symptoms across a variety of domains, including bodily sensations (e.g., fatigue, headaches), cognitive processes (e.g., difficulties with memory and attention), and behaviors (e.g., withdrawal, tantrums). Symptoms also significantly interfere with learning and social functioning.

In previous classifications (i.e., before the DSM-5), the broader category of mood disorders included both unipolar disorders (low mood only) and bipolar disorders (characterized by oscillation between high mood [mania] and low mood). Under the current DSM-5 nosology, the bipolar disorders are listed under a separate grouping from the unipolar depressive disorders. Childhood depression typically falls under the unipolar classification. Bipolar disorders are generally diagnosed in late adolescence or early adulthood (APA, 2013; Beardslee, Gladstone, & O'Connor, 2012; Gomez, Vance, & Miranjini Gomez, 2014). As the focus of this book is on elementary school children, only the unipolar depressive disorders will be discussed in this chapter, given their more direct relevance to that particular age group.

Depressive Disorders

Mr. Klein referred his student, Nick, a fourth-grader, to the school psychologist for evaluation. Mr. Klein was concerned about Nick's emotional presentation and poor academic progress.

Nick presents as a sad, quiet, and withdrawn child. In the classroom, he is well behaved and respectful, but primarily keeps to himself. He does not raise his hand in class and prefers doing work independently. He often seems disengaged and in his own world. Despite strong cognitive ability, last year, as academic demands increased, so did his resistance to completing assignments. Writing is particularly difficult for him, and work production has decreased significantly. He has not completed any homework for more than four months. In order to complete work, Nick needs someone with him, urging him to finish. He demonstrates very little motivation and drive. Socially, Nick does not have any strong friendships. He does not seek out play or peers, instead preferring to remain alone. At home, his family describes him as content to spend hours in his room alone, either reading or playing with Legos.

During the evaluation with the school psychologist, Nick indicated that he did not like school, but that he went because he had to. Nick reported that even when he tried hard, he felt as if he could not change things. He reported feeling like an inconvenience and often wishing that he were invisible.

The experience of sadness is part of the human condition. Children may experience sad mood in response to a temporary stressor or distress. However, when the stressor is removed, children are able to resume regular functioning and demonstrate an appropriate range of emotions and behaviors. In contrast, children who suffer from depressive disorders experience sustained mood disturbance that significantly impairs their emotional, social, and academic functioning.

As Maughan, Collishaw, and Stringaris (2013) indicate, less than three decades ago, depression was seen as a predominantly adult disorder. Children were considered too developmentally immature, with personalities insufficiently developed, to support the diagnosis of a depressive disorder. Adolescent low mood was considered part of the normal teenage experience, characterized by mood swings and irritability (Maughan et al., 2013). Current research highlights that children can and do experience depressive disorders. Not only do children experience depression, but this experience is a worldwide phenomenon. The World Health Organization (WHO) declared depression the leading cause of disability and the fourth leading cause of premature death worldwide for people ages 5 and older (WHO, 2003; Owens, Stevenson, Hadwin, & Norgate., 2012). One of the primary reasons depression stands out as a major public health problem is that the disorder is often chronic, recurrent, and increasingly harmful (Guerry & Hastings, 2011). Increased chronicity, severity, and impairment; high risk of relapse; and medical morbidity are particularly associated with childhood-onset depression (Beardslee et al., 2012; Brent & Maalouf, 2009; Eckshtain & Gaynor, 2011). Children and adolescents with depressive disorders are also at high risk of substance abuse, legal problems, negative life events, early pregnancy, and poor work functioning (Birmaher & Brent, 2007).

The statistics below highlight key information about the onset and prevalence of childhood depression. Given the chronic nature of depression, especially with earlier onset, as well as its quickly increasing prevalence beginning in middle childhood, early identification is critical.

- By the age of 18, approximately 15% to 25% of adolescents will have experienced a major depressive episode (Garber & Weersing, 2010; Lewinsohn & Essau, 2002, as cited in Auerbach & Ringo Ho, 2012).
- In prepubertal children, the rate of depression is approximately 1% to 2.5%, with similar rates for boys and girls. Average age of onset of major depression is between 11 and 14 years, with rising rates in the early teens and a near doubling of rates from 13 to 14 years (8.4%) to 17 to 18 years (15.4%; Goldman, 2012; Maughan et al., 2013; Merikangas et al., 2010).
- After the onset of puberty, girls have twice the risk of developing depression than boys (Auerbach & Ringo Ho, 2012; Brent & Maalouf, 2009).
- Twelve percent of children will relapse within one year, 40% will

relapse within two years, and 75% will experience a second episode within five years (Beardslee et al., 2012; Birmaher & Brent, 2007; Maughan et al., 2013).

WHAT CONTRIBUTES TO THE DEVELOPMENT OF DEPRESSIVE DISORDERS?

When children struggle with depressive disorders, it is often challenging to identify a primary reason leading to the diagnosis. Depressive disorders have their origins in the interaction between biology and life experiences. There are a number of risk factors that contribute to a child's presentation of depression, including those from the biological, neurobiological, psychological, and social realms (see Figure 3.1), and it is the interaction among those risk factors that leads to the disorder (Beardslee et al., 2012; Garber, 2006). Furthermore, chronic stressors affecting relationships appear to have a greater impact than isolated acute events, especially in females, in the development of depression (Maughan et al., 2013). The broader exploration of risk factors allows not only for a deeper understanding of the child's presentation, but also for more careful treatment planning that targets multiple areas contributing to symptomatology.

Biology

As with anxiety, depressive disorders run in families, with three- to fourfold elevation of rates of depression in the offspring of depressed parents (Maughan et al., 2013). Indeed, parental depression is one of the strongest risk factors for depression in children, with genetic factors accounting for anywhere between 24% and 65% of the major cause for development of childhood depression (Birmaher & Brent, 2007; Garber, 2006; Goldman, 2012). The risk of a child developing depression increases with greater family loading (i.e., multiple family members diagnosed with depression), earlier parental age of onset, and recurrent depression in parents (Brent & Maalouf, 2009). Genetic risk is also associated with the development of multiple disorders. In a 10-year longitudinal study, researchers found that offspring of depressed parents showed increased risk for both anxiety (five times more) and depression (eight times more) when compared to offspring of parents without psychiatric disorders (Dozois, Seeds, & Collins, 2009).

Factors Influencing the Development of Depressive Disorders in Children	
Biology	• Parental depression • Specific genes (e.g., 5-HTTLPR polymorphism)
Neurobiology	• Hypothalamic–pituitary–adrenal (HPA) axis dysfunction • Hormone imbalance
Temperament	• Negative affectivity • Behavioral inhibition • Low effortful control
Psychological Factors	• Global negative representation of self • Low sense of self-efficacy • Ineffective mood repair • Rumination in response to depressed mood • Passive and avoidant problem solving
Social Factors	• Parenting negatively impacted by psychopathology • Family conflict • Bereavement • Sexual abuse • Child maltreatment and neglect • Peer conflict and bullying • Poverty

FIGURE 3.1. Factors influencing the development of depressive disorders in children.

Specific genes have been identified as playing a prominent role in the transmission of depression from one generation to the next. The serotonin transporter gene variant *5-HTTLPR* has received significant attention, with "evidence that one variant of the gene increases risk for depression in those exposed to stressful life events or childhood maltreatment" (Maughan et al., 2013, p. 37). Some research has found that 10- to 12-year-old girls with this variance may be particularly sensitive to the effects of childhood adversity; however, research is still in its infancy, with inconsistent findings (Banducci et al., 2014; Beardslee et al., 2012).

Neurobiology

The hypothalamic–pituitary–adrenal (HPA) axis is one of the major biological stress response systems in humans. Hypothalamic dysfunction is associated with many of the key symptoms of depression, including disturbances in mood, appetite, sleep, and motivation. Additionally, serotonin and norepinephrine, the neurotransmitters associated with the development of depression, also regulate the functioning of the HPA axis (Guerry & Hastings, 2011). The literature on adult depression consistently finds chronic HPA axis hyperactivity and an inability to return to normal functioning following a stressor among these patients. The elevation in cortisol associated with HPA axis hyperactivity is associated with exhaustion and irritability, both hallmark symptoms of depressive disorders (Guerry & Hastings, 2011).

Although there is significantly less research examining HPA dysfunction and depressive disorders in children and adolescents, among youth, differences in HPA axis functioning are found most consistently in the context of increased exposure to psychological stress (Brent & Maalouf, 2009; Guerry & Hastings, 2011). Hankin, Badanes, Abela, and Watamura (2010) investigated HPA axis functioning among preschoolers, third-graders, sixth-graders, and ninth-graders, comparing children without symptoms of depression to those at risk for depression due to dysphoria. They found that among the dysphoric group, preschoolers and third-graders exhibited cortisol hyporeactivity, whereas the ninth-graders displayed cortisol hyperreactivity. Hankin and colleagues (2010) concluded that the developmental switch from a hyporeactive cortisol response to a hyperreactive one was explained by pubertal stage, possibly related to the increase in sex hormones during puberty affecting HPA axis activity (Hankin et al., 2010). The connection between HPA dysfunction and pediatric depression has been further established by findings that elevated levels of basal cortisol predict the onset and recurrence of depression, along with suicidality (Kovacs, Joormann, & Gotlib, 2008). In addition to cortisol level dysregulation, studies of depression in youth have found abnormalities in the secretion of growth hormone and prolactin, indicating that certain hormonal systems may be markers for depressive disorders (Garber, 2006).

Temperament

Temperament refers to aspects of a child's personality that are innate and that have an impact on how he or she responds to change or novelty, how intense his or her reactions to change may be, how persistent he or she may be with a new task; and how much attention he or she devotes to a person, thing, or activity. As with anxiety disorders, temperament characteristics, specifically negative affectivity, behavioral inhibition, and low effortful control, have been linked to depression (DeBoo & Spiering, 2010).

Negative affectivity refers to high levels of emotionality, sadness, withdrawal, and irritability. In contrast, positive affectivity refers to an approach orientation, energy, sociability, joy, and positive involvement with oneself, others, and activities (DeBoo & Spiering, 2010; Garber, 2006). In the face of emotional distress, children with positive affectivity are able to seek others for help, make attempts to change the situation or actively problem-solve, or recall positive experiences and memories to improve their mood and distract themselves from the distressing context. Children with negative affectivity tend to ruminate, or overly focus, on what is sad or wrong about the situation and feel helpless to change things; do not know how to employ positive emotions; and withdraw from others. As Garber (2006) indicates, according to the tripartite model of anxiety and depression, depression is characterized by high levels of negative affectivity and low levels of positive affectivity.

Children with a behaviorally inhibited temperament are shy, fearful, cautious, and resistant to change or new situations, and they tend to withdraw under stress or perceived threat. The behavioral avoidance so conspicuous in this temperamental style is a prominent feature of both anxiety and depressive disorders, but the focus of the avoidance is different. The avoidance that children with anxiety disorders demonstrate centers around feared events and stimuli, whereas the avoidance for children with depression centers around typical interactions and pleasurable activities (Dozois et al., 2009; E. K. Hughes et al., 2010). This type of temperament has been associated with prolonged symptomatology and with elevated rates of depressive disorders in adolescence, early adulthood, and middle adulthood (Dozois et al., 2009).

Effortful control refers to self-regulating processes such as attention focusing, inhibitory control, persistence, and constraint (DeBoo & Spiering, 2010). Children with high levels of effortful control are able to switch attention away from negative emotional experiences to more positive ones, are able to persist in the face of challenge, and are able to control their emotions in a distressful situation. Conversely, children with low levels of effortful control are not able to focus their attention away from their experience of distress, are not able to inhibit impulses to withdraw or escape from a distressing situation, and do not persist in finding ways to increase positive affect. Children with high levels of effortful control have been shown to have more effective coping and better psychological adjustment than children with low levels of effortful control. Furthermore, the combination of high behavioral inhibition and low effortful control has been associated with the highest levels of internalizing symptoms, including depressive disorders (DeBoo & Spiering, 2010; Sportel, Nauta, deHullu, deJong, & Hartman, 2011).

Psychological Factors

During middle childhood (ages 6–12), children develop a more sophisticated and stable sense of who they are. Their views of themselves are based less on concrete characteristics (e.g., "I am a boy," "I like to play baseball") and more on traits (e.g., "I am a good friend," "I am a hard worker"). Also during this developmental period, children begin to integrate past experiences in a way that informs their interpretations and predictions about themselves, others, and the world. For example, Michael, a third-grade student, was asked to create a drawing of an ocean animal for his art class assignment. He carefully studied pictures of the real animals, planned his drawing, and took his time in completing his assignment. His teacher praised him for his effort and hard work. She also submitted his drawing to an art show, and it was chosen to be displayed at a local public setting. Based on this experience, Michael began to form interpretations and predictions about himself, others, and the world that included a view of himself as a good student and artist, the belief that effort is important, the belief that others were there to support and recognize him and his work, and the belief that he had a template for how to work on assignments, problems, and situations in a way that brought positive results. Research indicates that these associations form as early as third grade, and with more stability by the sixth grade (Abela & Hankin, 2008; Auerbach & Ringo Ho, 2012).

How a child views herself, and how she interprets the world and the way in which she responds to it, are related to the development of depression. Children with depressive symptoms have negative views of themselves (e.g., "I'm not as smart as my friends"), perceive others and the world as critical and pessimistic (e.g., "No one is ever going to love me"), and have negative views of the future (e.g., "It doesn't matter what I do; nothing is ever going to change"). These perceptions lead to constant worry about social rejection and avoidance. Additionally, children experience feelings of helplessness, hopelessness, inadequacy, failure, and lack of self-worth (Abela & Hankin, 2008; Auerbach & Ringo Ho, 2012; Beardslee et al., 2012). Importantly, these negative representations of oneself, others, and the world are not specific to a particular situation, but rather are global and persistent. As mentioned earlier, children's attributions and self-definitions change during middle childhood to reflect more stable, traitlike characteristics. As these attributional styles become more entrenched and automatic, approximately at around age 12, there is a higher likelihood that children who already have negative attributions about themselves, the world, and the future will continue to experience negative affect and depressive symptoms.

When a person feels sad, is in a bad mood, or is in distress, there is a natural tendency to find ways to feel better—this is called mood repair. For example, when in a bad mood, children may do things such as play a video game for distraction, find a friend and go play, or talk to a parent or caretaker. All these strategies are employed to reduce feelings of distress and increase soothing and positive mood. Children who are vulnerable to depressive disorders have ineffective mood repair strategies. For example, when in a bad mood, they may withdraw to their rooms to be alone, may repeatedly think about the cause of the bad mood, or may yell at someone, blaming him or her for their distress. Indeed, research has found that poor mood repair is strongly associated with higher levels of self-rated depression in studies of 12- to 18-year-old students (Kovacs & Lopez-Duran, 2012).

Coping is part of emotional self-regulation and involves intentional responses to stress. Children may engage in active, or engagement, coping activities, including seeking help from others, problem solving, changing negative thoughts to positive ones, and distraction. For example, Ben, a fourth-grade student, was quite upset when he received a D on his science test. To manage his emotions, he employed active coping by asking the teacher to help him understand the questions he did not answer correctly; by telling himself that although he received a bad grade on this test, he still had opportunities to improve his overall grade; by asking his friend to study with him for the next test; and by going outside to play basketball until he felt better.

Alternatively, coping can be passive, or reliant on disengagement behaviors. Such coping is characterized by avoidance, blame of self and others, social withdrawal, venting, and rage reactions (Garber, 2006). If in response to his poor grade, Ben had employed passive coping strategies, his reactions might have included blaming the teacher for not giving fair tests, berating himself for being dumb, avoiding any discussion of his performance on the test, going alone into his room and tearing up his test paper, and avoiding offers for help or reassurance. Furthermore, Ben would likely have focused on that negative performance as an indication of his inability to be a good student and the high likelihood that he would fail the class.

Like Ben in the latter scenario, children struggling with depressive disorders are less likely to use active problem-solving strategies and less likely to change their negative thoughts to more positive ones. They also have lower levels of perceived self-efficacy in solving problems and higher levels of avoidance and passivity (Stegge & Meerum Terwogt, 2007). One particularly significant aspect of passive coping in relationship to depressive disorders is rumination. Rumination involves repetitive focusing on emotional distress as well as on the possible causes and consequences of the distress. Children who ruminate frequently are more likely to experience increased severity and duration of depressive symptoms (Abela & Hankin, 2008).

Thus far, the discussion has focused on how psychological vulnerabilities act as risk factors for, or predate, the development of depression. However, there is another perspective suggesting that an initial episode of depression in children may be caused by factors other than psychological vulnerabilities. That is, when a child experiences a severe stressor, his or her coping skills are overwhelmed, and therefore, he or she develops psychological vulnerabilities. Importantly, even after the depressive episode resolves, the child continues to experience the psychological vulnerabilities and is therefore vulnerable to further depressive episodes (Abela & Hankin, 2008). The particular psychological vulnerability of seeing oneself as flawed or deficient following severe stressors or negative events is especially salient in childhood depression. This relationship has been noted in children as young as third-graders (Cohen, Young, & Abela, 2012). The next section discusses the social factors that may tax children's coping and therefore lead to new, or interact with existing, psychological vulnerabilities, contributing to the development of depressive disorders.

Social Factors

Attachment

When children and their caregivers have secure attachment relationships, children can consistently count on their caregivers to provide safety, predictability, and comfort. When emotionally distressed, children can also rely on caregivers to provide help with regulation. When attachment relationships are insecure or disorganized, however, children's sense of safety, control, and emotional regulation are significantly impaired. When attachment relationships are disrupted by inconsistent parenting, children may develop internalizing disorders, including depression. Untreated parental psychopathology may lead to inconsistent parenting. Mothers with severe and chronic depression have insecurely attached children in the range of 55% to 87% across studies (Davies, 2011). Insecure attachment early in childhood has been linked with both anxiety and depression (Garber & Weersing, 2010; Madigan, Atkinson, Laurin, & Benoit, 2013).

Parenting

According to the Institute of Medicine, at least 15 million children are living with a depressed parent (Beardslee et al., 2012). Depression in parents presents an increased risk for depression in their children through both genetic and environmental influences (Brent & Maalouf, 2009). From a relational perspective, depression in parents may impact children through modeling of negative attributions; inconsistency in parenting; high levels of criticism, shaming, and rejection toward children; lack of physical and emotional involvement; and parent–child conflict. All these factors have been associated with increased depressive disorders in children (Abela & Hankin, 2008; Auerbach & Ringo

Ho, 2012; Beardslee et al., 2012; Brent & Maalouf, 2009; Burkhouse, Uhrlass, Stone, Knopik, & Gibb, 2012; E. M. Cummings, Cheung, & Davies, 2013; Dozois et al., 2009; Garber & Weersing, 2010; Madigan et al., 2013; Maughan et al., 2013). It is important to note; however, that parents who struggle with depression can be warm, effective, and wonderful parents. The factors impacting parenting listed below are typically the result of undiagnosed or untreated psychopathology.

The modeling of negative attributions (e.g., negative outcomes due to personal factors, low self-efficacy) and coping responses (e.g., withdrawal, rumination) may be one way in which children of depressed parents develop negative attributions themselves. Research has found that offspring of depressed mothers tend to exhibit negative attributional styles, greater hopelessness, and lower perceived self-worth than children of mothers without depression (Dozois et al., 2009). Beardslee and colleagues (2012) also found that among children ages 6 to 14, those who exhibited negative attributions and inferences were more likely to report increased depressive symptoms after an increase in their parents' depressive symptoms.

The quality and nature of parent-child interactions have been found to be of particular salience in children's development of depressive symptoms and disorders. Interactions between depressed mothers and their children tend to be characterized by high levels of inconsistency and criticism (Dozois et al., 2009). Criticism, in particular, has been found to be strongly associated with the onset, recurrence, and prolongation of depressive episodes in childhood (Brent & Maalouf, 2009). In a study conducted by Burkhouse and colleagues (2012), the researchers found that "maternal criticism predicts depression onset in children above and beyond that contributed by maternal depression" (p. 775). Chronic criticism may increase the frequency and intensity of children's negative affect and interfere with the development of emotional regulation skills.

Criticism is associated with shaming and rejection. Madigan and colleagues (2013) found that children who are shamed by their parents may be especially vulnerable to internalizing negative labels (e.g., *stupid, bad*) and therefore to developing self-criticism and shame. Following experiences of shaming and rejection, children may come to expect such treatment and as a result react to others in an antagonistic manner. Alternatively, children may perceive others as hostile and unsupportive, leading to passive withdrawal and internalization of negative affect (Garber & Weersing, 2010; Madigan et al., 2013). Both response patterns will likely elicit conflict, and parent–child conflict is associated with greater internalizing symptoms and subsequent depressive disorders (Auerbach & Ringo Ho, 2012).

The significant relationship between maternal and child mental health is highlighted by the direct influence one has on the other. Evidence suggests that treatment of maternal depression can help alleviate depression in children. Treatment studies of mothers struggling with depression showed that remission of maternal depression was associated with a significant improvement in children's depression, whereas persistence of maternal depression was associated with new onset of children's depression (Maughan et al., 2013).

Though the majority of research has focused on maternal depression, recent data indicate that both fathers' and mothers' depressive symptoms can impact child adjustment (E. M. Cummings et al., 2013). E. M. Cummings and colleagues (2013) found that "negative emotional expressiveness in the family by mothers and fathers were shown to both play roles in children's appraisals of security" (p. 705). Furthermore, they found that this connection was true even for young children, noting a pathway between parental depressive symptoms when children were in kindergarten and changes in children's internalizing symptoms in second grade (E. M. Cummings et al., 2013).

Adverse Life Events

As indicated in the previous chapter, adverse life events in childhood can have a significant and long-lasting negative impact on children's emotional health. A plethora of studies have found a strong association between adverse life events (e.g., family conflict, bereavement, sexual abuse, child maltreatment and neglect, peer conflict, bullying, poverty) and almost all mental disorders, including childhood depressive disorders (APA, 2013; Beesdo-Baum & Knappe, 2012; National Scientific Council on the Developing Child, 2012). All of these factors can lead either to subsyndromal levels of symptoms (i.e., child develops symptoms of a depressive disorder, but not enough to warrant a full diagnosis) or to a full disorder. In children and adolescents, subsyndromal levels of depressive symptoms significantly increase the risk of having a full major depressive episode (Garber, 2006). The worst risk is for those children who experience multiple adverse life events and/or prolonged exposure (Goldman, 2012).

In childhood, family disturbances of any kind, such as divorce, abandonment, or recurrent interparental conflict, can lead children to experience increased levels of sadness and helplessness (Abela & Hankin, 2008). In the context of divorce, it is often not the actual divorce that predicts how a child will adjust, but rather the level of marital conflict and acrimony the children witness and experience, with higher levels of conflict leading to poorer child outcomes (Beardslee et al., 2012).

One of the most traumatic family disturbances that can occur in a child's life is the loss of a parent. Children who lose a parent may have numerous and acute impairments, including major depression, suicidal ideation, and posttraumatic stress disorder. Children's outcomes are particularly severe if the parent dies traumatically (e.g., by suicide) or if the surviving parent has high levels of psychopathology (Beardslee et al., 2012; Brent & Maalouf, 2009).

One of the strongest predictors for childhood depression is maltreatment. The presence of childhood maltreatment, including sexual, emotional, and physical abuse, is associated with a two- to fivefold increase in the risk for depressive disorder (Beardslee et al., 2012; Gonzalez et al., 2012). Maltreatment is also associated with a poorer clinical course of depression, including earlier illness onset, greater symptom severity, and comorbidity (Tunnard et al., 2013). Once children endure an experience of maltreatment, they become more sensitive to adverse life events and therefore at higher risk for subsequent mental illness. That is, for these children, lower levels of acute life events trigger the onset of depressive episodes due to the persistent chronic stressors they have experienced in the past (Beardslee et al., 2012).

Disturbances in social development and peer relationships may also pose a risk for the development of childhood depression. Among children and adolescents, lower levels of social support and perceived rejection by peers are associated with higher levels of depressive symptoms (Auerbach, Bigda-Peyton, Eberhart, Webb, & Ringo Ho, 2011; Garber, 2006). Peer victimization has also been associated with depressive symptoms, particularly when there are loss and humiliation events (Auerbach et al., 2011; Galand & Hospel, 2013; Beesdo-Baum & Knappe, 2012).

Finally, exposure to poverty has a deep impact on children's current and long-term mental health outcomes. Results from a longitudinal study spanning 21 years revealed that children who were exposed to family poverty were more likely to report depression and anxiety in adolescence and young adulthood (Najman et al., 2010). Factors resulting from poverty, including limited access to medical and mental health care, limited resources, and burden on the family, likely all contribute to producing a state of pervasive distress for children.

HOW DOES DEPRESSION MANIFEST IN ELEMENTARY SCHOOL CHILDREN?

This section describes the manifestation of symptoms of depressive disorders in elementary school children. Symptoms manifest across several areas, including in children's emotional experience, how they

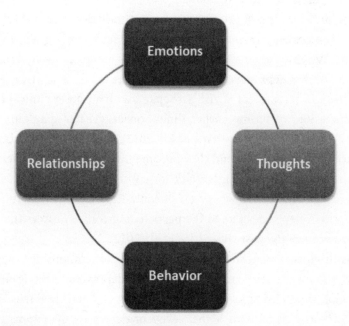

FIGURE 3.2. Depression has a direct impact on children's emotions, thoughts, behaviors, and relationships.

think about and interpret situations, how they behave in response to these interpretations, and how they function in relationships (see Figure 3.2). While the constellation of symptoms is difficult to tease apart, each domain is discussed separately to facilitate an understanding of what symptoms might look like in the school setting. It is important to note that the presence of individual symptoms is not sufficient to warrant a diagnosis. It is only when children exhibit numerous symptoms, over a prolonged period of time (e.g., two weeks or longer), and those symptoms impact social and/or academic functioning, that one should consider the presence of a depressive disorder.

Emotions

The symptom presentation can vary somewhat among younger children, but the core disturbances of dysphoria (a state of feeling unwell, unhappy, distressed, and anxious) and anhedonia (an inability to experience pleasure) are the most reliable symptoms. This overall sense of unhappiness can feel overwhelming and constantly intrudes into children's experiences. Recall that in young children, and even in adolescents, the dysphoria may be manifested as irritability. Importantly, though, children feel distressed, as though something is just profoundly wrong and they cannot escape the sadness. Some describe themselves as "broken" or "empty." The depression can lead to a sense of lack of wholeness or place in the world, with children feeling lost and alone. These feelings are also directly tied to an inability to experience pleasure. Especially in younger children, the anhedonia may be reported as persistent "boredom." Children who reject participating in activities or engaging with others because those things are "boring" may be expressing that they are having a hard time finding pleasure or fun in any activities or interactions with others.

Children without depressive disorders can experience dysphoria and irritability. However, these feelings are typically in response to a specific situation. For example, Luke (8 years old) was very sad when his pet hamster died. Luke was teary when he found him, when he and his family buried the hamster in the backyard, and for the rest of the day. When his younger sister tried to talk to him, he was cranky and asked to be left alone. In the evening, Luke's mom suggested that the family have a picnic in the living room where they could share pictures of the hamster and their favorite stories about him. Although still sad about the loss, Luke was able to engage in this family activity and even laughed while remembering the "cool tricks" his hamster could perform. Over the course of the next few days, Luke still had some moments when he felt sad when remembering his hamster, but this did not interfere with his ability to engage with peers or schoolwork.

In contrast, for children who struggle with depressive disorders, the experience of distress, unhappiness, and lack of pleasure is pervasive, intruding into all areas of functioning. Molly, an 11-year-old girl, was diagnosed with persistent depressive disorder. Molly's teacher was concerned about her lack of engagement in class, inconsistent completion of work, and withdrawal from peers, so she asked Molly to stay with her one day during recess to better understand how she might be able to help this student. When talking to her teacher, Molly reported not wanting to play in recess because everything was "so boring." She said, "The other kids just don't understand me, and anyway, they probably wouldn't want to hang out with me." Molly said she felt tired and had a hard time paying attention in class and was sure she was the "worst student" in the classroom. Molly told her teacher that she had tried to do some of her homework but had a hard time and couldn't do it. She further said, "No matter what I do, I can't figure it out." When Molly's teacher asked her about what she did outside school and how things were at home, Molly responded, "Nobody really understands me. My sister is always on my case and says I'm doing this on purpose to get attention." Molly indicated that her parents didn't understand what was going on, so they "keep asking me and I don't know what to say, so I just go to my room."

For children struggling with depression, one particularly distinctive feature of their emotional experience is a profound sense of shame. When faced with an accident, transgression, or negative situation, children with depression immediately conclude that it was somehow their fault. In other words, they believe negative situations or outcomes are the results of their perceived inefficiencies. The experience of shame is a combination of internal and external shame. With internal shame, the focus of the blame is on the self and perceived flaws. Internal shame is associated with high levels of self-criticism (e.g., "It's all my fault," "I'm so boring that everyone is having a bad time"). External shame relates to children's perception that others view them in a negative and judgmental light. Children come to believe that others perceive them as flawed, annoying, and a nuisance. External shame is associated with withdrawal behavior (e.g., "If I just stay in my room, they won't have to deal with me"). As a result of this shame, children also experience intense guilt, believing that "everything is my fault," or "if it wasn't for me, things would be better at home." This guilt is unfounded and out of proportion to actual situations. Children may also feel guilty for something in which they had no direct involvement or responsibility, such as parental divorce.

Cassie, a 12-year-old girl, wrote in her journal:

> After these past few days I have come to a conclusion, well more like a question, why do I always screw up? There have been so many times this week where I have messed things up. I almost ruined mom's computer, and I dropped a grocery bag that had eggs and a jar of spaghetti sauce in it, I was only trying to help. And I left the stove on too. What am I going to do? I make everyone's and my life miserable.
>
> P.S. I am so sorry Mom, Dad, Mark, and Jen for having to live with such a screw up.

Another area of difficulty for children with depressive disorders is the inability to decrease the experience of negative affect and to increase the experience of positive affect in order to regulate mood. When experiencing distress, children without mood disorders seek out ways to decrease the negative thoughts and feelings they may experience by using strategies such as talking to a parent or a friend, going outside to play, listening to music, or reminding themselves that they are able to manage problems and that in past situations everything has turned out fine. In this way, children seek to decrease the negative feelings and increase the positive feelings by engaging in soothing thoughts and pleasurable activities. In contrast, children with depressive disorders lack the ability to engage in more positive, action-focused coping and therefore stay "stuck" in the experience of negative feelings.

Emotions that children with anxiety disorders may exhibit include:

- Sadness
- Irritability
- Hopelessness ("Nothing will ever work out for me")
- Helplessness ("It doesn't matter if I try; I can't change anything")
- Worries and fears
- Lack of pleasure or interest in usual activities (may be reported as boredom)
- Shame
- Guilt

As noted earlier, emotions include a child's affective state as well as his or her physical responses. Depression hurts—children and adults who struggle with the disorder report a pain that is real and not made up or "in their heads." School-age children with depressive disorders will likely exhibit a number of body symptoms and will frequently present to the nurse's office.

Somatic complaints that children with depression may exhibit include:

- Headaches
- Stomachaches
- Chest pain
- Feeling like it is difficult to breathe or catch one's breath
- Rapid heartbeat
- Body aches
- Restlessness
- Low energy or exhaustion
- Nausea
- Gastrointestinal distress
- Muscle tension or pain

Thoughts

Negative thoughts and thinking traps characterize the thoughts of children struggling with depressive disorders. Because of these errors in thinking, children misinterpret situations, events, and interactions, leading to increased feelings of anxiety and sadness. Furthermore, the children make internal (e.g., "There is something wrong with me"), stable (e.g., "There is nothing I can do and this will never change"), and global (e.g., "I mess everything up") attributions for their perceived failures, leading to a sense of hopelessness (Garber & Weersing, 2010).

There are specific cognitive distortions, or thinking errors, that are associated with depression in school-age children (Goldman, 2012; Mennuti & Christner, 2012). While some thinking errors are present in children without mental illnesses, it is the high frequency, pervasiveness, and debilitating nature of these thoughts that characterize children with depressive disorders. The following is a list of the most commonly noted cognitive distortions:

- *Dichotomous or all-or-none thinking.* Things are either black or white, with no gradient or in-between options. A person may be viewed as good or evil, or a child may consider himself as a good baseball player or a terrible player.
- *Overgeneralization.* The child sees things as characteristic of how things will always be, rather than specific to a particular situation. This cognitive distortion is characterized by the frequent use of words such as *always* or *never*. A child may think, "I was picked last for the group project. I'm always going to be left out and unwanted."
- *Mind reading.* When children engage in mind reading, they are convinced that they know what others are thinking about them. For example, a child may think, "I know that Tess hates me. She wishes I wasn't in the class."
- *Catastrophizing.* When children engage in catastrophizing, they come to expect the worst possible outcome that will involve highly negative effects and intolerable distress. They may indicate that "everything is a total disaster" or may refuse to even try something for fear of complete distress, humiliation, or embarrassment.
- *Disqualifying the positive.* Because children with depressive disorders hold negative self-views that are internal, stable, and global, they come to believe that positive events occur purely by chance and are only temporary. For example, they may say, "I got that bas-

ket only because I was lucky," or "Tim picked me to be his science partner only because the teacher made him."

• *Personalization.* Children attribute situations to something they did wrong or to some faulty personal attribute. This occurs even when the situation has nothing at all to do with them. For example, June's mom seemed preoccupied and stressed in the morning. Her boss had called that morning and told her there was an emergency at the office and that she needed to come in immediately. Upon seeing her mom's facial expression and apparent distress, June assumed it was because of something she herself had done. Even after her mom told her about the phone call from work, June worried that her mom was just making that up to make her feel better.

• *Labeling.* Children may use global labels to describe themselves, rather than finding descriptors associated with a particular situation. For example, typically developing children may say, "I'm not a great student in math, but I'm really good in science. I'm also good at hockey, but not so great in volleyball." These labels of "good student" or "not so great" are related to specific situations. In contrast, children with depressive disorders may say "I'm a terrible student" or "I'm a bad friend" as general labels regardless of outcomes associated with specific situations.

• *Should/must statements.* Children may use *should* or *must* statements to describe how they or others should act. For example, they might say, "I should not show anger to anyone" or "People should always say sorry when they do something wrong." While having general expectations for behavior is not pathological, it is the inflexibility associated with these expectations that characterizes mood disorders. Also characteristic of mood disorders is the guilt and distress that follow not meeting such high expectations. For example, if a child's *should* statement is "I should always be nice" and he snaps at a friend due to the irritability associated with depression, he may become additionally distressed, thinking, "I shouldn't have snapped at him. I can't even do that right. I'm such a bad friend."

Children with depression also experience high levels of worry and anxiety. This pervasive sense of worry often leads to negative repetitive thinking, called rumination. Children who ruminate may continuously focus on past or present events, becoming stuck in the negative feelings and worries. They may continuously replay a negative interaction and ask themselves questions such as, "Why did this happen to me? Why do bad things always seem to happen? Why can't I feel better?" This replaying of the situation focuses on the negative feelings and lacks any active problem solving. Dozois and colleagues (2009) found that rumination is consistently associated with depression, as well as with longer and more severe mood, poorer problem solving, and excessive support seeking.

Another entry in Cassie's journal demonstrates the negative thinking associated with depression:

School is alright. The homework every night is a nightmare. What if I don't get it right? My friends seem to be better but I don't know if they're telling me the truth. I don't understand how people can tell me I am pretty when no guys like me, I hate it when people say that . . . I guess there are just too many bad things about me. What is wrong with me? How come nobody likes me?

Depression also has an impact on children's thoughts via deficits in cognitive-processing abilities. For example, children have difficulties with memory, processing, problem-solving skills, impulsivity, and attention problems (Mennuti & Christner, 2012). Given the similarity of these symptoms to those associated with learning disabilities, parents or teachers may initially erroneously attribute a child's difficulties to a learning issue rather than to an emotional one.

Finally, children may also have thoughts of suicide. These thoughts are associated with severe symptoms of depression and are significant risk factors for suicide attempts or completions. The special topics section discusses suicide in greater detail.

Thoughts that children with depression may exhibit include:

• Negative and abusive self-talk ("I'm not as smart as everyone else," "I'm just a burden on everyone")
• Cognitive errors

- Rumination
- Hopelessness
- Difficulty with organizing thoughts; high distractibility
- Thoughts of suicide

Behaviors

Regulating behavior is a difficult task for children with depressive disorders. The internal distress may manifest in withdrawal and isolation, in agitation and irritability, or in a mix of both. In young children, aggression is positively correlated with depression (Min et al., 2012). Some children may have decreased energy and may seem slowed in their responses and actions. For some children struggling with depression, engaging in typical routines such as taking a shower and getting dressed may feel exhausting. Their emotional energy is drained, and this, in turn, affects their physical energy.

Changes in eating and sleeping may occur, but are not consistently noted across all children. Increased appetite and weight gain should not be treated as indicators of depression in children or adolescents, given the many developmentally appropriate reasons for weight gain during this time. A decrease in appetite, weight loss, and failure to make expected weight gains are more indicative of the possible presence of a mood disorder (Cole et al., 2012; Kitts & Goldman, 2012). Children may also demonstrate a disruption in their sleeping patterns, with difficulty falling asleep or staying asleep, sleeping too much, or difficulty waking in the morning. These behavioral manifestations interact with one another, causing a cycle of increased difficulties and negative impact, which in turn further exacerbates symptoms of depression. For example, if a child is not eating well, she will not have appropriate energy to engage in routine activities. She may also have difficulty falling asleep, as she has too many negative thoughts and worries and has a hard time "shutting them off." The decreased energy due to lack of eating and sleeping contributes to poor academic performance. Poor academic performance, in turn, leads to more negative thoughts and increased emotional distress.

Behaviors that children with depression may exhibit include:

- Irritability ("short fuse," being quick to anger, being "mean" to others)
- Acting-out behavior (being rebellious, breaking rules, being defiant)
- Tantrums (particularly in younger children)
- Aggression (physical fighting or emotionally abusive behavior)
- Frequent blaming or accusation of others
- Isolation or withdrawal from friends
- Changes in appetite and weight (particularly decrease in appetite or weight loss)
- Changes in sleeping patterns
- Withdrawal from activities that were previously enjoyed
- Refusal to participate in family activities (not eating with the family, not going to family outings)
- Asking to go to the nurse's office due to multiple somatic complaints
- Asking to call parents to be taken home from school
- Crying
- Monotonic or quiet speech
- Whining
- Difficulties with transitions
- High sensitivity to perceived criticism
- Seeking frequent reassurance or assistance
- Difficulty concentrating
- Complaining of not being able to remember or understand new information

Relationships

The persistent feelings of sadness, irritability, and hopelessness associated with depression take a significant toll on children's individual functioning. Depression can also drastically impact children's relationships. Children struggling with depressive disorders have poorer communication and problem-solving skills; are more passive, irritable, and withdrawn; and are less supportive in friendships than children without depression (Garber, 2006). These characteristics often lead to neglect and rejection by peers. Peer relationships are pivotal for development during middle childhood, and a lack of peer engagement can have devastating emotional effects.

Recall that one of the hallmark symptoms of depression in childhood is irritability. Irritable mood, conflict, and acting out are other factors that impact children's ability to establish and maintain friendships. A negative cycle ensues, as the irritability associated with depression causes peers to distance themselves from the child with depression. This separation and rejection then lead to feelings of loneliness and lack of support, in turn increasing depressive symptoms (Birmaher & Brent, 2007). This cycle can also take place in the home, with increased conflict between the child, parents, and siblings.

Finally, the teacher–student relationship can also be impacted when children struggle with depression. The time before a child is diagnosed may be particularly challenging, as there may be a pattern of inconsistent behavior and academic performance that seems confusing within the classroom setting. Symptoms may also be confusing from a diagnostic perspective, as they might mirror those seen in other childhood disorders, including attention deficit hyperactivity disorder (ADHD) or oppositional defiant disorder (ODD).

Mrs. Smith was talking after school with colleagues. She mentioned that she was exhausted and that this group of third-graders was one of the most difficult she had had in her 10 years of teaching. One boy in particular, Alex, had significant behavioral issues, and in turn seemed to get others in class "all riled up." Either that, or Mrs. Smith had to spend most of her time trying to manage Alex's behaviors, leaving other students unattended. Alex was well known to staff in the school, as he had had difficulties since he began kindergarten. Testing at that time revealed a learning disability in reading. Behaviorally, he presented as an angry, defiant child. He had poor attention and concentration, refused to complete his work, was argumentative with adults and peers, and seemed unfazed by punishments. Socially, he could be quite hostile with other students, interrupting play or destroying materials. He did not seem to have much awareness of how his behavior impacted others. Alex generally did not establish close connections with adults in the school, but when he did, those relationships appeared strong and meaningful to him. With respect to his family, Mrs. Smith had met only his mom, and she had heard from other teachers who had Alex's siblings in their classrooms that the children came from a "chaotic" family environment.

As symptoms of depression disrupt functioning across multiple settings, supportive relationships that involve close communication and models for healthy coping are critical. For example, greater classmate support is associated with better clinical, academic, and personal adjustment in children (Auerbach et al., 2011). Strong student–teacher and parent–teacher relationships are also associated with positive child outcomes. Strategies for assisting children in the classroom are presented in Chapter 5.

HOW DOES CULTURE PLAY A ROLE IN THE MANIFESTATION OF CHILDREN'S DEPRESSION SYMPTOMS?

The symptom expression of childhood depression presented thus far follows a mental health disorder conceptualization largely guided by Western views and philosophies. Given the rich diversity of our population, however, one must also consider cultural differences in perceptions and approaches to mental illness that may influence how mood symptoms are expressed and interpreted (Varela & Hensley-Maloney, 2009). As Postert and colleagues (2012) indicate, the "categorization of emotional states and their subsequent verbal report is deeply embedded in culture-specific systems of meaning" (p. 186). Cultural differences are also observed in the behavioral manifestation of mood symptoms.

Cultural stigma associated with psychological illness may lead children and families to seek help for somatic symptoms, which are socially understood and accepted, rather than for symptoms of depression (Anderson & Mayes, 2010; Stewart, Simmons, & Habibpour, 2012). Among children, one of the most consistent findings in terms of cultural differences is somatic symptom presentation. Studies have found highest rates of somatic symptoms among Latino and Asian preadolescent children (Anderson & Mayes, 2010; Stein, Gonzalez, & Huq, 2012). For example, Chinese children with depressed mood do not report feeling sad, but may instead express boredom and symptoms of pain, dizziness, and fatigue (Postert et al., 2012).

Data from a study conducted in middle schools revealed cultural differences in children's affective and behavioral symptom endorsement. Specifically, among the study participants, African American preadolescents reported increased anger, aggression, and irritability with depression. Asian American students reported sad mood. Latino American youth endorsed diminished pleasure and energy, low self-esteem, crying, and difficulty concentrating (Anderson & Mayes, 2010).

As noted in Chapter 2, one must consider different social factors impacting minority populations that have a direct influence on their psychological functioning. Immigration-related factors include traumatic events (e.g., loss, separation, abuse) endured during travel into the United States, undocumented status, and poverty. These factors have been linked to significant anxiety and depression in children and adolescents (Stein et al., 2012). Perceived discrimination and racism are further associated with anxiety and depression symptoms (Martinez, Polo, & Smith Carter, 2012; Telzer & Vasquez Garcia, 2009).

WHAT ARE THE DIFFERENT KINDS OF DEPRESSIVE DISORDERS DIAGNOSED IN CHILDHOOD?

The American Psychiatric Association's *Diagnostic and Statistical Manual of Mental Disorders* (DSM) is the standard classification of mental disorders that mental health clinicians rely on for diagnosis. The most recent edition of the DSM is the DSM-5, and it is the depressive disorders listed in this edition that are identified below (APA, 2013). Common to these disorders is "the presence of sad, empty, or irritable mood, accompanied by somatic and cognitive changes that significantly affect the individual's capacity to function" (APA, 2013, p. 155). In this new classification, the depressive disorders are separated from bipolar and related disorders. Other disorders are listed in this general category and include premenstrual dysphoric disorder, substance/medication-induced depressive disorder, and unspecified depressive disorder. The aforementioned diagnoses are extremely rare among school-age children. Therefore, only the depressive disorders that most typically affect children and adolescents are described below.

• *Disruptive mood dysregulation disorder.* This new diagnosis is applied to children up to 12 years of age who present with "persistent irritability and frequent episodes of extreme behavioral dyscontrol" (APA, 2013, p. 155). As they mature, children with this presentation typically develop unipolar depression with or without anxiety, rather than bipolar disorder. Therefore, this new diagnosis attempts to capture this particular symptom presentation as well as reduce the potential overdiagnosis and treatment of bipolar disorder in children (APA, 2013).

The core feature of this disorder is chronic, severe, and persistent irritability. Children with disruptive mood dysregulation disorder have frequent temper outbursts that can be verbal or behavioral. The behavioral tantrum may include aggression against oneself, others, or property. The tantrums typically result from feelings of anger or frustration. When not exhibiting tantrums, children's behavior is characterized by a chronic irritable or angry mood that is present for most of the day, nearly every day, and is noticeable by others who interact with the child, including family, peers, and teachers. Children receive this diagnosis when the irritability and impairment in functioning have occurred for at least 12 months. What markedly distinguishes this diagnosis from bipolar disorder is the absence of a manic or hypomanic episode (APA, 2013). A diagnosis is made only if the child is between 7 and 18 years of age, and rates are expected to be higher in males and school-age children than in females and middle-school- and high-school-age youth (APA, 2013).

Possible manifestations in the classroom:

o What characterizes children with disruptive mood dysregulation is chronic irritability and anger. Therefore, their presentation will be consistent, without remission, for at least one calendar year. This indicates that teachers will see this presentation for the duration of the academic year, and that this will likely persist into the following academic year.
o Children will demonstrate extremely low frustration tolerance; therefore, situations like receiving feedback or correction, perceiving inability to complete an assignment, or receiving redirection of behavior will likely trigger a negative response or tantrum. Children may throw books, rip papers,

yell at peers or the teacher, hide under desks, get up from their seats and yell, or simply seem out of control behaviorally.

o Children struggling with this disorder have significantly impaired academic and social functioning. They have extreme difficulty participating in group activities and in play, and have trouble initiating or sustaining friendships.

o Extremely low frustration tolerance may lead to blaming others for unfair play or treatment, abruptly ending games, yelling at peers, or frequent fighting.

• *Major depressive disorder.* The essential feature of a major depressive episode is "a period of at least 2 weeks during which there is either depressed mood or the loss of pleasure in nearly all activities" (APA, 2013, p. 163). In children and adolescents, the hallmark may be irritability rather than sadness, though sad mood may also present. Other symptoms include changes in eating and sleeping, restlessness or decreased activity, difficulty concentrating and making decisions, fatigue or decreased energy, and recurrent thoughts of death, including of suicide. The symptoms must persist for most of the day, nearly every day, for at least two weeks, and denote a clear change from previous functioning. Loss of interest and pleasure is extremely common, and children may, for example, not engage in activities they previously used to enjoy. For children, the sleep disturbances may include difficulty falling asleep, or prolonged sleep episodes with difficulty waking. The weight changes in childhood most directly related to mood disorders are failure to make expected weight gain.

A sense of worthlessness or guilt is also typically seen, with unrealistic negative evaluations of oneself or preoccupations with past failures or negative interactions. Children may blame themselves for events in their lives (e.g., parents' divorce) or may feel they are the cause of others' distress or discomfort. If it is more severe in nature, the sense of blame may be delusional (e.g., the child may blame himself for world hunger). There are many cognitive symptoms that will interfere with functioning, including difficulties with memory, problem solving, concentrating, and decision making.

There are many specifiers that are used in recording the full diagnostic picture of the disorder that indicate severity, predominant symptoms, and context (e.g., mild, moderate, or severe; with anxious distress; with atypical features; with seasonal features). People diagnosed with major depressive episode may also develop psychotic features. The specifiers are particularly important in developing treatment plans.

Possible manifestations in the classroom:

- o Manifestation in the classroom correlates with symptom severity.
- o For example, some children with mild symptoms may function normally in the classroom. However, due to the additional effort they must employ during the school day, their parents may report that after school the children "crash," taking long naps or being unable to do much for the evening.
- o Children with more significant symptoms may demonstrate a decrease in grades precipitated by the cognitive symptoms (e.g., difficulties with concentration, problem solving, and processing). Also due to cognitive symptoms, children may struggle with writing, essays, or assignments that require sustained concentration, processing speed, and memory recall.
- o Children may also appear either restless (fidgety, unable to sit still) or tired and fatigued. For children with loss of energy, even simple transitions may seem to take double the usual time and effort.
- o Children may appear sleepy or to be daydreaming or not concentrating, and they may put their heads down on their desks.
- o There may be complaints and what seems like whining over unexpected changes or requests.
- o Children may tend to take even constructive criticisms or redirections quite personally.
- o Children may shy away from group projects, as feelings of guilt and/or worthlessness may lead them to think they will ruin the assignment or be the cause of peers' failure.
- o While some children may seem tearful, others may seem more cranky and irritable.

○ Externalizing behavior such as defiance, oppositionality, agitation, or disruptiveness may also be seen in children with depression. Such students may present with an agitated depression that features irritability and acting-out behaviors. They may blame others for perceived injustices, initiate arguments, or refuse to comply with rules.

○ Children struggling with major depression may make frequent requests to see the school nurse, reporting stomachaches, headaches, body aches and pains, nausea, or general fatigue.

• *Persistent depressive disorder (dysthymia).* This new diagnosis is a consolidation of the chronic major depressive disorder and dysthymic disorders found in the previous edition of the DSM, the DSM-IV. The essential feature of persistent depressive disorder is "a depressed mood that occurs for most of the day, for more days than not" for at least one year in children and adolescents, and there are no periods longer than two months without symptoms (APA, 2013, p. 169). As with major depressive disorder, mood can be primarily irritable in children and adolescents. Early onset of this disorder is defined in those who are diagnosed prior to age 21. Persistent depressive disorder often has an early onset and a chronic course. Symptoms include changes in appetite/weight, sleep disturbances, low energy and fatigue, low self-esteem, difficulty making decisions, poor concentration, and feelings of hopelessness (APA, 2013).

Possible manifestations in the classroom:

○ Given the chronicity of low mood associated with this disorder, some children may not be easily identified initially, especially if they do not pose any behavioral problems.

○ Children may have difficulty experiencing and maintaining positive affect, may feel "stuck" in the negative affect, may be sensitive to perceived criticism and rejection, may appear anxious, and may present with overall low self-esteem.

○ Children who struggle with pervasive low mood may experience difficulties with transitions, additional demands, or stressors, and may seem overall "down," speaking in a monotone voice.

○ Engaging in play and activities that require sustained activity and engagement with peers may be difficult. Therefore, children with such mood disturbances may withdraw and isolate themselves from peers.

Special Topics

NONSUICIDAL SELF-INJURY

Nonsuicidal self-injury (NSSI) is defined as deliberately harming oneself in the absence of suicidal intent (Guerry, Reilly, & Prinstein, 2011). NSSI includes repetitive and impulsive acts, including cutting, burning, picking or interfering with a wound, punching or hitting oneself or objects, inserting objects into one's skull, and hair pulling (Guan, Fox, & Prinstein, 2012). Nearly 7% of middle-school-age children and 14% of high-school-age adolescents have engaged in NSSI at some point (Guerry, Reilly, & Prinstein, 2011). Self-injury is a maladaptive coping mechanism used to relieve or deal with painful feelings and is generally not a suicide attempt. The injurer usually engages in self-harming behaviors in an effort to temporarily relieve the intense emotional pain evoked by distressing feelings such as hurt, sadness, disappointment, rejection, humiliation, loss, and abuse. Other reasons for self-injurious behaviors include (Angelkovska, Houghton, & Hopkins, 2012; Guan et al., 2012; Guerry, Reilly, & Prinstein, 2011; Reilly, 2011):

• To punish oneself
• To relieve tension
• To feel "real" by feeling pain or seeing evidence of injury
• To feel numb, calm, or at peace
• To experience euphoric feelings (associated with release of endorphins)
• To communicate pain, anger, or other emotions to others
• To nurture oneself (through the process of wound healing)
• To distract oneself from aversive rumination

The majority of the research on NSSI examines patterns in adolescent and adult populations, with relatively little being available on the NSSI patterns of preadolescent children. Researchers in England examined hospital data related to NSSI in youth ages 15 and under and found that the youngest patient with NSSI was 8 years old. A United States–based study of over three thousand 12- to 15-year-olds found a prevalence of NSSI of 3.7%, with higher rates among females. As with depressive disorders, the existence of NSSI is a global phenomenon. In a study examining data from over thirty thousand 14- to 17-year-olds from Australia, Belgium, England, Hungary, Ireland, the Netherlands, and Norway, 13.5% of females and 4.3% of males reported an episode of NSSI during their lifetime (Angelkovska et al., 2012). Negative affect and depressive symptoms appear to be among the strongest predictors of self-harming behaviors in children.

NSSI represents maladaptive attempts to cope with extreme distress. While initially suicidal thoughts and/or behaviors may not be present, NSSI is a significant risk factor for suicidal behaviors. There are high rates of comorbidity between suicidal behaviors and NSSI, and risk of suicide increases with a history of NSSI (Angelkovska et al., 2012). In a longitudinal study of the relationship between NSSI and suicide, Whitlock and colleagues (2013) found that NSSI preceded or co-occurred with suicide in 61.6% of cases. NSSI also heightened risk for later suicide independent of shared risk factors (Whitlock et al., 2013).

SUICIDE

> I don't care if anything happens to me, you know why? I think
> I know. I will never be happy. I can see the things I need and
> want to be happy but I will never have them because of who I
> am . . . because of who I am I will ruin it. It's like I can't handle
> life . . . everything makes me feel bad and I just fall apart. I always
> think everything is my fault and I just know I'm disappointing
> everyone . . . it's like people have to DEAL with me and I feel
> bad . . . I feel like a burden on everyone . . . I'm sure they would be
> happier without me.
>
> —Cassie, age 12

Suicidal behavior among children and adolescents is a serious public health concern, not just in the United States, but worldwide (C. M. Cummings, Caporino, & Kendall, 2013; World Health Organization,

2003). Suicidal behavior increases as children grow older, with adolescents being at higher risk than school-age children. Suicide does occur in children under 10, but such incidents are very rare (D. N. Miller & Eckert, 2009). In the United States, suicide is the fifth leading cause of death among children ages 5 to 14 and the third leading cause of death for adolescents between the ages of 15 and 24, behind only accidents and homicides (Guerry, Reilly, & Prinstein, 2011). As D.N. Miller and Eckert (2009) report, during 2003 and 2004, suicide rates for females ages 10 to 19 and males ages 15 to 19 increased significantly. Particularly alarming is the number of children ages 10 to 14 dying by suicide, with suicide rates among children in this age group increasing 51% between 1981 and 2004 (D. N. Miller & Eckert, 2009). Females report more suicidal ideation than males and attempt suicide at rates two to three times the rate of males; however, males die by suicide at a rate five times that of females (D. N. Miller & Eckert, 2009).

Suicide is an emotional crisis. Children do not wish to die as much as they wish to find a way to end their overwhelming emotional distress and pain. Most children who are suicidal actually very much want to live, but they struggle to see alternative solutions to their problems and feel hopeless about their likelihood of ever finding relief. There is a continuum of suicidal behaviors that includes the following (D. N. Miller & Eckert, 2009):

- *Suicidal ideation.* Ideation involves having serious thoughts of death by suicide. Ideation can be passive, where the child has passing thoughts of what it may be like to die but does not have any plans for how to die or does not engage in any behavior toward that end. Ideation may also be active, where the child has clearly defined thoughts of how to die and has a developed, articulated plan.
- *Suicidal intent.* This refers to the child's intentions at the time of his or her suicide attempt. That is, does the child intend to die, or is the child using a potentially lethal means to stop the emotional pain without explicitly intending to die?
- *Suicide attempt.* An attempt involves self-harming behaviors with the intent to die.
- *Suicide.* A self-inflicted fatal act.

Risk factors for suicide include mental illness; previous suicide attempts; access to firearms; genetic or familiar predisposition; past death of a friend or loved one, especially by suicide; adverse life experiences; and recent stressors or precipitating events (Guerry, Reilly, & Prinstein, 2011). It is important to note that although mental disorders are important risk factors for suicidal behavior, most people with mental disorders do not exhibit suicidal behavior (Bruffaerts et al., 2010). Therefore, not all children who struggle with depression will have suicidal behaviors. It is the acuity of symptoms and environmental stressors that act as combined risk factors for suicidal behavior.

A brief review of risk factors for youth suicide is presented below.

- A diagnosis of depression is a risk factor for suicidal behavior. Review studies have found that between 49% and 64% of adolescent suicide victims had a depressive disorder (Beardslee et al., 2012).
- Of those youth with depression, those with high suicidal ideation, previous suicide attempts, impulsivity, irritability, anger, and aggression are at higher risk for a suicidal event (Birmaher & Brent, 2007; Brent & Maalouf, 2009).
- A strong family history of suicide is associated with higher risk and earlier age of onset of suicidal behavior in children. Min and colleagues (2012) found that a suicide attempt in the mother was associated with a fivefold increase in risk of suicidal ideation and a ninefold increase in risk of suicide attempt in her offspring.
- Comorbidity with other disorders such as substance abuse and anxiety also increases risk (Goldman, 2012).
- The presence of childhood adversities increases the risk for suicidal behavior in childhood and longitudinally into adulthood. These include physical abuse, sexual abuse, neglect, parental death, other parental loss, family violence, physical illness, and financial adversity before the age of 18 (Bruffaerts et al., 2010).
- Research investigating data on childhood suicidal behavior across 21 countries found that childhood adversities had the strongest associations with attempt in childhood. Sexual abuse was an especially strong predictor. Specifically, a history of childhood sexual abuse was associated with a 10.9-fold increase in the likelihood of

an attempt between the ages of 4 and 12 years (Bruffaerts et al., 2010).

Risk factors are part of a child's history, and as such, teachers may not be aware of this information. In such cases, it is difficult to determine which children may be at active risk. In contrast to risk factors, *warning signs* for suicide are behavior based, more readily observable, and more proximal factors that suggest an increased probability for suicidal behavior (Guerry, Reilly, & Prinstein, 2011; D. N. Miller & Eckert, 2009). Warning signs include:

- Anger and rage
- Seeking revenge
- Engaging in reckless and risky behaviors (e.g., running out into traffic)
- Expressing feelings of being trapped or of being without any ways to feel better
- Significant withdrawal from friends and family
- Increases in observable signs of depression, including hopelessness and desperation
- Significant anxiety and agitation
- Changes in personality (e.g., a previously outgoing, spontaneous, and engaging child becoming quiet, withdrawn, and tearful)
- Saying good-bye to friends and family
- Giving away prized possessions
- Preoccupation with death-related topics
- Talking about suicide
- Erratic behavior changes
- Expression of significant and persistent guilt
- Collecting possible means (pills, firearms, etc.)

Guerry, Reilly, and Prinstein (2011) describe two profiles of youth who may engage in suicidal behaviors.

- *Impulsive-aggressive type.* These youth are often diagnosed with conduct disorder and demonstrate pronounced irritability, extreme sensitivity, intense reactions to frustration, and an impulsive approach to problem solving.

- *Depressed-perfectionistic type.* These youth are often diagnosed with depression and demonstrate strong feelings of hopelessness, self-defeat, shame, guilt, and loneliness. They often have an ambitious and rigid personality type, a high need for approval from others, high sensitivity to criticism, and strong reactions to failure or loss.

COMORBIDITY AND DEPRESSIVE DISORDERS

Comorbidity is the co-occurrence of mental health disorders. Research examining symptom patterns in school-age children has revealed that around two thirds of children with depression show at least one comorbid disorder, and over 10% show two or more (Maughan et al., 2013). Common diagnoses during this developmental period include ADHD, ODD, and conduct disorder (Maughan et al., 2013). In adolescence, comorbidity with substance abuse disorders also increases (Birmaher & Brent, 2007). Anxiety disorders are the most common comorbid disorders among children with depression, with comorbidity estimates ranging from 30% to 75% in preadolescents (C. M. Cummings et al., 2013; Garber, 2006). Clinical and research reports indicate that anxiety precedes the onset of mood disorders and therefore may be a risk factor for depression (Garber, 2006). A more mixed symptom presentation occurs in young children (third-graders), characterized by negative emotionality. Symptom presentation becomes more distinguishable for older children, around sixth grade (Garber & Weersing, 2010). Children with comorbid depression and anxiety generally experience depression at a younger age compared to those without comorbid anxiety. Additionally, as C. M. Cummings and colleagues (2013) indicate, the prognosis for comorbid anxiety and depression is worse than for either condition alone.

The Impact of Depression on Learning

Depression has a profound influence on children's learning, achievement, and school functioning in a number of ways. From a learning perspective, children struggling with depression have impaired motivation and concentration; demonstrate reduced processing speed, memory for verbal information, and set shifting; are slower at switching attention;

have higher levels of impulsivity and text anxiety; and exhibit decreased inhibition during tests of executive functioning (Brent & Maalouf, 2009; Brooks, Iverson, Sherman, & Roberge, 2010). Children's difficulties with concentration are exacerbated by two additional factors: (a) their tendency to ruminate over negative thoughts and situations, and (b) their interpretation of ambiguous situations as negative or threatening (Garber & Weersing, 2010). Rumination consumes a child's focus and prevents him or her from focusing on what the teacher is saying, and the interpretation of ambiguous situations as negative leads to more negative thoughts, which in turns begins another cycle of rumination. Imagine Jacob, a fifth-grader struggling with depression. In math class, he could not stop thinking about the test he had failed the previous week. He was sure that he would fail the next test. He noticed the teacher looking at him for a moment and concluded that she thought he was dumb. This made Jacob feel even more helpless and sad. When he tried to look at his math work again, he did not know what problem the class was on and was not able to focus at all. These kinds of neuropsychological difficulties, together with emotional distress, tap children's cognitive resources and make learning arduous.

Overall academic performance and school functioning are also more broadly impacted. Children with depression are often tardy and absent from school. In comparison to children without mental illness, children with depression are harder to wake up and have a harder time engaging in routines and in sustaining mental and emotional effort throughout the day (Abela & Hankin, 2008; Kitts & Goldman, 2012). Participation in class as well as in social activities throughout the day may be difficult as well. This sense of not belonging or of disconnection from schoolwork and from others leads to increased negative thoughts, impacting both academic and emotional functioning (Verboom, Sijtsema, Verhulst, Pennix, & Ornel, 2014).

Although a subset of children do not initially demonstrate significant difficulties in the classroom, the effort it takes them to sustain attention and participate in class drains their energy significantly, and parents often report that children "crash" when they get home, too exhausted to do anything else. Without intervention, sustaining this level of attention and focus in school becomes increasingly difficult, and eventually the child is no longer able to do so. This is when changes in grades, attitudes, and overall academic functioning become increasingly visible.

Diagnosis, Treatment, and Referral

DIAGNOSIS

As discussed in the previous chapter, the most reliable diagnoses are those that are based on various sources of data. Given that children's presentation fluctuates across settings, gathering qualitative observations and quantifiable measurements of symptoms from multiple reporters (e.g., the child, parents, teachers, and other caretakers) is important in gaining as comprehensive an understanding of the child's distress as possible. This broad-based perspective is important in determining the level of functional impairment and designing treatment goals accordingly.

TREATMENT

Treatment of depressive disorders in children can be broadly divided into three phases—acute, continuation, and maintenance—with recovery as the ultimate goal. The acute treatment phase begins immediately upon diagnosis and the goal is to achieve stabilization and response, defined as an at least 50% reduction in symptoms (Maalouf & Brent, 2012). During the continuation phase, the goal is to prevent relapse. Maintenance refers to continuation of a therapeutic alliance and "check-ins" to continue to develop coping skills that are appropriate as the child experiences new developmental or social experiences (Beardslee et al., 2012; Birhmaher & Brent, 2007). For example, if a child began treatment at age 10 and experienced remission (no or minimal symptoms), she should continue to go to therapy "booster sessions" to teach her new coping skills as she begins a new grade, as she transitions into middle school, or as she is faced with changes in her environment, such as moving to a new home. Recovery is the ultimate goal, and it is defined as the absence of symptoms for at least two months (Maalouf & Brent, 2012). A family component to treatment (e.g., family therapy) is helpful at every phase and level of symptom severity. The length of treatment for the family depends on the individual and the extent to which family dynamics are contributing to the child's struggles (Reilly, 2011).

The type of treatment plan created depends on the severity of the child's symptoms. Figure 3.3 outlines the type of treatment recommended based on symptom severity (Reilly, 2011).

Generally, if a child presents with mild depression (characterized by mild impairment, and lack of suicidality or psychosis), treatment may begin with education and support related to possible stressors in the family and school. The American Academy of Child and Adolescent Psychiatry suggests that in this category, response may be expected after four to six weeks of supportive therapy (Birmaher & Brent, 2007). For children with moderate to severe depression, (characterized by multiple episodes, significant impairment, suicidality, agitation, and/or psychosis) specific psychotherapy and pharmacological treatments are recommended (Birmaher & Brent, 2007). Ongoing screening for existing or developing comorbid disorders and risky behaviors should be a routine part of every treatment plan (Goldman, 2012). Family support and close communication with the school should also be integrated in treatment.

Severity of Symptoms	Type of Treatment	Average Length of Treatment
Mild	Individual outpatient therapy	Brief intervention lasting approximately eight weeks to longer-term interventions lasting months to years
	Group outpatient therapy	Typically 8 to 12 sessions
Moderate	Individual outpatient therapy	At least six months to years
	Medication	At least one year
Severe	Inpatient psychiatric hospitalization	Five to seven days on average; may require a longer stay
	Day treatment	One to two weeks
	Residential treatment	Months or years

FIGURE 3.3. Symptom severity and treatment indications.

Indeed, as Goldman (2012) indicates, family-based interventions have been demonstrated as efficacious interventions with all children, especially with younger children.

The three main evidence-based treatments for youth depression are cognitive behavioral therapy (CBT), interpersonal therapy (IPT), and medication with serotonin reuptake inhibitors (SSRIs). CBT aims to target the triad of negative emotions, thoughts, and behaviors that perpetuate the depression. CBT includes techniques such as behavior activation (getting children to participate in some physical activity, such as going outside for a walk or swimming), cognitive restructuring (changing negative thoughts to positive thoughts), emotion regulation (finding ways to increase positive feelings such as joy and pride), problem solving, and social skills training (Brent & Maalouf, 2009; Maalouf & Brent, 2012). CBT has also been found to be effective when treating children with depression and other comorbid disorders, especially anxiety and ADHD. From a prevention perspective, the use of CBT with children is effective in preventing symptoms of depression in children whose parents have a history of depression (Maalouf & Brent, 2012). While these skills follow a certain format in the clinical session, these principles can also be applied in the school setting. Classroom-based strategies based on these principles are found in Chapter 4 of this book.

IPT is another treatment approach that is increasingly being used with children to treat depressive disorders. Although initially created for treating adults, research has found IPT effective in treating depression among some older children and adolescents. The focus of IPT is how the symptoms of depression impact interpersonal relationships, and the aim is to reduce interpersonal conflicts. IPT treatment includes interpersonal problem-solving skills, effective communication strategies, and techniques for managing emotions in relational contexts (Maalouf & Brent, 2012).

With respect to medication, fluoxetine (commonly recognized under the brand name Prozac) is the only medication approved by the U.S. Food and Drug Administration (FDA) for the treatment of depression in preadolescent children (Birmaher & Brent, 2007; Goldman, 2012; Maalouf & Brent, 2012). For moderate and severe depression, combination treatment (i.e., medication and therapy) is generally recommended. As Goldman (2012) reports, with treatment, about 60% of the depressive disorders at least partially respond within three to four months, and over time about 15% to 20% more respond. These data are primarily based on an adolescent population, however, indicating a need for further investigation of treatment response among prepubertal children. In general, greater duration and severity of symptoms, multiple episodes, comorbidity, hopelessness, negative cognitive style, family problems, low socioeconomic status, past history of abuse, and exposure to ongoing negative events (e.g., abuse, family conflict) are associated with poorer outcomes and continuation of depressive episodes into adulthood (Birmaher & Brent, 2007; Maalouf & Brent, 2012).

REFERRAL

With respect to initiating a referral, the key message is, "The earlier, the better." Given the chronic and intermittent nature of depressive disorders, efforts at prevention and early identification are critical. If symptoms are identified early, when their severity is not at its most acute, there is a higher likelihood of response to treatment and reduction in symptomatology. In general, when children struggle with depressed (or irritable) mood in a manner that impedes their social or academic functioning for two weeks or longer, a referral is warranted. Recommendations for initiating a referral include the following:

- If you are concerned about a student, keep a record that documents:

  - A description of the behaviors of concern
  - How long the behaviors have been present
  - When the behaviors tend to occur
  - Which people, situations, or settings seem to trigger the behaviors
  - The child's description of his or her emotional state
  - How the behaviors are impacting the child's social and academic functioning

- Talk to other teachers or school personnel who interact with the child to determine how pervasive the change in the child's behavioral and emotional presentation may be.

- Reach out to parents as early as possible to communicate your observations. Ask whether they have also observed similar changes at home. When communicating with parents, it is often more useful to indicate how specific behaviors are impacting the child socially and academically than it is to attempt to identify the reason for the behavior or to diagnose the child's condition.
- Contact school administrators to determine your school's referral protocol. Whereas some schools have mental health practitioners on campus, other schools do not and different personnel are responsible for receiving and following up on referrals (e.g., guidance counselors).
- Be aware of your school's crisis protocols. If a child expresses suicidal ideation, it is your duty to inform school administrators immediately and to make sure you consult with the professionals in your building who are responsible for crisis intervention.

This careful observation, inquiry, and communication are invaluable for successful referrals. Treatment providers may use this information for diagnostic purposes as well as for the development of treatment goals. Furthermore, this process can facilitate a treatment plan where the teacher supports use and generalization of coping skills in the classroom.

Notice, Give, Nurture

WHAT CAN I NOTICE?

Noticing and assessing children's affect and behavior in the classroom should occur with intentionality. Intentionality refers to utilizing a knowledge base (e.g., of child development, of factors impacting development, and of how depression manifests in childhood) as a guiding principle for observation. Figure 3.4 indicates factors that foster positive emotional development during middle childhood. Figure 3.5 indicates the interruptions to this positive development that place children at risk for depressive disorders.

Careful monitoring of risk factors for depressive symptoms in children is critical for early identification. Typically developing children experience changes in mood that are congruent with their age and the particular situation. For example, Logan, a 12-year-old boy, proudly went into the basketball championship game. His team had an excellent season, and he was extremely excited about the prospect of winning the big trophy. The game started strong for his team, but during the second

Views of Self	Self-Regulation	Interactions with Environment
• A view of oneself that is more abstract and based on traits (e.g., "I am a good friend," "I am a good student") • Success in different areas that leads to positive self-esteem • Belief in oneself as capable of taking action and effecting change when necessary	• A broad range of mood repair skills • Active problem solving • Ability to shift attention effectively • Increased ability to tolerate strong feelings • Increased ability to inhibit impulsive reactions	• Secure attachments • Interactions with others that are generally predictable and stable • The existence of positive models for self-regulation and problem solving • The perception that help and support are available and consistent

FIGURE 3.4. Factors that foster positive emotional development during middle childhood.

Views of Self	Self-Regulation	Interactions with Environment
• View of oneself as inadequate, helpless, and hopeless • Globally negative view of onesel	• Poor mood repair • Rumination • High self-criticism • Difficulty with problem solving • Inability to shift attention from negative mood	• Insecure attachments • Significant stressors or trauma • Low social support • Dependency • Excessive reassurance seeking

FIGURE 3.5. Interruptions to positive emotional development during middle childhood.

half, the other team took the lead, eventually winning the game. Logan was sad, frustrated, and disappointed. Using the template in Figure 3.4, the following was true for Logan:

- *View of self.* Despite the loss, Logan still viewed himself as a good athlete. Success in other areas as well as a positive view of himself helped him to maintain his high self-esteem.
- *Self-regulation.* Logan shed a few tears of frustration, but he was able to inhibit this response in order to participate in the trophy award ceremony after the game. He tolerated his strong affect and sought out friends who had come to watch his game for support. He used humor to cope with the loss and engaged in conversation and play with his friends to feel better. He was able to tolerate his initial frustration and sadness, and once this passed, he successfully engaged in the rest of his day, even reframing negative thoughts to positive ones by saying things such as, "Well, we worked really hard and actually got to the championship. That's a big deal too."
- *Interactions with environment.* Logan sought out interactions with parents and friends, knowing that they would offer support and acceptance

If Logan struggled with depression, his responses would have been markedly different:

- *View of self.* The loss confirmed Logan's view of himself as a poor athlete and failure, further impacting his already low self-esteem. Instead of viewing his performance in the game as just one aspect of his abilities, he generalized his inability to perform to all contexts, such as the academic and social arenas.
- *Self-regulation.* Logan had a difficult time restraining his anger and frustration. He threw the basketball back at the referee and refused to participate in the team picture. He ignored teammates' words of congratulations for a successful season. On the ride home, he repeatedly blamed the referee for poor calls and called himself stupid for being on that team. His frustration persisted into the eve-

ning and he did not have dinner with his family, instead going to his room and shutting the door.

- *Interactions with environment.* Logan remembered his father saying that "second place isn't good enough." He worried that his father would come up to his room and point out all the errors he had made during the game. He was not able to express his feelings openly, as his father had often told him to "grow up and stop crying."

Noticing these patterns involves observing a child's responses, his or her ability to recover from negative situations, and his or her interactions with the environment. Understanding the different risk factors associated with childhood depression will further enlighten teachers about how a child's environment may serve to protect a child from depression, or alternatively, to further predispose him or her to it.

Additional patterns teachers may observe in the classroom include the following:

- *How does the child approach problem solving?* Active problem solving is associated with healthy emotional development, whereas passive problem solving or avoidance is associated with internalizing symptoms. Furthermore, girls more than boys tend to worry about problems rather than actively trying to solve them, using more passive problem solving approaches (Stark, Streusand, Krumholz, & Patel, 2010). Children who consistently have difficulties with initiating and implementing problem-solving strategies may be at risk. These children may not only ask others for help prior to attempting any problem solving, but they may also require frequent encouragement and reassurance.
- *Does the child seem alert and have sustained energy during the day?* Children who struggle with depression report more sleep difficulties than children without mental health disorders (Brent & Maalouf, 2009). Disrupted sleep predicts the onset and recurrence of depression, as well as a poorer response to treatment (Maalouf & Brent, 2012). As noted earlier, decreased appetite and weight loss are symptoms of depression in childhood. Therefore, noticing when

sleeping and eating patterns in students may be disrupted can be helpful in identifying early depressive symptoms.

• *Does the child consistently engage in pleasurable activities?* Children with depressive disorders are less likely to engage in pleasurable activities and report an overall less positive connection to school-work and school activities (Brent & Maalouf, 2009). If repeated attempts to engage children in activities fail, it is a warning sign for internalizing disorders. Furthermore, it is important to notice when a child is not engaging in pleasurable activities (such as playing during recess or completing a project on a favorite topic) because he is isolating himself or because he is being actively rejected by peers. Relational aggression and peer rejection are associated with internalizing symptoms (Kawabata, Crick, & Hamaguchi, 2010).

• *Is the child engaging in any risky or harmful behaviors?* For children struggling with depression, some self-harm behaviors may be used as a way to cope with significant emotional distress. Potential signs of self-injurious behaviors include:

  o Wearing long-sleeved shirts and long pants, even when hot, or other attempts to cover extremities
  o Unwillingness to participate in activities that require less clothing (e.g., gym class, swimming, sports)
  o Wearing large bandages
  o Wearing many bracelets to cover wrists
  o Unexplained burns, cuts, scars, or other markings on the skin

• *Does the child demonstrate any behaviors that may be warning signs of suicide?* Coming to terms with the reality that even young children can have thoughts of suicide is difficult for adults. To imagine such despair and desperation in a young child feels overwhelming. However, preadolescent children can develop suicidal thoughts and can have suicide attempts. Therefore, noticing any warning signs is critical. One of the prominent myths associated with suicide is that asking questions or talking about suicide with a child will put the thought into her head and therefore increase the probability of it happening. Research indicates that this is not true. In fact, the opposite has been found. Data suggest that open, direct, and supportive conversations with children about suicide can lead to beneficial outcomes (D. N. Miller & Eckert, 2009). A list of warning signs of suicide is found above in the special topics section of this chapter.

WHAT CAN I GIVE?

Despite the increased understanding of and scientific advancements associated with mental illness, a profound sense of stigma still remains. It is not unusual to hear words such as *crazy, overdramatic, manipulative,* and *weak* in reference to someone struggling with depression. It is also common to hear questions such as, "What does she have to be depressed about?" or "Why can't he just get over it?" Children are acutely aware of attitudes their families and society may have about mental illness. If these messages are negative or punishing, children may fear reporting their symptoms and may struggle in silence until reaching a crisis point. Therefore, any effort toward eradicating stigma is important and worthwhile. Attitudes, responses, and language that will foster children's early reporting of symptoms are paramount.

Power of Language

Teachers can give students the power of language to promote positive self-image and to decrease shame and stigma associated with mental illness. Language can be incredibly powerful in terms of the explicit and implicit messages it conveys, its potential to act as a trigger for negative affect, and its potential to positively impact self-image and school engagement. Below are suggestions for giving students the power of language:

- Depression should be explained as an illness, not a weakness, and not something that is "just in your head." Children should understand that depression is no one's fault, and that a combination of biological, social, and psychological factors contribute to its development. Children who struggle with depression are not being dramatic or manipulative.
- When children develop emotional disorders, they often worry that

others will judge or characterize them solely by the presence of the disorder rather than by other qualities, personality traits, or talents. How one refers to students with emotional disorders can reinforce this type of overgeneralization or stereotyping. For example, referring to a student as "the depressed child" implies that depression is the overarching, defining feature of the child. More appropriate language to use is "the child suffering from depression" or "the child with a depressive disorder." While on first look the differences may seem subtle, the impact of the language is significant. The latter phrasing indicates that there is a whole child, with other interests, talents, and unique qualities, who also happens to have depression.

• When discussing suicide, there is terminology that conveys the seriousness of the act in a respectful manner.

○ The phrase "died by suicide" should be used instead of "committed suicide." The terminology "died by suicide" objectively indicates cause of death without the more negative and criminal undertones of the phrase "committed suicide."

○ When referring to a death by suicide, it is more appropriate to say a "completed suicide" rather than a "successful suicide." Most will agree that the typical connotations of the word *successful* do not readily apply to suicide.

Invitations for Conversation

Teachers can also give their students invitations for conversations about emotions and coping. These invitations may be offered to students who are doing well. Letting students know that you notice their efforts to manage emotions appropriately and giving them ideas for continued coping can support their emotional health and well-being. The invitations may also be offered to students who are struggling emotionally. In such cases, it is important to use "I" statements to convey what you have observed and your thoughts about it. For example, you might say, "I noticed you are not playing with your friends anymore and you hardly talk to anyone during recess. I'm worried about you. If you want, you can talk to me about it. If you don't want to talk to me, I would be happy to help you find someone you feel comfortable talking to." The statements should include specific behavioral changes you have noticed and your feeling of concern, rather than general or diagnostic statements such as "You are having a really hard time emotionally lately; I think you may have symptoms of depression." It is important to note that children may not initially accept these invitations due to potential embarrassment or fear. Keep offering the invitations, as even if they do not respond, children still receive the message that you are concerned, and more importantly, are ready to talk about emotions.

Janis Whitlock and Barent Walsh, prominent self-injury researchers, recommend addressing children with "respectful curiosity" when asking them about potential self-harm. This nonjudgmental approach helps teachers to better understand children's experience. Examples of questions showing respectful curiosity include (Walsh, 2006; Whitlock et al., 2013):

- "How does self-injuring make you feel better?"
- "What kinds of situations or types of things make you want to injure?"
- "When did you begin injuring and why?"
- "What role does self-injury play in your life right now?"

What Can I Nurture?

Nurturing supportive, caring relationships with students is one of the most impactful prevention and intervention strategies that teachers can employ. A supportive relationship, with the sense of predictability and safety that it promotes, can serve as a powerful protective factor. For example, research shows that maltreated youth are less likely to develop depression if they have a supportive relationship with an adult (Beardslee et al., 2012). Among children struggling with depression, parental support is associated with reduced depressive symptoms, peer support is associated with higher academic self-efficacy and connection to school, and teacher support is associated with all three outcomes (Brent & Maalouf, 2009; Galand & Hospel, 2013).

Nurturing teacher–parent relationships is also vital when supporting children with depressive disorders. Parents' reports of their children's distress can assist teachers in their understanding and management of student behaviors. Similarly, teachers may share helpful strategies used in the classroom that parents may use at home to promote consistency and practice of coping skills.

Olivia is a 9-year-old girl struggling with symptoms of depression. Her father passed away from cancer recently, and Olivia has been tearful, despondent, and increasingly withdrawn. Her sleeping is completely dysregulated, and she has a very difficult time waking up in the morning. Getting ready for school is a struggle, and she has been tardy nearly every day since returning to school after her father's death. Olivia's mom called her teacher to share strategies that seem to help Olivia transition and manage her sadness. Olivia's teacher found that pairing Olivia with a class buddy and breaking classwork into smaller sections was helpful in maintaining Olivia's focus and engagement. This close communication facilitated Olivia's participation in class and helped her to continue to access important sources of support.

This chapter has offered a review of the development of depressive disorders in childhood as well as information regarding the manifestation of symptoms in the classroom, diagnosis, treatment, and referral. This notice, give, and nurture section has focused on factors that serve as scaffolds for additional classroom supports for children struggling with depressive disorders. Specific recommendations for accommodations and interventions are provided in Chapter 4.

CHAPTER FOUR

Practical Tools

Helping Children With Anxiety and Depression in the Classroom

Can you help me do my pinwheel breathing? My tummy is
starting to hurt.

—Luis, second-grader

THINK BACK TO THE students you have had in your class over the
years. Did you feel that some needed additional support or help around
their emotional well-being? How many students do you believe could
have been more successful academically had their emotional needs been
addressed? Among those students, how many actually received mental
health services? If you are able to recall a significant number of students who needed help but did not receive it, you are not alone. Unfortunately, despite the large number of children who struggle with mental
health disorders, the actual number of children who receive help is very
small. As many as 80% of the children and adolescents who need mental health services do not receive them (Essau, 2005). Several factors
account for this alarming figure, including lack of available therapists,
difficulty reaching providers due to physical distance, lack of transportation, long waiting lists, poor insurance coverage, and family factors
(e.g., parental illness, financial duress, lack of agreement between parents about need for treatment).

Given the number of obstacles impeding children from receiving
the help they need, it is imperative to find other avenues and settings
that will foster emotional support for students. Research demonstrates
that a teacher–student relationship characterized by warmth, closeness,
trust, and safety leads to better academic and social performance in students (Reeve & Jang, 2006). Therefore, an understanding of the particu-

lar emotional needs of students as well as of the skills that teachers can use and practice in the classroom can be important sources of support for children struggling with internalizing disorders.

This chapter presents tools (i.e., activities and strategies) that teachers can use in their classrooms to support students who are struggling with anxiety and/or depression. *It is critical to note that, in employing these tools, teachers are not expected to become diagnosticians or therapists.* Indeed, these tools do not take the place of therapy, nor should they be the only means used to support students. Instead, by employing these tools, teachers will use the knowledge of how anxiety and depression manifest in children to create a classroom environment that supports children's self-regulation and learning. This will support students who are already receiving treatment as well as those who are waiting to begin their therapeutic process. The tools presented in this chapter are based on cognitive behavioral techniques that are routinely used as part of intervention and prevention protocols. The use of these tools will not be harmful for children. However, to maximize supports for students, it is strongly recommended that the teacher, parents, and treatment providers communicate about the child's treatment protocol and coordinate efforts around how coping skills will be used across the office, home, and school settings.

The tools presented in this chapter are based on a transdiagnostic treatment framework. Transdiagnostic, or "unified," treatments are those that target common factors that produce symptoms in related classes of disorder, such as anxiety and depression (Ehrenreich-May & Bilek, 2012). As the reader may recall from Chapter 3, the coexistence of these disorders in childhood may be as high as 75%, and the disorders share the following symptoms:

- Sleep disturbance
- Fatigue
- Irritability
- Difficulty concentrating
- Worry (rumination)
- Restlessness
- Hopelessness

- Avoidance
- Withdrawal

Due to these similar overarching features, the tools offered will be helpful for children who struggle with both anxiety and depression. In instances where there is a primary difficulty (e.g., school refusal), that distinction will be highlighted.

Before we begin, let's consider some important questions that may be on your mind regarding the use of the tools and the measurement of their success.

1. *Will these tools immediately change my students' behavior?* Each tool individually will not immediately or entirely change children's feelings, thoughts, and behaviors. Remember that anxiety and depression are the result of the interaction of a number of domains, including genetic, temperament, family, psychological, and social factors. Therefore, the use of individual tools in the absence of addressing other domains of the child's life will not entirely cure a child of a mental disorder. Treatment that addresses multiple domains of a child's life is always recommended. However, the use of these tools allows the child to develop new skills, experiences, and behaviors that will lead to improvement and overall change. With continued practice and use in other settings (e.g., at home), the child can experience change and success. Importantly, the child will experience a sense of safety in the classroom, knowing that emotional well-being is just as important as academic progress.

2. *Will these tools work for all students?* Some tools will work better for some children than for others. One way to determine which tools may work well for a particular student is to try to use the ones that best fit the child's interests, learning style, and history. For example, a very active child may prefer more physically based tools (e.g., walking around the classroom to relieve distress); a child with language delays may prefer drawing or physical activities; and a child with a history marked by insecure attachment may not initially do well with tools that rely on social support and seeking others for help but may prefer to do individual journaling as a starting point.

In trying to determine whether a tool is working, it is critical to keep in mind where in the course of the illness the child may be. For example, when children are experiencing particularly acute symptoms, they may not demonstrate any improvement from classroom interventions, as they may require more intense treatment. Some children may show initial improvement but then experience an exacerbation of symptoms. This is not because the tools are failing, but rather because there may be outside circumstances at play (e.g., increased parental arguments at home, recent loss) that are impacting the child's functioning.

3. *How do I best support my students as I use these tools?* The best way to support students is to make sure you have support yourself. Seek out support from school mental health clinicians or administrators. Maintain close communication with parents if possible, and with treatment providers if they are available. Talk to other teachers and ask them what has been successful for them in the past. Teachers that are new to the profession will benefit greatly from seeking more experienced mentors who can guide and support them in their efforts to foster the emotional well-being of their students.

4. *I can use some tools to help my students with behavior and emotions, but what can I do to help them academically?* When students are struggling emotionally, their academic functioning will likely also suffer. Below are specific academic accommodations that may be used for students struggling with anxiety and depression. These accommodations seek to alleviate some of the disruptive effects that the cognitive symptoms of the disorders may have on learning. It is important to remember that when struggling with moderate to severe symptoms, children may simply not be able to keep the same pace as when their symptoms are milder or in remission. It is highly recommended that a team approach be employed, where teachers, parents, mental health clinicians, and school administrators work together to determine realistic work expectations for the child as well as the alternative assignments or grading methods that may be used to best support the child's progress.

Academic Accommodations

As noted in Chapters 2 and 3, anxiety and depression can negatively impact learning due to multiple factors, including decreased motivation and concentration, reduced processing speed, reduced memory for verbal information, decreased ability to switch attention from fear or worry, increased impulsivity, and decreased planning and problem solving (Brent & Maalouf, 2009; Brooks, Iverson, Sherman, & Roberge, 2010). The following accommodations seek to alleviate some of the negative effects of the cognitive symptoms associated with internalizing disorders.

- *Give movement breaks.* Breaks that allow for opportunities to engage in gross motor movements, such as whole-body stretching, jumping jacks, tall jumps, shooting hoops, or fast walking, can be very helpful for children struggling with internalizing disorders. When faced with distressing emotions, children without internalizing disorders are able to engage in self-distraction as a way of coping with their distress. They may think about something positive, change activities, or seek out someone's help. Children with anxiety and depression, however, can become stuck in their distress and rumination. Movement breaks can help distract children from their distress and stop the worry cycle. When opportunities for "large movement" are not available or possible, students can do other things such as running errands, helping the teacher distribute materials, and erasing the board. These activities offer movement breaks and have the added benefit of giving the child a sense of accomplishment. This sense of accomplishment is particularly important for children with internalizing disorders who have a hard time with up-regulation of positive feelings.
- *Use multiple modalities for instructions and reminders during transitions.* Students with anxiety and depression have difficulty shifting their attention from one task to another, especially when their thoughts are consumed by a particular worry or distress. Therefore, children may miss instructions and reminders if these are presented only verbally. Younger children may benefit from having a picture

schedule on their desk that the teacher can point to during transitions. All children may benefit from a gentle touch on the shoulder, or making sure that there is eye contact when the teacher offers a reminder.

- *Incorporate students' interests and/or areas of strength in assignments, projects, and classroom work.* To maximize attention, motivation, and concentration, teachers are encouraged to incorporate students' interests and/or areas of strength into their work. For example, a third-grader who is learning about biographies may be permitted to write about his favorite sports figure. A fifth-grader who enjoys science may be enlisted as the teacher's special aid when conducting experiments or demonstrations for the class.

- *Divide assignments into smaller segments.* Children struggling with internalizing disorders may not have the ability to pace their work in order to complete large or complex assignments. In addition to the cognitive symptoms listed, children may also struggle with fatigue, lack of interest or pleasure in activities, helplessness, and hopelessness. These symptoms can be paralyzing in the immediate moment, and can make long-term assignments seem daunting or impossible. For example, an assignment for a fourth-grader may include completing a book report and then creating a visual representation of a character from the story. While the entire assignment may be given at once with the expectation that the child pace his or her work over the time allotted, this expectation may not be realistic for children with internalizing disorders. Instead, the assignment can be broken down into distinct pieces, each with its own due date. Check-ins about the child's understanding of the components should occur at each juncture of the assignment. While this example is of a long-term assignment, some children may need even daily work broken down into smaller segments. For example, a typically developing child may be expected to participate in silent reading for 30 minutes. This expectation may need to be modified for a child struggling with an internalizing disorder, such that he is expected to read for 10 minutes, take a break, read for another 10 minutes, have another break, and then read for the final 10 minutes.

- *Figure out what in the current instructions may be making the child anxious.* While in general there are some commonalities to the difficulties that children with internalizing disorders experience, some of the fears or worries may be idiosyncratic to a particular child. When children appear distressed in the context of an assignment or task, it is important to ask what aspect of the task is worrisome for the child rather than assuming the source of the worry. For example, Nicole, a third-grader, became very tearful when she was not able to complete her timed multiplication facts test. While she knew her times tables, she became very frustrated and distressed while trying to complete the practice test, telling the teacher, "I just can't do it!" The teacher initially thought that Nicole was distressed by the timed component of the test. Upon further investigation, however, the teacher discovered that Nicole was getting "stuck" when trying to complete the match problems by following the rows. The teacher worked together with Nicole and asked, "How else could we work on the math facts?" When Nicole tried completing the math facts by working in columns rather than rows, this seemed to help her, and she was able to complete the timed test without difficulty. From that moment on, Nicole's teacher used that experience as an opportunity to offer Nicole gentle reminders and encouragement before tests by saying, "Up and down—you can do it!"

- *Offer additional ways for the child to have full instructions and notes.* When children's symptoms are moderate to severe, other factors may impact their attention and participation in class, including fatigue, restlessness, sadness, slower processing, and frequent tardiness or absences. Offering other ways for students to "catch up" or have the material readily available can be very helpful. This includes videorecording the class, recording specific instructions, asking a peer to share his or her notes, or pairing the child with a "study buddy" who can help him or her with in-class assignments.
- *Support desensitization plans.* Some students may find it very difficult to complete assignments that require presentations in front of others. This is particularly true for students with social anxiety disorder. Tasks such as reading a speech in front of the class, presenting a project at a science fair, or writing on the board may seem especially daunting, with students experiencing an intense fear of doing something that will be embarrassing or humiliating. Men-

tal health providers will likely develop a desensitization plan for a child with such struggles, where the child is gradually exposed to the feared situation while simultaneously practicing relaxation techniques and addressing her negative thoughts. As children progress through the desensitization plan, teachers can help by supporting each step as the child practices it in the classroom. For example, for a child who is afraid of reading her creative writing assignment in front of the class, she may begin the process of desensitization by making a recording of herself and then turning it in to her teacher. She may then ask a friend to read her creative writing assignment in class, and so on, until she is able to read aloud by herself in front of the class. Each of these steps can be very difficult to complete for a child with significant anxiety. Therefore, understanding, flexibility in modifying the assignment, and support of the student's coping skills can all be extremely helpful.

• *Structure the timing of assignments from less demanding in the morning to more demanding in the afternoon.* For students struggling with school refusal, morning time can be quite difficult, as that is the time when they must transition into the school setting. Children may be late due to attempts to stay home from school, they may have a difficult time entering the classroom, or they may not make it to the classroom at all in the morning. Therefore, scheduling less demanding subjects or tasks for the morning may allow for an easier transition into the classroom.

Students struggling with depression may also have a hard time in the morning. Some children experience sleep disturbances that make it difficult to wake up in the morning. They may also be fatigued, as what appear to be simple tasks, such as getting dressed and ready for school in the morning, can be difficult and exhausting for children struggling with depression. Having less demanding subjects or tasks in the morning may allow them to transition more easily, experience success more readily, and have an opportunity to rally more energy for later.

• *Enlist the student's input for all interventions.* Ask the student whether he feels comfortable asking for help in the classroom or whether he would prefer to communicate with you individually.

Creating a special signal between you and the student can be helpful. This signal will indicate to you that the student needs additional help or might be feeling overwhelmed without attracting undue attention from peers.

• *Provide test accommodations.* Certain test accommodations may be helpful in allowing children to better access and process information.

- o Ease the transition into the test by asking the child to do a brief relaxation exercise. This can be taking three deep breaths, doing muscle relaxation for the back and neck, or repeating a calming mantra.
- o Children with internalizing disorders may have difficulty completing open-response essays due to memory and processing impairments. They may be more successful with multiple-choice exams, as these assist with recall.
- o Adjust time expectations in timed tests if possible to allow students additional time to complete the test.

Emotional and Behavioral Tools

Sometimes understanding a child with anxiety or depression can be difficult. The source of distress or worries may not be readily apparent, yet the behavioral manifestation is clear. The child's resulting withdrawal, reticence, irritability, or inability to verbalize what he or she is experiencing may feel frustrating for those trying to help. At times, teachers may wonder whether the child's behavior is consciously manipulative. In order to better understand and empathize with a child's experience, it will be important to reframe "won't" to "can't." "Won't" implies conscious manipulation—a child is doing something on purpose for a particular outcome. "Can't" implies there is something impeding the child from being able to engage, comply, or explain. From a child's point of view, anxiety and depression get in the way, and here are the things that "I can't" do:

• Say how I feel
• Make my body stop
• Make my mind stop

- Control my feelings
- Find other things to do

As one might imagine, the feeling of "I can't" is frustrating, embarrassing, and difficult for children. These feelings may also lead to helplessness and hopelessness. The activities listed below target each of these "can't" domains in order to help the child feel more empowered and successful. The tools follow a scaffolding model, where initial skills form the foundation to support more complex skills as the children grow in multiple domains (e.g., cognitive, language, emotional).

While these activities are designed to assist students with anxiety and depression, the skills learned can be helpful for all students. Teachers are encouraged to use some activities with their entire class to avoid singling out individual students as the only ones who need help, and to create a common emotions language for the class.

Domain	Grade	Activity
Identifying Feelings and Managing Somatic Symptoms	K–3	Finding the Body Clues
	4–5	Clue
Cognitive Restructuring	K–5	Thought Bubble
	K–3	Stop Those Thoughts!
	K–3	Sticky Thoughts
	4–5	The Roadblock Crew
	4–5	The NASTY Trap
Contingency Management	K–5	Pick a Prize
	K–5	The Nurse Pass
Behavior Support	K–5	Safe People and Spaces
	K–5	Deescalating Anger

FIGURE 4.1. Classroom-based tools to help students struggling with anxiety and depression.

Increasing Positive Affect	K–5	Process Finders
	K–5	Art Gallery
	K–5	Thank-You Notes
	K–5	Mantra Cards
	1–5	Peer Leadership
	3–5	Goal Setting
Active Coping	K–3	The Sponge
	K–5	Journaling
	K–5	What Would You Do?
	K–5	Sensory Box
	K–5	Worry Stones
	4–5	Mindfulness
Relaxation Skills	K–5	Breathing Exercises
	K–5	Progressive Muscle Relaxation
	3–5	Guided Imagery
	3–5	Visualization
Social Support	K–5	Power of the Group
	K–5	Buddy Up
	4–5	"You Can Do It" Messages

FIGURE 4.1 *Continued*

Figure 4.1 lists the different emotional and behavioral domains each activity addresses, as well as the general age range for which each activity is appropriate. The recommended age range should be used as a guideline rather than as an absolute. It will be important to consider the child's developmental stage, language abilities, cognitive abilities, and overall understanding of concepts in choosing appropriate activities. For example, some third-graders may be able to use more complex language or begin to use abstract concepts, whereas other third-graders may have a more difficult time doing so. Each activity listed in Figure 4.1 is described in detail, including instructions for use and accompanying materials. While a general script is offered, teachers should feel free to revise and adapt instructions as they feel is most appropriate for their students.

Activities

Domain	Grade	Activity
Identifying Feelings and Managing Somatic-Symptoms	K–3	Finding the Body Clues
	4–5	Clue

IDENTIFYING FEELINGS AND MANAGING SOMATIC SYMPTOMS

An important foundational skill for children is to understand different emotions. Children are generally able to identify core emotions such as happiness, anger, and sadness. However, they need further instruction and modeling around the identification of a wider range of emotions (e.g., frustration, bewilderment, confusion, apprehension). Teachers are encouraged to promote children's continued learning of emotion states by labeling facial expressions, linking tone of voice and body language to particular emotions, and wondering aloud how someone may be feeling. Emotion awareness and recognition is a lifelong skill and should therefore be promoted at all stages of child development. Incorporating this skill regularly into classroom discussion helps in removing any stigma associated with feelings and allows for continued practice and skill development. Activities in the classroom that promote emotion identification include:

- Identifying for a child what his or her tone of voice and body language are indicating (e.g. "Mark, you are speaking very softly and you are looking down. I wonder how you are feeling").
- When reading a story, asking children for clues that let them know how a particular character may be feeling.
- Cutting out pictures from magazines, showing them to the children, and asking the children to label them with what the different people may be feeling.
- Emotions charades: Children can "act out" what they are feeling, and their peers have to guess what the emotion may be.

Children with internalizing disorders also often complain of multiple somatic symptoms, including stomachaches, headaches, nausea, dizziness, body pains, rapid heartbeat, and difficulty catching their breath. It is important to note that the pain they feel is real and not "in their heads." The pain is also indicative of psychological distress. Therefore, when children report somatic concerns, it is important to validate the pain as real, yet guide them to the link to psychological connections (Warner et al., 2011). Younger children may first need assistance in identifying the somatic complaints, whereas older children will need assistance in making the connection between the physical and the psychological.

Finding the Body Clues (Grades K–3)

This activity helps children identify somatic sensations and connect them to particular feelings. Body scans are techniques used in treatment to help patients discover where in their bodies they are holding tension, are feeling particular sensations, or may be storing different emotions. In this activity, children will use the concept of a body scan but in a fun, interactive way. Helping children to identify their body cues and develop the language to describe them can be helpful in linking the body cues to feelings. For example, in supporting a student who complains of tummy aches, a teacher may say, "It sounds like the queasy tummy is acting up. I wonder if there is something that is making you worried?"

Materials Needed
- Large sheets of paper for students to do whole-body tracings *or* small sheets of paper
- Drawing instruments (e.g., markers, crayons, colored pencils)
- Construction paper
- Scissors
- Tape

Instructions
- If using the large roll of paper, cut out enough paper for the children to be able to trace their bodies. If using small sheets of paper, ask the children to draw an outline of their bodies.

- Using the script below as a guide, ask the children to draw the body sensations they notice and where in the body they are (e.g., pain in tummy, red ears, sweaty palms). Encourage them to find funny or silly names for these sensations to make them less threatening (e.g., "tummy tweaks" or "gassy tummy," "twitchy legs," "wobbly arms").

Script

(The language should be adjusted to meet the children's developmental level.)

We have a mystery on our hands today. Who is ready to be a detective and help me find some clues to solve that mystery? The mystery is figuring out how our bodies talk to us to let us know how we are feeling. Sometimes our bodies can be very loud to let us know how we're feeling. If you're very excited, you may feel like jumping up and down and moving your arms about. Sometimes our bodies can be a little quieter, and we have to listen closely to know what's going on.

What does your body tell you when you're feeling happy? (Use this as a practice question so students understand the concept.)

Great! Those were great examples. Now, let's go find clues to our mystery. Today's mystery is, how does your body tell you that you are feeling nervous or worried? (Note: You can use this activity multiple times by changing the "mystery" to address different feelings, such as *scared, happy,* or *frustrated.*) *Think of something that makes you a little nervous or worried. OK, now, on your paper, draw what your body is telling you. Listen for the clues and draw them on your paper.*

- Once all children have completed their drawings, post the drawings around the room. Ask the children to share their drawings with peers and explain what sensations they identified. This is important in creating a language the class will understand (e.g., all the kids will know what the "gurgling tummy" is) as well as in allowing children to know that others experience similar feelings.
- Next, ask the children to come up with ideas about what might be

useful for decreasing the body sensations or making them go away. Cut up the construction paper into pieces, and on each piece have the children either write words (e.g., "relax") or draw a picture (e.g., someone exercising) pertaining to something that can be helpful in making the tummy tweaks or twitchy legs (use their own words) feel better.

- Have the children walk around the room and match the construction paper solutions to the drawings of the body sensations. Ask the children to explain why they chose that solution and how they think it might work.
- If time allows, choose a few of the solutions the children identified and have the whole class practice them. For example, if one of the identified solutions was deep breathing, have the whole class practice a deep-breathing exercise. The student who identified that solution may lead the class in practicing.

Clue (Grades 4–5)

This activity helps children identify somatic sensations and connect them to particular feelings. It also helps them identify particular situations or people that may trigger these feelings.

Materials Needed

- 3x5 index cards or pieces of paper cut roughly into 3x5 dimensions (approximately 10 cards or pieces of paper per child)
- Envelopes (one for each child)
- Pencils or pens

Instructions

- Distribute cards (or paper) and envelopes to all students.
- Give the following instructions:

Have any of you ever played the game Clue? In that game, the object is to solve a murder mystery by identifying the correct person, weapon, and place of the murder. Today we're going to play a game that resembles Clue, but you are not solving a murder mystery. Instead, you're solving your own feelings mystery.

Let's get our Clue material ready. Take three cards and label them

"People." Now, take three other cards and label them "Places." Now take another three cards and label them "Body cues."

Now I want you to think something or someone that makes you feel nervous or worried. (Note: You can use this activity multiple times by changing the "mystery" to address different feelings, such as *angry, unhappy, overwhelmed, betrayed,* or *frustrated.*) *Using your "People" cards, write down the people that may make you nervous or worried. Using your "Places" cards, write down the places or situations that make you nervous or worried. Now, using your "Body cues" cards, write down the feelings you get in your body that let you know you are nervous or worried.* (You can give examples here, such as blushing, headaches, or shallow breathing.)

Now pick the one "People" card, the one "Places" card, and the one "Body cues" card that are associated with the most nervousness or worry. Put the three cards in your envelope.

- At this point, you have options about how to engage students in a discussion:

    o Ask students to find a partner and exchange envelopes. Partners can ask each other about what's written on the cards and help each other find solutions for how to manage their worries and the body symptoms.
    o Ask students to share with the larger group what their three cards say. Ask the group to offer solutions for managing the worry and the body symptoms.

- Potential discussion questions include the following:

    o "Are there other ways that your body lets you know when you're feeling nervous or worried?"
    o "What do you do when you get these signals? What's been most helpful? What's been least helpful?"
    o "If the situation that is making you nervous can be changed (e.g., a bad grade on a test), what can you do differently? If the situation can't be changed (e.g., a parent is ill), what can you do to feel better? Whom could you talk to?"

Domain	Grade	Activity
Cognitive Restructuring	K–5	Thought Bubble
	K–3	Stop Those Thoughts!
	K–3	Sticky Thoughts
	4–5	The Roadblock Crew
	4–5	The NASTY Trap

COGNITIVE RESTRUCTURING

Cognitive restructuring is one of the most commonly used strategies in prevention and intervention programs for childhood anxiety and depression (Dozois, Seeds, & Collins, 2009; Garber, 2006; Kingery et al., 2006). It refers to modifying the negative thoughts and thinking errors about oneself, people, events, and the future. Understanding one's thoughts, challenging them, finding evidence for their validity, and changing them is not an easy process. It requires practice, but also abstract thinking. Therefore, consideration of the child's developmental stage is critical in implementing cognitive restructuring techniques.

The goal of cognitive restructuring is to first identify self-talk. Next, a connection is made between self-talk and feelings. For example, if a child's self-talk before a test is, "I studied really hard and am ready for this test; I'm sure I'll do a great job," she will likely feel confident and calm. However, if the self-talk is, "I don't think I can do this; I can never remember how the teacher taught me to do this," she will likely feel worried and scared. The next step in the sequence is to challenge the negative self-talk that children may have. In the example where the child's self-talk is "I can never remember how the teacher taught me to do this," the word to challenge is "never," as it represents an all-or-none thinking error. Children need help with this type of challenging negative self-talk, but the goal is for them to be able to increasingly identify their own negative thoughts and challenge their thinking errors. Importantly, challenging thoughts does not mean simply discounting thoughts (e.g., by saying "that would never happen" or "that's just not true") or changing negative thoughts to positive thoughts. Cognitive restructuring involves questioning the thoughts and using evidence to prove or disprove unrealistic thoughts. The following are techniques that may be used when helping children understand their self-talk.

Thought Bubble (Grades K–5)

Phillip Kendall, a renowned psychologist, has a famous technique called the "thought bubble." It is a great tool to use when helping children identify their negative self-talk. It can be difficult for children to think about their thoughts. However, an external representation, such as the thought bubble, can help children identify their thoughts more easily. This technique may be used with children in Grades K through 5.

Materials Needed

Handout in Appendix A

Instructions

Teachers can help students begin to identify their self-talk by starting with the question, "What's in your thought bubble?" Artistic ability is not a must; a simple stick figure with a thought bubble is perfect.

- This technique may be used individually or with the whole class. You can encourage students to practice identifying their self-talk by asking them to think about different situations. For example, using the thought bubble handout in Appendix A, ask students to fill out what their self-talk might be during these situations:

  - When they are asked to do chores
  - When they are at the playground and other kids are using the swing they want to use
  - At a birthday party
  - In class before a test
  - Coming back to school after a vacation
  - When someone is looking at them kind of funny and they don't know why
  - When they have made a mistake on an assignment

- Once children have practiced identifying their self-talk, an introduction of the different thinking errors can begin. Children can be encouraged to look for the thinking errors in their thought bubbles. The following is a list of the most commonly noted thinking errors among school-age children:

  o *All-or-none thinking.* Children view things as either black or white, with no gradient or in-between options.
    Example: "All the kids in the class think I'm stupid."
  o *Overgeneralization.* Children see things as characteristic of how things will always be, rather than specific to a particular situation; this cognitive error is characterized by the frequent use of words such as *always* or *never.*
    Example: "I'm always going to be left out."
  o *Mind reading.* When children engage in mind reading, they are convinced that they know what others are thinking about them.
    Example: "She looked at me but did not say hello. She must be mad at me."
  o *Catastrophizing.* Children expect the worst possible outcome.
    Example: "If I go to the party, everyone will make fun of me."
  o *Disqualifying the positive.* Children believe that positive events occur only by luck and are not due to something they did.
    Example: "I got a good grade just because I guessed the right answers."
  o *Personalization.* Children attribute negative situations or outcomes to something they did wrong, or to some faulty personal attribute, even if the situation had nothing to do with them.
    Example: "Mrs. Thomson is absent because she's so tired of having to deal with me."
  o *Labeling.* Children may use global labels to describe themselves rather than finding descriptors that are associated with a particular situation.
    Example: "I'm just a failure."

o *Should/must statements.* Children use *should* or *must* statements to describe how they or others should act.
  Example: "I should have known better."

• Once students are familiar with the concept of identifying their self-talk, you can introduce how to challenge the negative self-talk or thinking errors. This process may generally begin with students in third grade, but will require practice and assistance. Helpful questions that you can ask students include:

  o "What is another way to think about this?"
  o "Is there another way to look at this?"
  o "Has this happened before?"
  o "Would it be so bad if it happened?"
  o "What else could you tell yourself about this?"

Stop Those Thoughts! (Grades K–3)

Younger children (i.e., third grade and below) may have difficulty challenging their negative thoughts and finding evidence for or against their accuracy. A technique that may be more helpful for younger students is using thought stopping. Thought stopping involves identifying negative self-talk, such as "I'm a loser" or "I can't do anything right" or "Nobody likes me," and then picturing a stop sign or some other visual cue as a reminder to stop those negative thoughts. Some students like to name their worry or their negative thoughts. You can ask younger students to draw their worry or their negative thoughts and give them a name. I worked with a 7-year old boy, Sam, who drew his worry as a hairy monster and called it Harold. Every time Sam did something to get rid of his negative thoughts or his worry, he erased a little bit of Harold, until eventually, Harold was gone. Sam took great delight in erasing Harold and saying, "See ya! Don't come back!" Like Sam, students can "talk back" to their negative thoughts, erase them, or tell them to stop or to go away. The thought stopping or talking back to the worry should be paired with some activity that is relaxing or enjoyable, such as deep breathing, doing jumping jacks, or drawing, to help children distract themselves and stop the potential cycle of rumination.

Sticky Thoughts (Grades K–3)

This activity helps children identify their negative self-talk and thinking traps. Because it is done in a group setting, it can benefit all children, even those who do not struggle with internalizing disorders. Furthermore, the activity helps to build a common language (e.g., "sticky thoughts") and encourages peers to be a source of support for each other.

Materials Needed
- Post-its (of different colors if possible)
- Markers

Instructions
- Divide students into groups of four or five.
- Distribute Post-its and markers.
- Ask students to come up with different examples of negative self-talk that kids might have (e.g., "I'll always be picked last at recess") and write them on the Post-its. (Kindergarten students should come up with three examples, first-graders with five examples, second-graders with seven examples, and third-graders with 10 examples.)
- One member of each group will be the designated "sticky stick," and he or she will have all the Post-its stuck on him or her.
- The challenge is on! The first group to replace all the negative self-talk Post-its on the "sticky sticks" with positive self-talk Post-its wins. (Examples of positive self-talk: "I messed up this time, but next time I will be prepared and will do better. I can succeed at this if I try. It's OK to make mistakes; no one is perfect.")
- The winning group can share their new Post-its with the rest of the class. If time allows, all groups can share what they wrote as their positive self-statements.
- The Post-its with the positive self-statements can be posted around the room to provide a reminder for students of how to challenge negative thoughts.

Variation
This activity can also be used for individual children as a way to externalize their negative thoughts. Children may at times have recur-

rent negative thoughts that interfere with their ability to concentrate or work on assignments. When you know this is an area of difficulty for your student, you can give him a packet of Post-it notes. He can then write the "sticky thought" on the Post-it. This serves as a way of externalizing, or bringing out of himself, the distressing thought. It can also give you a better understanding of what the student is thinking at the moment. Based on the particular sticky thought identified, you may suggest a technique that might help, such as a movement break, assistance with transition, taking deep breaths, or working with a partner.

The Roadblock Crew (Grades 4–5)

This activity encourages students to think more critically about how particular situations may lead to negative self-talk and thinking traps. The thoughts, in turn, impact how they feel about the situation and how they respond. This activity is best done individually.

Materials Needed

Handout from Appendix B

Instructions

- Introduce the activity:

   Some situations can make us feel difficult emotions, like worry, anger, or sadness. These emotions can put up roadblocks in our minds, so that we have a hard time thinking things through and fig-uring out what to do. Sometimes we just feel like giving up and not doing anything. It sounds like you're struggling with some of those roadblocks now. Let's use this handout to help us figure this out.

- Ask the student, "What is your tough situation?" The student might reply, "I'm invited to a party but I don't know if I should go." Continue your script: *What emotion is strongest for you right now? OK, I want you to imagine that emotion as a construction worker that keeps putting up roadblocks and blocking your path.*

- Ask the student, "In this situation, who's the construction worker?" The student may reply, for example, "Worry." Continue your script:

OK, what do you think the roadblocks the construction worker is putting up would say? Let's fill that in on your worksheet.

- The student might reply, for example, "You shouldn't go to the party; nobody there will talk to you. You were just invited because someone felt sorry for you. If you go, you'll do something embarrassing and people will talk about you." Continue your script:

   When these roadblocks are up, it makes you feel like you can't get over them, but you know what? There are ways we can figure out how to jump right over them. What could you think? What could you do?

- This is a good place to help the child find evidence against negative thoughts such as "You were just invited because someone felt sorry for you." Another helpful tip is to help the child think about possible actions he or she can take. For example, if the child is worried about doing something embarrassing, help her talk through what she thinks would be embarrassing. Ask questions such as, "And if you dropped your food, what would be the worst possible thing that could happen? How could you handle that situation?"

- In response to the question, "How do you get over the roadblocks?" the student may reply, "I could go with my friend. She knows how nervous I get at parties and she'll help me. If I do something embarrassing, like dropping my food, I could just laugh it off and say, 'Woops, butterfingers!'"

- Encourage the child to review the answers she wrote on the handout when facing the identified situation. Having written reminders can be helpful. These handouts can also be used later when trying to figure out how to handle similar situations.

The NASTY Trap (Grades 4–5)

This activity helps students understand the connection between thoughts, feelings, and actions. The activity also helps students to learn "cue words" that signal when they are falling into thinking traps.

Materials Needed

Board and chalk *or* dry erase board and markers

Instructions

This activity can be done individually, in small groups, or with the whole class. The script below is for use with the whole class.

Picture yourself at a soccer game. Your team is about to have the final game of the season. Everyone is excited and the coach praises everyone for how hard they've been working, tells the players they're ready, and says that everyone is going to have a great time. Everyone is cheering and laughing.

What kinds of thoughts do you think are going through the team members' minds? How do you think they are feeling? How do you think they'll behave? (On the board, write down three columns: one labeled "Thoughts," the second labeled "Feelings," and the third labeled "Behaviors." As students respond, ask them in which column their responses might belong.)

Now imagine this: Your teacher just handed you a makeup exam to make up for the one you missed while you were absent. She tells you this test is harder than the original one, and says you will probably be confused and not understand all the questions.

What kinds of thoughts might be going through your head? How might you be feeling? What might you do?" (As students respond, again record their answers on the three columns labeled "Thoughts," "Feelings," and "Behaviors.")

As you can see, the kinds of thoughts we have can affect how we feel and how we act. If we have positive thoughts, we are likely to be in a good mood and to do things that keep our good mood going. If we have negative thoughts, we are likely to feel worried, anxious, angry, or sad. When we feel sad, anxious, worried, frustrated, or angry, we can fall into some "thought traps." Once we fall into those thought traps, we are likely to keep having more negative thoughts and then even more negative feelings. We might also behave in ways that continue to make us feel bad, such as staying away from friends or arguing with family members. It's like a circle that keeps going unless we do something to stop it. These traps can be nasty, so we have to figure out ways to keep from getting caught in them. There are some words that act as signals that we may be starting to fall into the nasty traps. Let's look at what those words are:

N: NEVER ("I'm never going to figure out this problem.")

A: ALWAYS ("I always mess things up.")

S: SHOULD HAVE ("I should have known that; how could I be so stupid?")

T: TOTAL DISASTER ("I don't want to go up to the board. I'm going to trip and everyone will laugh; it'll be a total disaster!")

Y: WHY BOTHER ("Things will always be bad, so why bother to do anything?")

Whenever you get caught in the NASTY trap, it can be difficult to think of how to change the situation or to find ways to make you feel better. So, let's think together for a moment. What can you do to feel better and stay away from the traps? You can learn to listen carefully for those words like never, always, *and* total disaster. *Then challenge those negative thoughts. You can ask yourself questions like:*

- *"What is another way to think about this?"*
- *"Is there another way to look at this?"*
- *"Has this happened before?"*
- *"Would it be so bad if it happened?"*
- *"What else can I tell myself about this?"*

What else can you do to keep away from the NASTY trap? (Elicit responses from students about coping skills they might use to help themselves manage their mood.)

Domain	Grade	Activity
Contingency Management	K–5	Pick a Prize
	K–5	The Nurse Pass

CONTINGENCY MANAGEMENT

Contingency management refers to the examination of antecedents and consequences of behaviors to understand what is reinforcing a particular behavior. When helping children with anxiety and depression, we aim to reduce any reinforcement of maladaptive behavior, such as avoidance, and to increase reinforcement of adaptive behavior, such as asking for help without having a tantrum.

Avoidant behaviors are often unintentionally reinforced for children struggling with anxiety and depression. For example, if a child is nervous about speaking in front of the class, she may ask to go to the nurse's office because she has a stomachache. By leaving the classroom to go to the nurse's office, her anxiety temporarily decreases. This reinforces the pattern of avoiding anxiety-provoking situations. Avoidance can also be reinforced by the child's having access to something that is more pleasurable than facing the feared situation or place. For example, a child may refuse to go to school because she is anxious about being in class. If she is permitted to stay home, she will receive extra attention from her mom and will be able to play with her toys or watch TV. These are all pleasurable activities, and access to them has reinforced the behavior of refusing to go to school.

Pick a Prize (Grades K–5)

By being mindful of not reinforcing avoidance but instead reinforcing brave behavior, teachers can help children shift their behavior patterns. Approach behaviors earn rewards that are motivating or interesting for children. The rewards should be individualized per child, but generally things such as small toys, extra computer time, being line leader, or being the teacher's helper for the day may be offered.

Example: A child struggling with depression is irritable and refuses to complete an assignment. Rather than allowing the child to not do the assignment (and therefore reinforcing the avoidance), the teacher reinforces any step toward completion of the assignment. Writing down his name earns acknowledgement, completing one problem earns acknowledgment, and so forth. The child can earn a particular reward if a portion of the assignment is completed. He may earn another reward if the whole assignment is completed.

Example: A child struggling with generalized anxiety disorder worries about tornadoes and about pieces falling off the playground equipment. She worries that if she goes outside, one of these things might happen and she will be hurt. She avoids going outside to recess. Rewards should be given for attempts to go outside and for the brave behavior of leaving the classroom and going to the playground (even if she needs an adult to accompany her).

The Nurse Pass (Grades K–5)

Because children experience so many somatic symptoms as part of their internalizing distress, going to the nurse's office is one strategy that children often try to use to manage feelings of anxiety. While receiving some kind attention and temporary relief from stress does not sound like a bad thing, the difficulty is that retreating to the nurse's office reinforces avoidance. To minimize opportunities for avoidance associated with going to the nurse's office, you, together with your student, may create a "nurse pass."

Materials Needed

Any representation of a pass (e.g., an index card, a written paper)

Instructions

- Together with your student, create a scale to indicate the level of anxiety the child is feeling.

  With younger children you can use symbols:

  With older children, you can use numbers:

  0 = feeling fine

  3 = having a hard time but can stay in class

  5 = very anxious

- Create a list of things the child can do to manage anxiety (younger children may label this as worry or nervousness). Examples include taking three deep breaths, taking a movement break, helping the teacher with a particular task, or using positive self-statements. These ideas should be written down on a card.

- When the child asks to go to the nurse's office, ask him to tell you (using faces or numbers) how he is feeling. If he is at either of the first two faces, or if he is below 5, ask him to use a skill from his card to help him feel less anxious. Any use of these coping skills earns a reward (e.g., praise, a point toward earning a prize, an extra minute of computer time).

- The child can use the nurse pass only when he is at the third face or at 5.
- For the first week of this intervention, the pass can be used only once a day.
- Gradually, access to the pass should be made more limited. For example, for the second week, the pass can be used only three days out of the week.

Domain	Grade	Activity
Behavior Support	K–5	Safe People and Spaces
	K–5	Deescalating Anger

BEHAVIOR SUPPORT

Behavioral structures can help children maintain self-regulation throughout the school day. For example, all students benefit from knowing the routines around transitions and from understanding behavioral expectations while in the classroom. Children struggling with anxiety and depression especially benefit from behavioral supports as, given the helplessness and avoidance associated with their disorders, they often are not able to independently devise strategies for behavioral regulation.

A key component in developing and facilitating behavioral regulation in children is the experience of emotional safety. As noted in Chapters 2 and 3, children struggling with internalizing disorders may have a history of trauma that compromises their experience of safety related to people and situations. Traumatic experiences can form emotional memories that are extremely powerful and long lasting. These memories are relived when cues or signals in the environment activate those memories (National Scientific Council on the Developing Child, 2010). Therefore, an important intervention to support children's behavior in the classroom is to understand what teacher behaviors or classroom routines may be triggering children's trauma responses and thereby decreasing their experience of safety. Examples of actions that may trigger children's trauma include:

- Clapping to focus the students' attention back on the teacher (for some children, the sound of clapping may remind them of being hit)
- Turning lights on and off to signal a transition (this may be triggering for children who were victims of emotional or sexual abuse)
- Yelling (this may be triggering for children who were victims of emotional or physical abuse)

For an excellent example of a classroom-based, trauma-informed intervention, see the PAX Good Behavior Game at http://goodbehaviorgame.org.

Safe People and Spaces (Grades K–5)

Students who struggle with poor attendance, frequent tardiness, or school refusal benefit from having a designated school staff member who can meet them upon arrival at school. The "safe" person may be a teacher, the school nurse, a teacher's aide, or a school secretary. This person acts like a coach, praising the child for arriving at school and encouraging her to go to class. This person facilitates transitions for the child by walking her to different classrooms as needed, or to the lunch room or recess. An assistant coach should also be identified in case the coach is absent or not able to meet the child on a particular day. The parents, the child, and the school staff member should predetermine where the "safe space" to meet will be. Safe spaces may include the drop-off site for the school, the front door, or the main office.

The coach may wish to have a particular responsibility or task that the child helps with before school. For example, if the coach is a teacher's aide, he or she may be responsible for delivering notes or materials to teachers before classes begin. The child can have the special responsibility of assisting the coach in these deliveries. Other special responsibilities may be feeding a class pet, setting up the computer lab, or delivering attendance sheets. By having a special responsibility, the child can be distracted from the initial distress of starting school. Furthermore, feeling entrusted with a responsibility, as well as experiencing the success of completing the responsibility, can promote positive self-esteem in the child.

Deescalating Anger (Grades K–5)

One of the hallmarks of depressive disorders is sad mood. In children, sadness and overall emotional distress may be manifested as irritability. Children struggling with anxiety disorders may also exhibit irritability, frustration, and anger that result in behavioral acting out. Younger children with internalizing disorders may have more tantrums than their typically developing peers. Older school children may have short tempers, may have some oppositional behaviors, or may express significant anger. Therefore, having clear interventions for helping children manage and deescalate anger is an important component of supporting students' behavioral regulation. This activity describes how to create an anger management plan as well as strategies teachers can use in the moment when the child is experiencing anger and distress.

As in the management of other symptom presentations, prevention and planning are always recommended. That is, do not wait until a crisis arises to create an intervention or to try to rationalize the situation with the student. Instead, find opportunities when the student is calm and receptive and engage him in creating an anger management plan. This plan helps him know how to identify his anger and how to rate its intensity, and has him list actions he can take to decrease the anger. For children whose anger escalates very quickly or may involve dangerous behaviors, it will be important to identify safe places to deescalate. For example, the student may move to a different seat, to a different part of the classroom, or to another location (e.g., an office). Staff that the teacher may call on for assistance should also be identified. These conversations should occur in private, and if possible, should include the child's parent or therapist to ensure that consistent expectations, responses, and rewards are used across settings.

Materials Needed
- Student journal for writing strategies for anger management
- Handout from Appendix C (for Grades K–3) or Appendix D (for Grades 4–5)

Instructions

- The handouts in Appendices C and D are guides for helping a student "talk through" his experience of anger. Giving the child a way to break down the experience based on what he is feeling in his body and having him determine what his thoughts might be, make an assessment of the intensity of the experience, and think about what to do all build self-awareness and self-management skills.
- When the child is angry, find a peaceful area where you may speak more privately. Kneel down to be on the same level as the child and speak slowly and calmly. Acknowledge that the child may be experiencing intense feelings inside and that it may be difficult for him to manage them all at once or even to verbalize everything at once. For children who are struggling with finding words to express how they feel, you may offer prompts such as, "It looks like you're pretty frustrated."
- Allow the child some time to calm down. Wait to ask clarifying questions or to find out more about the situation until the child seems calmer. For some children, continued questioning may feel either judgmental or accusatory and may further escalate their anger.
- For many children struggling with internalizing disorders, the anger is a behavioral manifestation of other distress, including sadness, fear, anxiety, or helplessness. If the child is able to engage in a conversation, encourage him to think about what other emotions he might be feeling. For example, a child may push a peer in the playground due to sadness about being left out of games. Exploring what else the child may be experiencing helps to increase his self-awareness, and also will help you to better understand children who might otherwise be labeled as "behavior problems."
- Think together with the child about what actions he may take to cope with the strong feelings. Examples might include writing in a journal, playing with clay, squeezing a stress ball, shooting hoops, crumbling or ripping paper, or listening to music.
- Allow the student opportunities for a "do-over." That is, if a student behaves in a way that is disruptive, allow him the opportunity to correct the behavior. For example, if a student crumbles up his paper out of frustration, allow him to straighten out the paper and begin anew.

- Notice appropriate behaviors or use of coping skills and provide praise and encouragement for the child. Identify the behavior you noted and let the child know why that behavior is important. For example, you might say, "I noticed that when you were feeling angry, you walked to the corner of the room to find a stress ball. Thank you for finding something to help manage how you are feeling and for doing so quietly so that the other students can continue to focus on their work."
- If the child appears unable to settle down and presents with behaviors that are dangerous to himself or others, ask for assistance immediately.

As discussed in the section on contingency management, when assisting children who struggle with internalizing disorders, it is important to understand which antecedents and consequences are reinforcing specific maladaptive behaviors (e.g., withdrawal). In this case, we want to reduce any responses that are unintentionally reinforcing a child's disruptive behavior. Leflot, van Lier, Onghena, and Colpin (2010) found that teachers' negative reactions to child problem behaviors, combined with a lack of positive responses to appropriate child behaviors, may unintentionally reinforce the child's disruptive behavior. Interestingly, they found that this link between negative teacher–child interactions and child behavior problems is stronger for boys than for girls.

To avoid the cycle of escalating anger and unintentionally reinforcing problem behavior, the following recommendations are offered:

- It is fine to ask a few questions such as, "Are you OK? Will you let me know when you are feeling calmer?" However, avoid asking too many questions too rapidly. This may feel overwhelming for the child. The child will not be able to process the entire situation until he has had an opportunity to calm down. Anger is a very intense emotion that involves activation of the stress response system. Children are not able to properly process complex or abstract information until their internal alarm system has deactivated.
- Redirect the child to engage in a different behavior. Asking the child to stop without offering alternatives will likely be unsuccessful.
- Do not blame or accuse the child. It is very likely that the child's distress and subsequent anger stems from self-blame or judgment.

External blame will reinforce the negative thoughts the child may be having.

- Avoid reprimanding the child in front of others.
- Do not enlist peers' help in deescalating the child's anger.

Domain	Grade	Activity
Increasing Positive Affect	K–5	Process Finders
	K–5	Art Gallery
	K–5	Thank-You Notes
	K–5	Mantra Cards
	1–5	Peer Leadership
	3–5	Goal Setting

INCREASING POSITIVE AFFECT

Positive emotions in children, such as hope, joy, and pride, have been associated with academic interest, effort, achievement, and problem solving (Valiente, Swanson, & Eisenberg, 2012). Positive emotions are also associated with self-efficacy, or a child's perceived ability to produce a particular action regardless of actual abilities (i.e., "I can do it if I try"; Bandura & Shunck, 1981). Typically developing children seek out situations and people that lead to positive emotions, and they seek out ways to maintain that positive affect. Picture a kindergarten student who loves to be with her friends. She seeks them out at the playground and tries to find ways to maintain continued engagement with them. She knows that when she plays with her friends, she feels happiness, excitement, and fun. Picture that same child as she tries the monkey bars for the first time. Even if she is not able to make it across the whole thing, she feels pride and joy at her ability to try and succeed, even if it's only one or two bars at a time.

Children struggling with internalizing disorders have difficulty regulating their experiences of positive affect. While they may feel positive emotions, they struggle with finding ways to initiate and maintain those emotions. Furthermore, children with anxiety and depression have low perceived self-efficacy. They do not feel confident about their competence, skills, or ability to effect change. This sense of helplessness leads to avoidance and giving up. The activities in this domain are designed to help children find opportunities to feel and maintain positive emotions. As positive affect is such an abstract notion, the activities aim to create experiential and visual representations that are concrete enough for even younger children to understand.

Process Finders (Grades K–5)

Internalizing disorders are characterized by avoidance, significant difficulties with flexibility (i.e., finding new solutions to emotionally distressing situations), and inability to use past successes as a way to approach new situations and promote positive affect. Therefore, it is important for teachers to notice when students demonstrate more flexibility and give praise for appropriate risk taking and tolerance of novelty. In this activity, teachers are the process finders.

Instructions

- When students go out of their comfort zone, approach something new, or take a good risk (e.g., approaching a new peer), highlight the importance of that process for the student. Use language that focuses on the process rather than on evaluation or judgment of the end result. Focusing on the process highlights that it is trying that connotes success, not just the end product. As you may recall from Chapter 1, promotion of a growth mindset focuses on the attempt rather than on the product. For example, you might say:

   1. "You weren't sure what to do, but you thought about it and made a decision."
   2. "You worked really hard on that drawing!"
   3. "You are very curious about that."
   4. "You tried something new."
   5. "You tried different ways to finish that project—way to go!"

Art Gallery (Grades K–5)

Art Gallery focuses on another area of difficulty for students with internalizing disorders: identifying success and positive affect, and using these experiences to maintain positive affect. This activity seeks to reinforce the experiencing and maintaining of positive affect through visual representations.

Materials Needed
- Paper
- Drawing materials
- Stickers and other decorating materials (e.g., glitter)

Instructions
- Notice when a student experiences a success (e.g., completing an assignment, participating in class, making a new friend, getting through a whole class without asking to go to the nurse's office, asking for help).
- Ask the child what the success or positive experience looks like. You can also ask what it sounds like, feels like, and even smells like.
- Ask the student to draw what he just described. Emphasize that it can be anything—a shape, a color, an object, a sound. It does not have to make sense to anyone but him.
- Have the student keep that visual representation on his desk for the rest of the day as a reminder of the positive accomplishment.
- To create the art gallery, you can ask all students to do this so that they have constant reminders of what their positive feelings look like. A fun added component is to have an art show, where kids can talk to each other about their drawings. Encourage students to not only talk about their drawings, but also to help each other think about how to experience more positive feelings that they can capture and show on their growing art gallery.

Thank-You Notes (Grades K–5)

Children struggling with anxiety and depression often worry about how others perceive them. It is not unusual for them to make negative assumptions about how adults and peers feel about them. In order to challenge these negative assumptions, having concrete and tangible proof of how others feel about them can be very helpful. This activity offers a fun way for children to share their positive regard of each other.

Materials Needed
- Cardstock, colored paper, construction paper, or regular paper
- Markers

Instructions
- Distribute a piece of paper and a marker to each student.
- Ask students to fold their paper in half. This will make a card that opens up. On the outside of the card, ask students to write their names. They may decorate the name or write it in whichever way they wish.
- Once they have completed their cards, ask students to get up and visit each other student's desk. It is critical that they understand that they must write on every child's card. On their peers' cards, they are to write any of the following things:

    o A nice memory of the person
    o An attribute or quality they appreciate about the person
    o An example of how the person was helpful to them or someone else
    o A positive message they wish to share

- Once all students have finished, have them read what their peers wrote on their cards. If you have time, you may ask students to share some of what was written on their cards. You can also encourage further discussion by asking, "How did it make you feel to read that on your card?" "Did you know people felt that way about you?" "Was there anything that surprised you? Why?"

Variation

Try doing this activity at your next faculty meeting. Adults can benefit from positive regard just as much as children can!

Mantra Cards (Grades K–5)

Mantra comes from the Buddhist or Hindu tradition and is defined as a word or a sound that is repeated to help maintain concentration and focus while praying or meditating. The definition of *mantra* can be expanded to include a word or phrase that captures belief in something or helps to maintain a particular feeling. For example, in my home, we have a card that looks like this:

> *"I can figure this out."*
>
> *"I will try my best."*
>
> *"I will be proud."*

Whenever there is a particular project that needs to be completed, a test to study for, or a difficult situation to face, the person facing the challenge uses the card and keeps it with him or her as long as it is needed.

This activity helps students develop their own mantras to help motivate and encourage them.

Materials Needed
Index cards

Instructions
- Distribute several cards to each student.
- Ask them to write down a mantra, or special message, that helps them feel good, motivated, or positive.
- They can ask other peers for ideas, or share ones they like.
- Encourage students to keep the mantra cards on their desks. You can begin your morning routine with a deep breath for grounding (see the relaxation skills section in this chapter) and having your students read their mantra.
- If possible, laminate the cards for students so that they last longer.

Peer Leadership (Grades 1–5)

As Davies (2011) states, "prosocial children gain the admiration of their peers; in turn, being appreciated for helpfulness, kindness, and altruism increases their self-esteem" (p. 338). Students struggling with anxiety and depression have low self-esteem. While they very much desire connection with others, these students may not know how to initiate helpful interactions. Alternatively, they may avoid opportunities to participate or help, worrying about not knowing what to do or how others will perceive them. Therefore, creating structured opportunities for children to help others represents an opportunity to promote positive self-esteem and regard. Below are ideas for giving children helping opportunities.

Instructions

- Find a special job or task for the child (e.g., distributing papers, caring for the class pet).
- Have the student be a "reading buddy" to a younger student.
- Have the student be a "study buddy" to someone who may need help with an assignment, or to catch someone up after an absence.

Variation

Some older students (e.g., fourth- and fifth-graders) may feel comfortable sharing their experiences with worry or fear. If appropriate (as deemed by the parents and therapist if applicable), the child may share with other students his or her experiences and how he or she overcame that challenge. For example, a student may share how she often worried about what others thought of her and how that made her shy away from peers and reject invitations to social gatherings. She can then explain what coping skills she used to help her overcome those challenges.

Some coaching will need to occur before this sharing in order to make sure diagnoses are not discussed and to figure out how the worry will be explained. While this preparation is important, it is equally important to remember that sharing such experiences will not make the anxiety "contagious." Instead, it will initiate an important conversation about feelings and coping, and will emphasize to students that learning about emotional health and wellness is very important.

Goal Setting (Grades 3–5)

Research indicates that "children who experience discrepancies in their goal striving and actual performance tend to evidence greater psychopathology" (Grills-Taquechel, Fletcher, Vaughn, Denton, & Taylor, p. 405). Children who struggle with internalizing disorders often experience such discrepancies because of perfectionism, having little energy and feeling as if any action toward a goal is impossible, setting unrealistically high goals and then feeling disappointed and sad when they cannot meet the goals, and rumination and worry that get in the way of identifying goals.

Instructions

- Help children struggling with anxiety and depression to set goals that are realistic for their current symptom presentation. For example, if a child is experiencing severe symptoms of depression, he may need to set goals around attendance rather than around completing assignments. If a child is experiencing difficulties with perfectionism, a goal may be to simply create an outline or rough draft of a project. By doing this, you break up the large assignment into smaller, more manageable goals and (a) teach that "rough drafts" are helpful and positive and (b) show the child a way to stop the cycle of becoming paralyzed by things needing to be perfect.
- Reward the student for minor achievements as well as for partial successes. Any effort to proceed toward a goal should be rewarded rather than only the final product.
- Failures should be celebrated as wonderful opportunities to learn, and perfection should never be the goal. It is therefore critical to be cognizant of what explicit and implicit messages are shared in the classroom about what constitutes failure versus success.

Domain	Grade	Activity
Active Coping	K–3	The Sponge
	K–5	Journaling
	K–5	What Would You Do?
	K–5	Sensory Box
	K–5	Worry Stones
	4–5	Mindfulness

PROMOTING ACTIVE COPING

Finding active, approach-related ways of coping is an area of great difficulty for children struggling with internalizing disorders. The following set of activities aims to help children develop a repertoire of skills to use that involve thinking about possible solutions, keep a visual and tangible set of soothing mechanisms, and keep a record of their new skills to reference and use in the future.

The Sponge (Grades K–3)

The concept of emotions is quite a complex and abstract one. Younger children benefit from understanding the concept in a more concrete and accessible manner. Therefore, developing vocabulary around emotional understanding is an active way for them to develop coping and self-regulation. This activity offers one idea for explaining the concept of emotions to younger students. Teachers should feel free to use their own metaphors and ideas as appropriate for their students.

Materials
- Sponges
- Water table or buckets
- Paper towels

Instructions
- Introduce the activity:

    Today we're going to talk about feelings.

    Can anyone tell me what feelings are? (It is important to make the connection here that feelings are something we experience in our bodies, minds, and actions.)

    What kinds of feelings can people have? (Encourage students to list as many as possible.)

    Where do feelings come from? Feelings can come from inside of us—our bodies and minds let us know what feelings we might have. We can also be like sponges, soaking up feelings and energy from all around us.

    Has anyone used a sponge? How does it work? What happens if it's completely dry—will it work? No, it doesn't work too well. What if it's too wet? That's right—when the sponge gets really wet and we don't squeeze water out of it, it gets heavy and drips—not too easy to use then either, right? So what do you do? You squeeze out the extra water but keep enough in the sponge so that the sponge works well and you can use it to help you clean. This same thing happens with our feelings.

If we have too many and we don't know what to do with them, we can feel heavy, with feelings just dripping out of us, spilling and getting in the way of our figuring out what to do. But what do you think would happen if you figured out a way to squeeze out some of those extra feelings? That's right—you can use them to help you understand what's going on, ask for help, and feel good. Remember our sponge? What happens if it's too dry? (It won't work and is not easy to use.) Same thing with your feelings! You don't want to be completely without feelings, because feelings help you connect to others, feel good about yourself, and understand your world. We want just the right amount. So, how can we squeeze the excess water out of our sponges?

- Have fun with this! Have the students engage in water play to figure out good ways to squeeze their sponges. Have them compare what the sponge looks like when it's completely dry, too wet, and just right. Ask the students what they look and feel like when they're too dry or too wet (regarding feelings).

- You can label the different sponges with different emotions (e.g., the angry sponge, the happy sponge, the worried sponge) and ask the children what too dry, too wet, or just right would look like for those emotions.

- Think about ways to continue this conversation with your students. For example, if a child seems to be struggling emotionally one day, you can ask, "Is your sponge dry?" or "Too much water in your sponge today? What can we do?"

- Another example of continuing to use this metaphor is to have a special "sponge" award each week or month for students who demonstrate good self-regulation.

Journaling (Grades K–5)

Children with internalizing disorders struggle with three emotion-related competencies: awareness, expression, and coping (Thomassin, Morelen, & Suveg, 2012). Journaling has been used as a tool to help develop and promote these emotion-related competencies. The use of journaling is based on the self-regulation theory of expressive writing, which suggests that attending to emotions while writing helps to build mastery and increase self-efficacy for emotion regulation (Frattaroli, 2006). This connection was highlighted in a study by Thomassin and colleagues (2012), where the researchers found a reduction in anxiety symptoms among school-age girls (7–12 years) who used electronic journaling.

Materials

Notebooks, cards bound by a ring, folders with papers inside, or any other medium that may serve as a journal

Instructions

- When using journals in the classroom, it is helpful to integrate their use into a regular routine. For example, the child can begin the day with a brief scan of how she is feeling and write that down in her journal. At the end of the day, she may refer to the journal again to briefly write down what helped during the day and what was challenging. The handouts in the appendices may also be incorporated into the journals.
- Below are ideas for journal prompts that can be used with students of different ages:

  o For younger students (Grades K–3):

    □ My feelings are . . .
    □ Things I notice in my body are . . .
    □ My thoughts are . . .
    □ Bad self-talk that I have is . . .
    □ Good self-talk that I have is . . .
    □ Good things that happened today are . . .
    □ Some things that were hard today were . . .
    □ What I feel the best about today is . . .

  o For older students (Grades 4–5):

    □ What situations or people make me feel most stressed?
    □ How do those people or places affect me (in terms of my feelings, thoughts, and actions)?
    □ What have I noticed and learned about myself when I get stressed?

- □ When I felt stressed, was it helpful to talk to someone? Who was helpful?
- □ What kinds of things help me feel successful, as if I can manage my stress?

  o For older students (Grades 4-5) who have identified struggles with anxiety and/or depression:

  - □ What is my anxiety about? (this involves psychoeducation about anxiety)
  - □ What causes my anxiety? (triggers; for example, particular situations or fears)
  - □ How do I know when I'm feeling anxious? (bodily sensations, thoughts, actions, feelings)
  - □ What do I do when I feel anxious? (coping skills)
  - □ My top five coping skills; things I can do (individualized to each student)
  - □ How and when can I use these? (real-world practice)

- An important part of journaling also involves monitoring participation in enjoyable activities. Prompts in the journal may include:

  o For younger children (Grades K–2):

  - □ Three fun things I did today were . . .
  - □ When I did those things, I felt . . .
    ☺   ☺   ☺

  o For older children (Grades 3–5):

  - □ Three fun things I did today were . . .
  - □ When I did those things, I felt . . .
    1 = OK
    3 = good
    5 = great

What Would You Do? (Grades K–5)

Students struggling with internalizing disorders may find particular emotions (e.g., fear, sadness) unacceptable or aversive, so they may suppress their emotional expression in an attempt to (a) avoid the emotional experience and (b) minimize potential negative evaluations by others (E.K.Hughes, Gullone, & Watson, 2011). Suppression of emotions typically involves avoidance. That is, rather than dealing with a particular emotional experience, children avoid the situation altogether. This activity helps students anticipate possible difficulties that may arise and to develop coping scenarios for those difficulties in order to decrease avoidance and increase active coping.

Materials Needed
- Student journal
- Index cards with different scenarios

Instructions
- Through individual conversations, help students identify situations that make them feel worried, scared, sad, or overwhelmed. For example, a student might say, "I'm afraid I'll start crying if I have to go up and write on the board."
- Once the student identifies the situations, offer competing responses to negative thoughts or behaviors. For example, you might say, "If you start to feel like you are going to cry, what could you do? Could you take some deep breaths and repeat to yourself 'I have gone to the board before and I have not cried.'?"
- Help the student identify other coping skills he or she may use and write these down in his or her journal.

Variation
These skills are ones that all students, not just those struggling with anxiety and depression, would benefit from practicing. You can encourage all students to participate through role plays.

- Ask the students to identify situations that may make them feel angry, sad, worried, and so forth, and write each one on an index card.

- Divide up the class into groups of three to five students.
- Give each group a scenario, and ask them to come up with a role play of how they might handle that situation. After a role play is presented, encourage discussion by asking questions such as:

  o What do you think was most helpful?
  o Is there anything you might do differently?
  o What else could you do in that situation?
  o How can we help each other to remember and practice those great ideas?

Sensory Box (Grades K–5)

When students are struggling emotionally, it can be difficult to immediately remember and implement the coping skills they have developed. For example, when a child is very anxious about entering the classroom, it may be challenging for him to stop, identify his thoughts, and challenge them. At that moment, he may need something more immediate and tangible to help him with soothing and calming. A sensory box is a portable collection of soothing techniques that children can use to calm down prior to using more cognitive-based coping skills.

Materials Needed
- Shoebox
- Materials as identified by the student that will go into the box

Instructions
- Explain to the student that in his box, he will put things that can help him feel calm and safe when he is having a hard time. Encourage the student to decorate the box any way he chooses. Also choose a name for the box—it can be something like "My Toolbox," "My Calming Box," or "My Happy Box."
- Identify objects that will go into the sensory box. Make sure that the objects represent all senses (smell, taste, touch, sound, sight). Objects might include things like pictures of loved ones, a picture of a calming scene, a scented candle, a bit of perfume, a worry stone or crystal, a CD of soothing music, or a piece of a favorite fabric.

For sounds, you might identify things that are available in the classroom. It is important to identify things that are calming for the child, that will easily fit into the box, and that will not be too distracting when used in school.

• Once the student has a completed sensory box, remind him to use it when he feels anxious, fearful, sad, or overwhelmed.

Worry Stones (Grades K–5)

You may recall observing someone who used his or her hands to maintain focus or a state of calm; people who knit, squeeze a stress ball, or doodle during meetings come to mind. For many people, engaging in some constant, rhythmic activity can be calming and can help focus their attention. One way to help children release their worries and refocus their attention is by offering a worry stone.

Materials Needed
• A flat stone (can be purchased as a worry stone or can be made by getting the stone and writing a particular word on it)
• Permanent marker

Instructions
• Give the child a stone. If you have stones that have words already printed on them, ask the student to choose the one she feels would be most fitting or helpful. If the stone has no words, ask the child to identify the word that she would like to use and then write it for her on the stone using a permanent marker.
• The child can place the stone on her desk. Whenever she feels nervous, worried, sad, or distracted, she can use the stone to "rub" these emotions away. As she rubs the stone, ask her to imagine all her worries being rubbed away, with the reassurance that they cannot reenter her body.

Variation
If you feel stones are unsafe to use with your students, you can alter this activity by using stress balls or by cutting a piece of fabric (e.g., felt)

and writing the word on the fabric. You can make stress balls by using a strong balloon and filling it with flour.

Mindfulness (Grades 4–5)

The previous activities promote awareness of emotions and use of active skills to manage them. The progression of awareness and management of emotions offers a scaffold for the more complex process of awareness described in this activity: mindfulness. Kabat-Zinn (1994) defines mindfulness as "paying attention in a particular way: on purpose, in the present moment, and nonjudgmentally"(p. 4). When used to decrease symptoms of anxiety and depression specifically, the aim of mindfulness is to improve emotion awareness, promote acceptance of experiences, and dissuade "against maladaptive attempts of regulation" to "allow for more flexible responses" (Amstadter, 2008, p. 219). A number of studies have investigated the effect of mindfulness-oriented therapies for children, with promising results. For example, Gould, Dariotis, Mendelson, and Greenberg (2012) used mindfulness-based techniques for decreasing depression symptoms among fourth- and fifth-grade students (primarily of African American and Latino decent). The researchers found that among children who reported low or medium levels of baseline depressive symptoms, the intervention reduced rumination, impulsive response, and intrusive thoughts (Gould et al., 2012). This activity describes prompts that can be used with students to help them be more mindfully aware of their emotions. It also begins to introduce the concept of the nonjudgmental approach that is a cornerstone of mindfulness.

Materials Needed
Student journal

Instructions
- Begin this conversation individually with the student when he is calm and receptive. It is not helpful to try to introduce this activity when the student is experiencing a heightened level of emotional distress.
- Ask the student what he thinks being *mindful* means. You can describe mindfulness as the process of focusing on something—

just noticing it, while not trying to explain it or solve it. You can have him practice being mindful by offering a piece of candy or something from his snack. Ask him to notice everything about it as he eats it. What does it feel like in his mouth? What does it taste like? What does he notice about its texture? How does it change?

- Have the student practice mindfulness by asking him to identify a situation. This can be anything, such as watching his friends play or being in math class.

  o *Focus.* Have the student choose one spot to focus on—maybe a picture, or a spot on the wall.

  o *Breathe.* Have the student focus on his breathing, noticing the inhale and exhale.

  o *Observe.* Have the student just notice the experience, watching his feelings and thoughts come and go. Tell him not to push his feelings or thoughts away, but just to let them happen.

  o *Describe.* Have the student put his experience into words (e.g.," I feel sadness in my chest"); have him be specific and honest.

  o *Participate.* Have the student be a part of the experience, keeping his attention focused in this one moment and forgetting about other stories and other times.

  o *Don't judge.* Have the student observe and notice what is going on and what he feels, but refrain from evaluating it, from giving labels like "good" or "bad," and from trying to solve anything.

- Encourage the student to describe what this experience was like. Ask about how this impacted his feelings.
- These prompts can be written into the student's journal as a reminder of the process of mindfulness.

Domain	Grade	Activity
Relaxation Skills	K–5	Breathing Exercises
	K–5	Progressive Muscle Relaxation
	3–5	Guided Imagery
	3–5	Visualization

RELAXATION SKILLS

Relaxation training is an essential component of the treatment of children with anxiety and depression. "Relaxation training helps the child recognize that he or she does have control over physical reactions" and includes breathing exercises and muscle relaxation (Kendall, Furr, & Podell, 2010, p. 48). Other techniques can also be used to help the child feel calm and in control, including guided imagery and visualization. The activities described below offer examples of scripts and exercises that may be conducted with children. It is important to note that what may work for one child may not work for another. Therefore, the child's comfort level and interests must be taken into account when choosing a relaxation skill.

Breathing Exercises (Grades K–5)

Breathing exercises are helpful to use when the child is experiencing anxiety, is having a difficult time concentrating or focusing, or is feeling angry or overwhelmed, or when several somatic symptoms (e.g., stomachache, shaking, nausea) are active. It is not unusual for students to giggle and get a bit silly when learning breathing exercises. They are likely to look around the room, wonder what others are doing, and laugh. Acknowledge that sometimes it can feel a bit strange or even silly as one begins to learn breathing exercises, but that with practice, it gets easier and is one of the best ways to help when one feels angry, scared, anxious, or stressed.

Instructions

- For students in Grades K through 3: Pinwheel and Cookie Exercise

  - Deliver the following script:
    Imagine that you are at the park outside. It's a bright, sunny day, and at a table in front of you is a big plate of cookies. Choose the cookie you like most and pick it up with your hand. Also on the table are lots of different pinwheels. Choose the pinwheel you like most and pick it up with your other hand. Now smell the cookie with a nice deep breath, and now blow on the pinwheel slowly to make it move. If you blow on

the pinwheel too fast, it won't move, and if you don't blow on it long enough, it won't move either. It has to be just right. Let's practice. Smell the cookie; now blow on the pinwheel. (Repeat three times.)

   o Discussion questions:

      □ What was that like?
      □ What kind of cookie did you choose?
      □ What does your pinwheel look like?
      □ How do you feel after doing some pinwheel breathing?

• For students in Grades K through 5: Calming Words Exercise

   o Deliver the following script:
      Take a slow, deep breath through your nose and exhale out your mouth. Take another deep breath in, feeling your tummy expanding. Now exhale through your mouth, letting all the air out. Let's practice one more time. Deep breath in through your nose, feeling that tummy get large, and deep breath out your mouth, letting out all the air. Now, as you breathe in through your nose, think of a special calming word to yourself. It can be any word you want. As you breathe out your mouth, think of another calming word. It can be any word you like that makes you feel calm and safe. Let's practice the deep breathing again, this time with your special words. Ready? Deep breath in through your nose, think of your word, and breathe out your mouth, thinking of your other special word. Let's do this two more times. (Note: For older children, you can use the words *inhale* and *exhale*.)

   o Discussion questions:

      □ What was that like?
      □ How does your body feel?
      □ How does your mind feel?

☐ Were you able to think of two special words?

☐ Would anyone like to share their words?

• For students in Grades 4 and 5: Gray Mist Exercise

    ○ Deliver the following script:

        Sit back in your chair, as relaxed as you can. If you feel comfortable, close your eyes. If you prefer not to close your eyes, keep them fixed on a spot on the floor in front of you. Now take a nice, deep breath in through your nose, and exhale out your mouth. Let's try that one more time. Deep breath in through your nose, exhale out your mouth. Now as you breathe in, try to count to three, and as you exhale, count to three. Ready? Inhale—one, two, three; now exhale—one, two, three. Let's do that one more time. Inhale—one, two, three; now exhale— one, two, three. Notice the feeling of calm and relaxation. Now imagine any worries or negative thoughts or fears that are bothering you as gray mist that leaves your body every time you exhale. Take a nice deep breath in, and as you exhale, let go of any gray mist that you may be holding in your heart, your mind, and your body. Imagine there is a pouch in front of you. The pouch can look any way you wish. As you breathe out the gray mist, it goes into that pouch. Take deep breaths in, exhale the gray mist, and watch it go into the pouch. Once all the gray mist is out of your heart, mind, and body, close the pouch. Feel safe in knowing that the gray mist cannot reenter your body. It is in the pouch and gone. Continue to take three deep breaths. Remember to breathe in through your nose and out your mouth. Open your eyes when you're ready.

    ○ Discussion questions:

        ☐ What was that like?

        ☐ How does your body feel?

        ☐ How does your mind feel?

        ☐ Were you able to breathe out the gray mist?

Progressive Muscle Relaxation (Grades K–5)

This exercise helps students identify areas of their bodies that may be tense and use progressive muscle relaxation to feel calmer and more relaxed. For younger students, you may wish to focus on just one or two muscle groups. With older students, use as much or as little of the script as you have time for. Always end with the deep breaths and noticing of relaxation.

Instructions

Deliver the following script:

This exercise is used to help you feel more relaxed by focusing on groups of muscles that may be tense or tight. Sometimes when we're feeling nervous, stressed, angry, or worried, our bodies can feel very tight and our muscles get tense. We are going to learn how to relax our bodies by focusing on specific groups of muscles at one time. When I tell you to tense the muscles, I want you to make them as tight as you can. Want to try it? Take your hands and make fists. Tense them—scrunch them up as tight as you can. Now let them go. Do you feel that difference?

OK, now let's get started. I will ask you to tense, or tighten, a specific muscle group for 5 seconds, and then relax it for 5 seconds. When you tighten your muscles, do it as hard as you can. When you relax you muscles, let the muscle go completely limp. While relaxing, try to remember the pleasant feeling of the moment.

Hold your right arm straight out in front of you and bend your hand upward, pointing your fingers toward the ceiling. Make your arm as straight and stiff as you can. Hold that tension for one, two, three, four, five. (Count 5 seconds.) *Now relax and let your arm drop to your side for one, two, three, four, five.* (Count 5 seconds.)

Hold your left arm straight out in front of you and bend your hand upward, pointing your fingers toward the ceiling. Hold that tension. (Count 5 seconds.) *Now relax and let your arm drop to your side.* (Count 5 seconds.)

Shrug your shoulders, raising them as high as possible. (Count 5 seconds.) *Now relax and let your shoulders drop down.* (Count 5 seconds.)

Sit up straight in your chair. Arch your back as much as you can. (Count 5 seconds.) *Now relax and sit back in your chair.* (Count 5 seconds.)

Close your eyes tightly. (Count 5 seconds.) *Now relax and leave them closed, but softly.* (Count 5 seconds.)

Tighten your jaw muscles as much as you can, clenching your teeth together. (Count 5 seconds.) *Now relax your jaw muscles and unclench your teeth.* (Count 5 seconds.)

Bend your neck forward, trying to touch your chin to your chest. (Count 5 seconds.) *Now slowly bring your neck back upright.* (Count 5 seconds.)

Straighten both legs out in front of you, stretching them outward and tensing all the muscles. (Count 5 seconds.) *Now let them relax and slowly bring them back down to the floor.* (Count 5 seconds.)

Take three nice deep breaths, and remember that feeling of relaxation and calm.

Guided Imagery (Grades 3–5)

Guided imagery is a mind-body technique that engages all of the senses to bring about individual changes in behavior, perception, or physiologic responses (Menzies & Jallo, 2011). In treatment with various populations, guided imagery has been shown to relieve stress and anxiety as well as increase sense of self-efficacy for managing symptoms (Menzies & Jallo, 2011). For example, in a study assessing pain levels of 6- to 11-year-old children with sickle cell disease, results showed that after use of guided imagery, the children reported significant increases in self-efficacy and reductions in pain intensity (Dobson & Byrne, 2014). The activities described below aim to help students experience reduced levels of stress and anxiety as well as increase their self-efficacy around symptom management. Guided imagery scripts can be created to best fit the metaphors the student understands, taking into consideration his or her developmental level. Teachers should feel free to create their own scripts to use with students.

Instructions

Deliver the following scripts (or your own) as appropriate to the situation.

- *Script for Managing Headaches*

    Imagine your headache as a bucket full of hot water. What color is your bucket? How large is it? With 1 being just a little uncomfortable and 5 being really uncomfortable, what number do you feel with your headache right now? OK, now imagine that you have another bucket, but this one has cool, soothing water. Imagine yourself pouring that cold water onto your headache. Feel the cool water over your head, making it feel more relaxed and making the pain wash away. Pour some more cool water, slowly, feeling the change in temperature and feeling the cooling sensation. What number does your headache feel now? (Continue with the image of pouring cool water until the child notices a difference from the initial discomfort as indicated by a lower number on the rating scale.) *Notice that feeling of comfort, soothing, and how the pain was washed away. Remember that you always have that bucket of cool water ready to help you feel refreshed and safe.*

• *Script for Managing Stomachaches*

Imagine your stomachache (or tummy ache) as a big twisty jumble of knots. Can you see them? What are the knots made of? With 1 being just a few loose knots and 5 being too many really tight knots, what number are your knots right now? Now picture your hands touching the knots. You find one and start to loosen it. Your fingers are working quickly, finding ways to make the knot loosen and untie. When that knot is gone, you feel your tummy getting calmer, and the pain going away. Now find another knot, letting your fingers work quickly over it, loosening it and untying it. Another knot is gone and your tummy is feeling better, less tight, and calmer. (Continue with the image of untying knots until the child notices a difference from the initial discomfort as indicated by a lower number on the rating scale.) *Notice that feeling of comfort, soothing, and how the pain goes away each time you untie the knots. Remember that you always have the power to untie the knots, no matter how tight they may be. Your hands hold the power to make you feel better, stronger, and calmer.*

• *Script for Managing Anger*

Imagine your anger as a thick sheet of ice. It is slippery and hard, and it is so cold so that it makes your body shake and it's hard to think about much else but being warm. With 1 being just a little angry and 5 being so angry it's hard to control it, what number is your anger right now? Now in your mind, picture your hands. Look at your palms, and see that there is a soft, warm green light that slowly melts the ice. Put your palms where you want to start melting the ice, feeling the warm sensation in your hands and arms. See the green light as it spreads, melting the ice and making you feel warmer and calmer. Keep using the light from your palms, touching any ice you want to melt. Watch the ice turning to water, feeling warmer and safer. (Continue with the image of the green light melting the ice until the child notices a difference from the initial discomfort as indicated by a lower number on the rating scale.) *Notice that feeling of comfort, calming, warmth, and how the anger has melted away. Remember that you always have that warm soft light in you, ready to help you feel warm and safe.*

• **Script for Managing Worries**

Imagine your worries as swirls of light surrounding you. They look like lightning bugs, moving move around and close to you, touching your head and your heart and your body. With 1 being just a few worries and 5 being too many worries to keep track of, what number are your worries right now? Now imagine that you have a jar and that with this jar you can capture each swirl of light in the jar. What color is your jar? How do the lights look in the jar? Use your jar and look around in front, behind, next to you. Notice any lights and simply catch them in your jar. You can do this easily and without any difficulties. With each light that you catch you feel calmer and more peaceful. As your jar fills with light, you feel stronger, safer, and more peaceful. (Continue with the image of catching lights in the jar until the child notices a difference from the initial discomfort as indicated by a lower number on the rating scale.) *Notice that feeling of comfort, calm, and freedom as all the lights are in the jar and cannot touch your head, heart, or body. Remember that you always have that jar, ready to help you catch worries to feel safe and in charge.*

Visualization (Grades 3–5)

Visualization exercises can be used to help students find a time to be mindful and in the moment, with the goal of reducing negative emotions. Engaging in visualization breaks the cycle of rumination and helps students feel more in control of their bodies and minds.

Instructions
- Deliver the following script:

Something that can be very helpful when you are feeling stressed is to picture, or visualize, yourself in a place that feels relaxing and peaceful to you. This could be the beach, outdoors, or the most relaxing place you've ever been. It could even be an imaginary place that only you know about.

Before we start using our imaginations, let's talk a little bit about how imagination works. Did you know that your imagination works in a different way than someone else's? Maybe some kids can see pictures in their minds first, but other kids can hear sounds or even smell things first in their imaginations. The great thing is that there is no right or wrong way to use your imagination. Just let your special place show up in your imagination, piece by piece, as works best for you.

To help you figure out which of the senses might be easiest for you to start with, let's try this quick exercise. Close your eyes, take three deep breaths, and try to imagine the following things:

- ○ *The smell of pizza*
- ○ *The feel of your favorite stuffed animal*
- ○ *Looking out over a field of snow*
- ○ *The smell of fresh-baked cookies*
- ○ *The smell of a freshly quartered orange*
- ○ *The sound of popcorn popping*
- ○ *The feel of sticky cotton candy on your fingers*
- ○ *The sound of your favorite song*
- ○ *The taste of your favorite food*
- ○ *The touch of bumpy brick*

What came to your mind first? (Encourage students to share what they pictured, felt, smelled, or heard first in their imaginations.)
Great! Now that you know which sense to start with, use that as you begin to create your relaxing space. Once your place starts to develop, try to use other senses—sight, sound, touch, smell, and taste. The more senses you try to use, the stronger your place will be.

Now take a piece of paper and write down what you see, hear, feel, smell and taste. Describe your relaxing place in as much detail as you can. Now that you have written about your relaxing place, let's practice the exercise in silence. Take a few deep breaths, and go through your relaxing place in your mind. (Allow students about 10 minutes to practice.)

You can practice your visualization during a study period, for example, or on your way to school. Try to practice at least two times per day, so that the place becomes stronger and clearer. Anytime you feel stressed, worried, frustrated, or overwhelmed, go to your relaxing place to help you find peace and calm.

• If you have time, ask students about what the experience was like for them. Ask whether they may wish to share about their special place, or how they felt once they were there.

Domain	Grade	Activity
Social Support	K–5	Power of the Group
	K–5	Buddy Up
	4–5	"You Can Do It" Messages

SOCIAL SUPPORT

During middle childhood, interactions with peers are critical for development. Peers can serve as sources of joy, support, and encouragement. Interactions with peers also offer scaffolding opportunities for development of social, athletic, and academic skills. Many children struggling with internalizing disorders do not know how to actively engage in recreational activities, especially activities that include friends. Therefore, creating opportunities to promote social support among peers is critical in supporting students struggling with anxiety and depression.

Power of the Group (Grades K–5)

Children struggling with anxiety and depression often have difficulties with transitions and change. It takes a long time to establish trust and safety, and big changes in their environment pose a perceived threat to that trust and safety. Therefore, if students with internalizing disorders have found a group of peers with whom they feel comfortable, it can be helpful to maintain those students with the same peer group during big transitions if possible (e.g., during next-grade classroom assignment).

Buddy Up (Grades K–5)

Children with internalizing disorders benefit from having a peer or group of peers who can model appropriate self-regulation. This modeling should occur across different settings to promote generalization of skills.

Instructions

- When finding seat assignments, ask the child to identify the peers with whom she feels most comfortable and allow her to sit next to them.
- During projects or class assignments, partner the student with a child who exhibits good emotional regulation. Ask them to come up with a "partner plan" for how they will work together on the assignment.
- More-unstructured times, such as lunch or recess, can be particularly anxiety provoking for some students. To support such students, create a "lunch group" that will support and include the child. During recess, find partners that can help the student transition into and out of the unstructured activities.

"You Can Do It" Messages (Grades 4–5)

Children often feel a sense of pride and accomplishment when they are able to help others. This help, in turn, earns the admiration of others, leading to increased self-esteem. For students who have experienced symptoms of anxiety or depression, being able to help others or encourage them to practice coping skills may foster a great sense of achievement. Several years ago, I had the honor of working with teens and young adults who shared their stories of struggling with depression on the documentary *Break Free From Depression* (Reilly, 2011). These individuals decided to share their stories so that other youth watching the film could learn about depression, how to seek help for themselves, and how to help their friends. The response of youth who see the documentary is almost uniform in the sense of gratitude they express for being able to learn directly from actual stories of youth so similar to them.

Instructions

- Older students (fourth and fifth grade) who have experienced symptoms of anxiety or depression and found helpful coping skills may wish to share their experiences with others and teach the skills that were helpful to them.
- Sharing can happen informally in the classroom or through more formal settings, including:

  o Presentations to the class that include psychoeducation (e.g., what is anxiety?) and suggestions for coping skills (e.g., deep breathing exercises)
  o Panel discussions during a wellness fair
  o Filming brief "you can do it" messages that include ideas for coping and words of encouragement

- As these activities require self-disclosure, it is important to obtain parental consent. Furthermore, if a child is still actively in treatment, it is prudent to discuss the child's self-disclosure with the therapist to ensure that such an activity would be therapeutic and not counterproductive for the child.

Special Topics

REENTRY FOLLOWING PSYCHIATRIC HOSPITALIZATION

A carefully thought out plan for reentry is critical when a student returns to school following a psychiatric hospitalization. Generally, students are still quiet vulnerable upon discharge. While ideally stabilized, the students will still likely struggle with significant symptoms. Creating a plan that takes into account current symptom presentation, individual needs, and school accommodations can make this transition more tolerable for students. Following are recommendations to consider when creating a student's reentry plan. Every child is different, and so will be his or her needs. However, having a structure in mind as well as a clear plan for parent-teacher-clinician communication promotes a preventive, rather than reactive, approach to supporting the child.

Note: Children may be cared for by different adult figures. In the sections that follow, the term *parent* will be used generally, with the understanding that parental figures may include other caretakers or legal guardians.

Meeting With Parents

Prior to the student's discharge, it is helpful to arrange a meeting with the parents and school staff (e.g., adjustment or guidance counselor, teacher, nurse, principal) to assess the following information:

- *What information about the child's illness do parents feel comfortable sharing, and with whom?* When children struggle with a psychiatric illness, parents or guardians often worry about the child's privacy and who will know the details of his or her illness and treatment. While this worry develops for many possible reasons (e.g., the child will be constantly asked about how he or she is feeling; other children may reject the child due to the illness), it is important to openly ask the family about how they wish to share information and what factors may lead to hesitation about sharing information, especially with school staff.

- *How are parents explaining the student's absence from school? What should be said if others ask about the student's absence?* Some parents may not feel comfortable openly discussing the child's psychiatric hospitalization and may request that another explanation be given when others ask about the child's absence (e.g., physical illness, surgery). While it is important to respect the family's privacy and wishes regarding the child's reentry plan, it is also important to invite them to think about what impact the alternative explanation may have on their child. For example, will the child feel additionally stressed or burdened by having to share a different story than what actually occurred? Will the child feel relieved by not having to explain the hospitalization? Again, an individualized approach that takes all child factors into consideration is warranted and recommended.

- *Will parents grant permission for school personnel to speak with the student's mental health clinician(s)?* At times, parents may feel quite hesitant to grant permission for school personnel to speak with the child's mental health providers. Worries about confidentiality and appropriateness of such contact may arise. For example, parents may worry about too many school personnel having access to a child's private information, potentially leading to mixed messages or to intervention by staff who may not have the expertise to help the child. Alternatively, parents may wish to grant permission for such communication, asking that school personnel actively contact mental health providers. Parents may ask for daily communication with treatment providers or implementation of complex treatment plans in the school setting. In either case, it is important to have a clear conversation about possible worries parents may have and determine how those worries will be addressed. It is also important to address expectations parents may have of the school and determine which expectations are reasonable and may be appropriately implemented by the school.
- *If applicable, will parents share information about their child's medications and dosages?* There are clear benefits to informing school staff about a child's use of medication. Knowledge of the type of medication, dosage, and possible side effects can be helpful in monitoring the child's physical and psychological health. For teachers, understanding possible side effects of medication can be helpful in creating classroom supports for the child. For example, some medications may cause gastrointestinal distress. Using this knowledge, the teacher can create a signal to use with the student that facilitates discreet communication about needing to use the bathroom. The teacher can also allow the student more bathroom breaks as needed, thereby decreasing the student's anxiety around this side effect. Again, parents may express some concern about sharing information related to medication and somehow compromising

the child's confidentiality or how he or she is regarded or treated at school. Having a clear rationale for why this information is helpful (e.g., to monitor potential side effects, to be able to better respond to a possible medical emergency, and to create classroom supports) may help to alleviate parents' fears in this regard.

• *What concerns do parents have in terms of their child's reentry into the school? Whom should they call to check on their child's progress while in school?* When a child returns to school, it is ideal to have a team that will help facilitate the transition and address any concerns the child and the family may have. For example, the school nurse, the child's teacher, a guidance counselor, a school mental health clinician (if available), and an administrator may make up the support team for the child. An identified member of this team should take the lead in communicating with parents about the plan for the child's reentry, addressing any concerns the family may have, and reporting back about the child's progress. Perhaps parents worry about the child's level of fatigue, or about receptivity to their calling to find out how the child is doing. Perhaps parents worry about workload or how the child's grades will be impacted. Asking careful questions during the reentry meeting about the parents' concerns for the child's reentry process can help facilitate this transition.

Communication With Treatment Providers

Communication with the student's treatment providers can assist in determining the particular needs the child will have in the school setting.

• *Is the student safe to return to school? Is he or she at any risk for harm to self or others?* When students have been hospitalized due to concerns about risk for harm to self or others, schools may have a protocol that indicates that the child needs documented clearance from a mental health clinician prior to returning to school. It is critical to review your school's protocol for such situations. If one does not exist, it is strongly recommended that one be created to avoid possible confusion should such a situation arise in the school.

- *Is there a concern about possible flight risk with this student?* Some students may have a difficult time remaining in the school setting, either due to acute anxiety or to some other symptom presentation. If it is possible that the student may attempt to leave the school setting, school staff will need to implement additional supports (e.g., a one-on-one aide) to help the student remain safely in the classroom.

- *Will the student be able to handle a full day, or will he or she need to reenter gradually?* Depending on the student's current symptom presentation, he or she may not be able to handle a full day back in school. Understanding how much the child can handle upon reentry will help in creating a gradual return plan as well as a modified academic workload. This information will also assist in determining when the student might be ready for full days.

- *Will the student need more individualized attention during specific times?* Students may need particular attention during different times of the school day, depending on the type and acuteness of their symptoms. For example, children may need additional assistance in the morning or at the end of the day, when they are most fatigued and have little energy. Some children may need individualized attention during unstructured times, such as lunch and recess. Communication with the treatment provider will help to identify times of heightened vulnerability for the child, as well as techniques that may be helpful for assisting the child.

- *What are the recommendations to be followed in school?* During a hospitalization, coping strategies are identified that help the child manage his or her symptoms. During outpatient treatment, the provider continues to identify coping strategies and teaches the child to use them in the context of a particular treatment plan. There may be coping skills the child can use in the school setting, or perhaps certain situations in the school are part of the treatment plan (e.g., remaining in the classroom for one hour without asking to go to the nurse's office). Communication between the teacher and treatment provider can facilitate the child's use of specific skills, promote reinforcement of skill use, and create continuity between the office, home, and school settings.

School Staff Meeting

Once school personnel have met with the parents and received information and recommendations from the treating clinician(s), a meeting should be held to create an individualized reentry plan for the student. During this meeting, the following questions may be addressed:

- Who will be a part of the student's support team in school?
- How will the reentry plan be documented? Who will be in charge of ensuring that the plan is accurately implemented and that any necessary adjustments are made?
- Which support team member will be the primary liaison for communicating with parents and treatment providers?
- If treatment components are recommended as part of the reentry plan (e.g., gradual exposure to feared stimuli in school), who will be able to implement and monitor this?
- If the student is absent or needs a modified schedule, how will assignments be modified? Who will share the assignments and work materials with the parents?
- What additional in-school supports may be mobilized (e.g., modified grading structure, tutoring, technology-related support, regular visits to the guidance/adjustment counselor or school mental health clinician)?

NONSUICIDAL SELF-INJURY (NSSI)

NSSI is characterized by maladaptive attempts to cope with extreme distress. It can be shocking to think about a child being in such distress that he or she uses self-harm as a way to cope. It can also be difficult to understand how this happens and how to talk to children about it. Following are some helpful tips for communicating with a student who may be struggling with NSSI. This information is based on findings from the Cornell Research Program on Self-Injury and Recovery (http://www.selfinjury.bctr.cornell.edu/).

- If you are worried that a student is engaging in self-injurious behavior, set aside time for a private meeting where the child may feel more comfortable discussing his or her experience, feelings, and behaviors.

- Do not be afraid to talk about self-injury. Adults often worry that by initiating a conversation with a child about self-injury, or by asking a child about his or her experience with self-injury, one will introduce new (i.e., harmful) ideas to the child or will place him or her at risk by triggering negative thoughts or increased symptoms. Addressing this topic directly with children in a developmentally appropriate, calm, and caring manner will not put them at risk and will not cause harm.

- When conveying your concern to the student, use clear indicators of what you have noticed (e.g., "I notice scratches on your arm") and avoid diagnosing or interpreting why the student is engaging in such behavior. Approach the student in a gentle, nonjudgmental, and nonpunitive manner. Often people show shock or disbelief at the behavior or report it as a discipline problem. This is likely to make the student feel judged, ashamed, and misunderstood, and will not promote open conversation. Let the student know that you want to talk so that you can figure out how to help. Dr. Janis Whitlock, an expert on NSSI, recommends showing "respectful curiosity" by inviting the student to speak freely about his or her experience. Ask questions such as, "How does injuring help you feel better?" or "Are there particular people or situations that make you think about injuring or want to injure?"

- Students may worry about how you might use the information about their self-injury. Be open and honest, and convey that it will be important to talk to the student's parents and to seek support from staff in school who may be able to help (e.g., the school's mental health clinician or adjustment counselor). Do not promise to keep secrets about self-injury. Students may plead, "Please, I only do it once in a while; I promise I won't do it anymore if you don't say anything." NSSI is difficult to simply stop without support and active intervention. Keeping a secret about the behavior prevents the child from obtaining appropriate treatment.

- Consult your school protocol about how to make a referral for a student who may be self-injuring.

- If you wish to learn more about self-injury, below are helpful websites:

  o S.A.F.E. Alternatives (www.selfinjury.com)
  o Cornell Research Program on Self-injurious Behavior (www.selfinjury.bctr.cornell.edu)

SUICIDE

If a student feels safe with a specific teacher, it may be that teacher who first hears of the student's suicidal thoughts. As with NSSI, imagining that a child may be in such distress and is resorting to such extreme measures to find relief is alarming. Offering appropriate responses; however, can help the child communicate and access help. Discussing suicide with a student will not introduce new ideas and will not place the child at risk. Below are recommendations for communicating with a child who is expressing suicidal thoughts or behaviors:

- Listen carefully, without interrupting the student to ask for too many clarifying questions. Do not panic or act shocked. Approach the student in a gentle, nonjudgmental, and nonpunitive manner.
- If the child talks about suicidal thoughts, ask the child directly about whether he or she has a plan.
- It may be tempting to try to convince the child out of such thoughts, or to convince the child about the helpfulness of other options. When a child is in a suicidal crisis, he or she feels extremely hopeless and may feel as though nothing has helped or ever will help. Trying to convince the child otherwise is counterproductive. Instead, validate the child's distress (e.g., "Things are very hard for you right now, and it's hard to see how to make the pain stop") and reinforce that you care about him or her and will assist in finding help.
- Do not promise to keep a secret about suicidal thoughts, even if the student promises not to act upon them.
- Do not leave the student alone, and seek assistance immediately. Follow your school's protocol around how to handle psychiatric emergencies.

NOTICE, GIVE, NURTURE

Supporting students with internalizing disorders can be challenging and emotionally taxing. Teachers may find themselves questioning the appropriateness or helpfulness of their support, or else they may encounter frustration if things do not appear to help. This notice, give, and nurture section encourages teachers to focus on their own experience to promote self-reflection, self-awareness, and self-care.

What Can I Notice?

Comfort levels around discussing emotional concerns and helping students vary among different people. Notice which aspects of talking to children about their emotional experiences or about helping them may be most challenging for you.

- *How comfortable are you with asking open and direct questions about children's symptoms?* Do you find yourself using complex words, unclear metaphors, or referring to symptoms in a roundabout way? Elementary school children may not fully understand their emotional experiences, especially if they are just starting to develop symptoms of depression and/or anxiety. Using complex terms or unclear explanations may lead to further confusion or shame in the child. Use simple, clear words and confirm with the child that he or she understands (e.g., "It sounds like you are feeling very sad and angry at times. Did I get that right?")
- *Is it difficult to engage in active listening and resist the urge to engage in immediate problem solving?* It may be quite challenging to avoid giving advice and engaging in immediate problem solving, as teachers are caring, compassionate individuals for whom it is hard to see a child in distress. However, active, empathic listening is very important when working with both the child and his or her family. There is a palpable sense of isolation that families experience when a member struggles with a psychiatric illness. Whether it is due to shame, fear, or just not knowing what to do, it is easy to feel lost and alone. Therefore, it can be incredibly supportive and validating to

the child and his or her family to simply listen without rushing to potential solutions.

- *What factors may be impeding your ability to stay focused in active listening?* There are certain topics that may be particularly difficult for us to manage, and this is due to our own history, experiences, and interactions. Certain students may remind you of a loved one, interactions with a parent may remind you of difficult past experiences, or you may find yourself additionally invested in a particular child because he or she is going through the same struggles you encountered. These responses are not wrong, but it is important to be mindful of how personal factors may impact your interactions with a child. In my own work, I try to listen to the "chatter" in my head. When the chatter, characterized by many questions, self-doubt, or intrusive thoughts, becomes extra loud, I know that I have to reflect upon what may be turning up the volume. Chatter can also come about due to stigma and may contribute to reluctance to talk about mental health issues. For example, the chatter may sound like this:

  ○ "Working with this child is difficult because it is exactly what I am going through with my own daughter. I'm worried people will find out what my daughter is going through."
  ○ "I am struggling with anxiety myself and I worry that the parents will not think I am able to support their child."

- *Which of your own behaviors may be inadvertently impeding student progress?* As mentioned in Chapters 2 and 3, certain parent behaviors (e.g., openly discussing their own fears or approaching new things as dangerous) may inadvertently reinforce maladaptive patterns of negative behavior or avoidance in children struggling with internalizing disorders. Similarly, certain teacher behaviors may contribute to reinforcement of negative behaviors in students. For example, Leflot and colleagues (2010) found that teachers' use of negative remarks was associated with higher levels of off-task and oppositional behavior among second-grade children. An intervention focusing on reducing the use of negative remarks and reinforcement for positive behavior resulted in more on-task and compliant behavior among the second-graders (Leflot et al., 2010).

What Can I Give?

Giving students concrete tools and accommodations is useful in supporting them. However, giving empathy, hope, and safety can be just as, if not more, important in promoting student progress.

- *Offer students genuine, empathic interactions.* Even very young children understand when adults are "talking at" or "talking down" to them, or labeling their behavior as manipulative. Interactions characterized by empathy for and understanding of the child's experience foster mutual respect and communication. In contrast, it can be very difficult for a child to respond to an adult when the child hears, "I cannot read your mind," or "I'm trying to help you, but you won't talk, so there isn't anything I can do." Nonverbal cues from adults, such as eye rolling, hand waving, and looking down at the child with arms crossed, convey judgment and lack of understanding.

  It is important to acknowledge that sometimes communicating with children who are under emotional duress can be trying. They are not always able to articulate how they feel, or they may seem to just give up or may even act out. Adults must remember that these behaviors are not targeted at them; the behaviors are manifestations of the child's own distress and frustration. When it is challenging to understand what the child is trying to convey, you may ask questions such as, "I'm trying to understand what you're thinking and feeling. Are you able to tell me how you feel? If you can't, are you able to show me? Can you draw it for me?" Other approaches may also be helpful, including saying things like, "Sometimes it can be hard to know what you're feeling; can you start by telling me what your body feels? Would you like to practice your breathing exercises to help you feel calmer?" Recall that when children are particularly distressed, it is important to regulate their stress response system through relaxation and physical calming down. Until this is achieved, children will have more difficulty accessing language, processing, and planning.

• *Give students some TLC!*

      o Teachers Love their Children
      o Teachers Look for Connection
      o Teachers Live with Compassion

Many students experience significantly adverse life circumstances, including abuse, neglect, poverty, separation, and illness. They may have little stability in their home or may not have access to resources. Connection and compassion for each child's circumstances as well as those of his or her family promotes empathy and reduces fear or shame that the child may experience.

• *Be a source of advocacy for the child.* Some circumstances may prevent children from accessing the help and support they need. For example, schools may not have access to mental health resources; a child's behavior may be misdiagnosed as behavioral acting out without consideration of the co-occurrence of an internalizing disorder, or the family may not know how to access services. Learn about your school's referral protocol, communicate with the school staff managing mental health concerns in children, and learn about the mental health resources available in your community. Advocate for appropriate supports for your students.

What Can I Nurture?

Hope, self-care, and communication are extremely important, not just for students with emotional disorders but for all students. Think about the culture in your classroom. How do you promote these factors on a daily basis?

• *Instilling hope.* Children with anxiety and depression have a diminished sense of hope, not only in themselves, but also in others and in the future. How do your students understand the concept of hope? How can you bring this abstract concept to life in your classroom? What does hope mean to you as a teacher, and how can you incorporate that into your teaching?

- *Self-care.* This chapter has offered different activities that promote self-care and support in students struggling with internalizing disorders. This section invites you to look for opportunities to reflect on your own self-care.

  o Do you acknowledge the intensity of your feelings when managing students' emotional needs, or do you try to ignore or suppress your emotions?
  o Are you trying to support your students without help or consultation for yourself?
  o Do you feel like you are primarily responsible for the child's emotional well-being?
  o How do you process your experiences in trying to help your students?
  o What do you do on a daily basis for self-care?
  o Do you find there are particular times when your self-care diminishes or disappears?
  o Whom can you enlist to support your efforts around self-care?

- *Communication.* Fostering open and safe communication around emotions is an important way to support students. This communication does not always have to be via serious, individual conversations. It can happen through fun group activities like the ones mentioned in this chapter, or through written stories (e.g., bibliotherapy). Below are recommended books to use with children to foster continued understanding and communication around mental health needs. These books are available through the American Psychological Association's Magination Press (http://www.apa.org/pubs/magination/).

  o *Nobody's Perfect: A Story for Children About Perfectionism* by Ellen Flanagan Burns (ages 8–12)
  o *Understanding Myself: A Kid's Guide to Intense Emotions and Strong Feelings* by Mary C. Lamia (ages 8–13)

- o *Mookey the Monkey Gets Over Being Teased* by Heather Suzanne Lonczak (ages 4–8)
- o *A Terrible Thing Happened: A Story for Children Who Have Witnessed Violence or Trauma* by Margaret M. Holmes (ages 4–8)
- o *Blue Cheese Breath and Stinky Feet: How to Deal With Bullies* by Catherine DePino (ages 6–12)
- o *Mind Over Basketball: Coach Yourself to Handle Stress* by Jane Weierbach and Elizabeth Phillips-Hershey (ages 8–12)
- o *Wishing Wellness: A Workbook for Children of Parents With Mental Illness* by Lisa Anne Clarke (ages 6–12)
- o *Why Are You So Sad? A Child's Book About Parental Depression* by Beth Andrews (ages 3–8)
- o *What to Do When You Grumble Too Much: A Kid's Guide to Overcoming Negativity* by Dawn Huebner (ages 6–12)
- o *What to Do When You Worry Too Much: A Kid's Guide to Overcoming Anxiety* by Dawn Huebner (ages 6–12)
- o *The Boy Who Didn't Want to Be Sad* by Rob Goldblatt (ages 4–8)
- o *Double-Dip Feelings: Stories to Help Children Understand Emotions* by Barbara Cain (ages 4–8)

CHAPTER FIVE

Fostering Emotional Wellness in All Students

Ms. P is the best teacher. She's nice, funny, helps us understand stuff if we don't, and says it's OK if we get stuff wrong. She asks us how we feel, and she lets us study real tadpoles!

—Michael, third-grader

MRS. HANNAH'S SECOND-GRADE CLASS is buzzing with excitement about their new project—learning about ocean animals. They started the day by reviewing the class values and sharing examples of how they would demonstrate those values when the visitors came to the classroom to show them live sea creatures. Mrs. Hannah reviewed the schedule for the day and made sure everyone understood the activity for the moment. She showed the picture reminder and asked for a call-back response when she finished the directions. All students knew where to go in the classroom and what the expectations were. A big sign on the side of the board said, "Mistakes and questions always welcome." A few minutes before the visitors were scheduled to arrive, the students were giddy with anticipation. Mrs. Hannah reminded them of how to get their wiggles out and calm their minds by doing two minutes of muscle relaxation and breathing exercises. Once their bodies were calm, their minds were ready to learn. All agreed to be mindful of every moment and enjoy each sight, sound, and smell of the animals before moving on to the next. Happily they welcomed the visitors, ready to meet new friends.

Does that sound like the way you would like your classroom to be? It can happen. Even more exciting is that such synchrony, behavior, and well-being is not limited to individual points in time. When you integrate skills that foster emotional health and wellness, you give your students skills that promote regulation, social, and academic success for a lifetime.

- "Sound mental health provides an essential foundation of stability that supports all other aspects of human development—from the formation of friendships and the ability to cope with adversity to the achievement of success in school, work, and community life" (National Scientific Council on the Developing Child, 2012, p. 1).
- The Report of the Surgeon General's Conference on Children's Mental Health highlighted the importance of mental health promotion and social emotional learning for optimal child development and school performance by indicating that "mental health is a critical component of children's learning and general health" (Durlak, Weissberg, Dymnicki, Taylor, & Schellinger, 2011).
- Results from meta-analyses indicate that social emotional learning programs for students enhance their classroom behavior, academic achievement, and positive emotional connection to school (Durlak et al., 2011).
- A strength-based approach that focuses on well-being is important for children's mental health. Factors that promote life satisfaction and emotional well-being include hope, gratitude, self-efficacy, belongingness, prosocial activities, school engagement, strong relationships with adults, and self-regulation (Howell, Keyes, & Passmore, 2013). These factors can be taught and practiced within multiple settings, including the classroom.

The previous chapter focused on how to support children struggling with internalizing disorders to promote learning and self-regulation. This chapter presents tools (i.e., activities and strategies) that teachers can use in their classrooms to promote self-regulation and emotional wellness in all children. The tools in this chapter are based on the concepts of prevention science and use a social emotional learning framework as described by the Collaborative for Academic, Social, and Emotional Learning (CASEL; www.casel.org).

Emotional and Behavioral Tools

As with the activities presented in the previous chapter, it is important to keep a few points in mind:

- These activities do not translate into immediate behavioral compliance after one use. However, participation in these activities allows the child to develop new skills, experiences, and behaviors that will lead to improvement and overall change. With continued practice and use in other settings (e.g., at home), the child can experience change and success.
- Some tools will work better for some children than for others. One way to determine which tools may work well for a particular student is to try to use the ones that best fit the child's interests, learning style, and history. Teachers should feel free to adjust the activities to meet the developmental levels and specific needs of their students.
- If students do not understand the concepts right away, it does not mean failure on your part. It often takes young students some time to fully understand the abstract concept of emotions. Continue to promote discussions about emotions. It is important to send the message to your students that their emotions are important to you and that the classroom is an emotionally safe environment.

Figure 5.1 lists the different emotional and behavioral domains each activity addresses, as well as the general age range for which each activity is appropriate. The recommended age range should be used as a guideline rather than as an absolute. It will be important to consider the child's developmental stage, language abilities, cognitive abilities, and overall understanding of concepts in choosing appropriate activities. For example, some third-graders may be able to use more complex language or begin to use abstract concepts, whereas other third-graders may have a more difficult time doing so. Each activity listed in Figure 5.1 is described in detail, including instructions for use and accompanying materials. While a general script is offered, teachers should feel free to revise and adapt their instructions as they feel is most appropriate for their students.

Domain	Grade	Activity
Classroom Culture	K–5	Physical Layout
	K–5	Our Values
Promoting Behavioral Regulation	K–3	Green Light, Red Light
	K–3	Clap and Snap
	K–3	Freeze Dance
	K–3	Head, Shoulders, Knees and Toes
	K–3	Silent Bell
	K–5	Simon Says
Identifying and Managing Feelings	K–2	Breezy and Calm Scarves
	K–5	Feelings Charades
	1–5	Freeze the Action
	4–5	Emotion Debit Card
Understanding Connections Between Thoughts and Emotions	K–5	Bibliotherapy
	4–5	The Emotions Daily
Problem Solving	3–5	Problems, Ideas, Plans: Let's Do the PIP!
Increasing Positive Affect	K–1	Friendship Soup
	2–5	My Strengths
Active Coping	K–5	Sweet Dreams
	2–5	Surfing the Waves
	3–5	Here's My Card
Relaxation Skills	K–5	The Chill Zone

FIGURE 5.1. Classroom-based tools to promote students' self-regulation.

Activities

Domain	Grade	Activity
Classroom Culture	K–5	Physical Layout
	K–5	Our Values

CLASSROOM CULTURE

Physical Layout (Grades K–5)

The culture of a classroom has a powerful impact on children's emotional health. Culture is reflected in the physical layout, in expectations of how people will behave and treat others, in directly articulated values around emotions, and in the unspoken ways in which emotions are addressed. A bright, cheerful space with different materials and arrangements of learning centers to minimize distraction is conducive to learning. Clearly posted classroom rules, values, and routines, with visual cues, are also helpful in offering children reminders and stability. Finally, clearly articulated as well as unspoken messages help children understand the values associated with identifying, talking about, and honoring feelings. For example, classroom rules focusing on the importance of friendship, honoring others' opinions, and respecting others' perspectives promote a value of emotional safety. Unspoken messages include how teachers respond to students (e.g., "You seem upset; I'm interested in knowing more about how you feel") as well as materials in the classroom (e.g., books about social emotional topics; charts with "feeling faces" so children have additional ways to convey how they are feeling).

Our Values (K–5)

There are many school rules by which children must abide. Students typically have no direct say in these rules, and therefore, they comply with them simply as part of a routine. When children have the opportunity to create rules and values for their classroom, these rules become more than routine; they become a set of internally valued expectations. Clearly articulated classroom rules can serve as a road map for the group's values. In this activity, teachers will guide students in creating classroom rules that focus on emotional and relational expectations. This activity addresses all social and emotional learning core competencies identified by CASEL: self-awareness, self-management, social awareness, relationship skills, and responsible decision making.

Materials Needed
- Poster board
- Markers

Instructions
- This activity can be tailored to meet the developmental stage of your students. The key is to hold a conversation with students so that they can cocreate the social emotional rules and values of the classroom. Ideally, this activity should take place during the first week of school. However, it is never too late to introduce this concept to students.
- Some suggestions for guiding this conversation:

  o "How we talk to and treat each other in this classroom is very important. Can you help me think of some ways of how we should talk to and treat each other?"
  o "In our classroom, it will be important for everyone to feel valued and safe. What rules can we come up with together so that all students in the class will feel safe?"

- Rules and values should be stated in a positive form. For example, rather than saying, "Don't shout," the rule should be stated, "Use quiet voices."
- Once you have developed your set of classroom rules and values, post them somewhere where they are visible to all students.
- The rules and values that you develop should be a living document. That is, the rules should not be absolute, but rather may be amended or added to. Have periodic check-in moments about the rules (e.g., every semester). Ask students whether they think the rules are working and whether anything needs to be added or changed. This

emphasizes an important process of continued self-reflection and the understanding that emotional awareness is not a static concept.
• It will be important to "catch the positive" often by highlighting when a student is following one of the classroom values. Praising these behaviors will continue to reinforce the use of social emotional skills.

Domain	Grade	Activity
Promoting Behavioral Regulation	K–3	Green Light, Red Light
	K–3	Clap and Snap
	K–3	Freeze Dance
	K–3	Head, Shoulders, Knees and Toes
	K–3	Silent Bell
	K–5	Simon Says

PROMOTING BEHAVIORAL REGULATION

Children's behavioral self-regulation skills are critical in the classroom, as these skills (e.g., attention, working memory, and inhibitory control) enable students to successfully follow rules, pay attention to teacher instructions, and engage in learning (McClelland et al., 2007). Behavioral self-regulation is also associated with academic outcomes, including better reading, writing, and math skills (McClelland et al., 2007; von Suchodoletz et al., 2013). Unfortunately, many children entering formal schooling do not have basic regulatory competencies needed for positive school adjustment. Rimm-Kaufman, Pianta, and Cox (2000) found that as many as 46% of teachers reported that more than half of children entering their kindergarten classes did not have basic behavioral self-regulation. These children are at significantly greater risk for low academic achievement and poor social functioning (McClelland et al., 2007).

The activities in this section aim to increase behavioral regulation in children. These skills translate into better classroom and academic functioning, as well as into better social functioning. Children with strong behavioral self-regulation "are better able to apply social rules and standards as guidelines for their behavior and, as such, are more functional in all contexts" (von Suchodoletz et al., 2013, p. 62).

Green Light, Red Light (Grades K–3)

This activity is a classic children's game where children are asked to stop or go based on the light color. Children must use their attention, working memory, and inhibitory control to successfully engage in this game.

Materials Needed

None

Instructions

- This game should take place in a setting where there is enough space for children to move freely.
- Designate one student to be the "traffic light" leader. This student will be in front of the rest of the students. With her back turned to the other students, she calls, "Green light!" and the students are able to move closer to her. She then calls, "Red light!" and turns toward her peers. Those students who move when "Red light!" is called are out of the game. The student that reaches the "traffic light" leader first wins and becomes the new "traffic light" leader.
- You may make this game more challenging by adding new components that target working memory and inhibitory control. For example, you may indicate that students must stop when the leader calls "Orange light" *or* "Blue light" and may go when the leader calls "Pink light" *or* "Yellow light." In this variation, students must hold in working memory the new colors that are associated with the motions, without relying on the more well-established cues of red and green as stop and go, respectively.

Clap and Snap (Grades K–3)

This activity promotes behavioral regulation by requiring children to pay attention to a specific attribute of an object or situation while ignoring other attributes.

Materials Needed
None

Instructions
- This game can be played in any setting, with the teacher adjusting the clap and snap rules.
- *Sample variation:* While outside on recess, children are asked to pay attention to the cars going by. When they see a red car, they clap, and when they see a gray car, they snap.
- *Sample variation:* While in the classroom, children are asked to pay attention to a particular vocabulary word. When the teacher says that word, they clap. When the teacher says another identified vocabulary word, they snap.
- *Sample variation:* You can make this more challenging by adding more motions to specific words, actions, or situations.

Freeze Dance (Grades K–3)

This is a popular and fun activity that will help behavioral regulation as well as emotional regulation by allowing students a break and letting them move. In this activity, students dance while a song plays and must "freeze" when the song stops. This activity targets attention and behavioral inhibition.

Materials Needed
Device to play music

Instructions
Tell your students that you will have a fun dance party. In this party, though, there are special instructions. When the music is going, they can dance any way they want. Have fun and let all the wiggles out while the music is playing! When the music stops, though, they have to freeze in place. If someone is still moving when the music stops, he or she is out and must wait until the next round. The last person on the dance floor is the winner.

Head, Shoulders, Knees and Toes (Grades K–3)

This activity is based on the popular "Head, Shoulders, Knees and Toes" song. It targets attention, working memory, and behavioral inhibition.

Materials Needed

None

Instructions

- Ask students to get up from their seats and have a big stretch. Ask them to get any wiggles out of their bodies because they'll have to pay attention in this fun game.
- Have all students sing the song "Head, Shoulders, Knees and Toes" and do the corresponding motions. Start out by doing it slowly. Repeat the song, this time singing it a bit faster. Sing it for a third time, this time even faster.
- Now that the students have practiced the motions and completed them at a fast pace, you can add variations, including the following:

  o Sing the song normally, with the order of "head, shoulders, knees, and toes," but for the motions, instead of starting with the head, start at the toes and go upward instead of downward (so that the movements will actually be toes, knees, shoulders, and head).
  o Indicate that when you sing "head and shoulders," you will touch only the head, and that when you sing "knees and toes," you will touch only the toes.
  o There are no winners or losers in this game. The fun will be in everyone trying to remember the new rules.
  o After the game is over, ask the students, "What was most challenging about that? What did you do to help yourself remember the new rules?" This processing can help them become more aware of the strategies they use to improve behavioral regulation.

Silent Bell (Grades K–3)

This activity is based the concept of mindful walking meditation as described by Diamond and Lee (2011) and on an activity described in the *Parents Magazine* March 2014 edition. In this activity, the student is asked to walk across the classroom carrying a bell, but without making noise. If the bell rings, the student has to come back and begin again. This activity targets mindful awareness of an action, behavioral inhibition, and attention.

Materials Needed
- Bell
- Spoon
- Water
- Small ball

Instructions
- Give the bell to a student and ask him or her to walk across the room without ringing the bell. If the bell rings, the student has to return and start over again.
- *Sample variation:* Draw a line on the floor (it may be straight or curved) and ask the student to walk on the line without ringing the bell.
- *Sample variation:* Give the student a spoon with water in it and ask him or her to walk across the room without spilling the water. If the water is spilled, the student has to return and start over again.
- *Sample variation:* Draw a line on the floor (it may be straight or curved) and ask the student to balance a ball on the palm of his or her hand while walking the line. If the ball falls, the student must start over.
- You may use any variation that you wish. The intent of the activity is to have the student focus his or her attention, resist distractions, and focus mindfully on the activity until it is completed.

Simon Says (Grades K–5)

This activity is based on the popular game of "Simon Says." It targets attention, working memory, and behavioral inhibition.

Materials Needed
None

Instructions

- Introduce the game of Simon Says. Ask for a volunteer to be Simon for a practice round. Students who follow the rules when the caller says "Simon says" may stay, but anyone who follows the rule when the caller does not say "Simon says" is out and must wait for the next round.
- Play a few practice rounds so that different students may take a turn being Simon.
- Now the teacher becomes Simon. This time, when saying "Simon Says," do a different action than what Simon has called for. For example, say "Simon says touch your head" while you touch your ears. This variation makes it more difficult for students to play, as they now must learn to pay attention to what "Simon" is saying to do versus what he or she is doing.

Domain	Grade	Activity
Identifying and Managing Feelings	K–2	Breezy and Calm Scarves
	K–5	Feelings Charades
	1–5	Freeze the Action
	4–5	Emotion Debit Card

IDENTIFYING AND MANAGING FEELINGS

Strong self-regulation also involves an ability to identify and manage one's feelings. Two of CASEL's social and emotional learning core competencies are particularly important in this regard: *self-awareness* ("the ability to accurately recognize one's emotions and thoughts and their influence on behavior") and *self-management* ("the ability to regulate one's emotions, thoughts, and behaviors effectively in different situations"; CASEL, n.d.). The activities described in this section focus on offering students different formats for learning how to identify and manage emotions. Students have different learning styles and ways of accessing emotion-related concepts. Therefore, the activities in this section use movement, humor, and metaphors to extend students' options for talking about emotions.

BREEZY AND CALM SCARVES (GRADES K–2)

This activity is used with younger children to help them develop a greater understanding of how to manage emotions as well as an understanding of how one's emotions touch, or impact, others. The scarves are used as a metaphor to symbolize emotions. Metaphors can give students another way to identify an emotional state, especially for those children whose language skills or emotional distress may make it difficult for them to articulate how they are feeling. For example, a student may be able to tell you that he has "a lot of scarves moving around" as a way to indicate distress.

Materials Needed

Two scarves per student

Instructions

- Give two scarves to each student. Explain what the scarves mean: "Pretend that these scarves are feelings that you have. What kinds of feelings do you have today?" Elicit responses from the students. Refer to the scarves as the feelings mentioned so that the students understand the concept and associate the scarves with those feelings (e.g., "So you mentioned happy and excited; which scarf is the happy one, and which is the excited one?").
- Ask students to hold one scarf in each hand, then extend their arms. They may twirl their arms around or move the scarves with their hands.
- As the students walk around and move their scarves, narrate for them what is happening. For example, you may say something like, "Notice how when you walk around, your feelings are touching others. Tom's excited just bumped into Mark's frustrated."
- After students have walked around and interacted, ask them to stop in place but with their arms still outstretched.
- Ask students to take a deep breath and, as they exhale, to slowly bring their arms down. Have them take another deep breath, again bringing their arms down, and then a third breath, bringing their arms all the way down to their sides.
- Ask the students to sit down and close their eyes. When their eyes are closed, have them touch the scarves that they have. Ask them to

examine what they feel like: What is their texture like? How do the scarves feel in their hands?

- Now ask the students to take another deep breath and notice what may be going on in their bodies. Starting from the top of their head, have them notice if there is anything different or new. Move down to their necks, shoulders, backs, arms, legs, and feet.
- Now ask them to take another deep breath and open their eyes.
- Follow this activity with a discussion:

  o "The scarves that we used today are like our feelings. Did you notice how when we walked around, they touched other people? Our feelings can touch, or have an effect on, other people. Like when you get really mad—how do others act? Or how about when you get really sad—what do others do? Why do you think it's important to know that our feelings touch other people?"

  o "What was it like when you took deep breaths and brought your scarves down to your sides?"

  o "Did you notice what the scarf was like when you had your eyes closed? The way you were noticing the scarf is the way we can stop for a moment to notice how we are feeling. Remember when you checked your body? Our feelings can sit in different parts of our bodies, so when we stop for a moment to check each part, it can give us clues about how we are feeling. Did any of you discover a feeling when you were checking your bodies? Where did you notice it? What was that like?"

Feelings Charades (Grades K–5)

In this activity, children participate in the charades game, but with a focus on emotions. This activity allows children to use movement to express emotion.

Materials Needed

3x5 cards with a different emotion written on each one (e.g., *anger, sadness, happiness, frustration, fear, jealousy*)

Instructions
- Divide the class into two teams.
- Ask each team to select a person who will act out the charade. That person will draw a card from the emotion cards pile.
- Each person will have two minutes to act out the emotion (you may wish to allow a longer time for younger students).
- The team with the most correct guesses wins.
- You can follow the game with a discussion about a time when students felt each of those emotions:

  o "Can you remember a time when you felt _____?"
  o "What did you do?"
  o "Is there something you wish you had done differently?"
  o "How have others managed _____?"

Freeze the Action (Grades 1–5)

Often, when asked directly about how they feel or how they might handle an emotion, students may respond with a resounding "I don't know." This activity eliminates the "I don't know" by allowing students to be the directors in different skits.

Materials Needed
- Paper and pencil to write down the scenarios
- Props (optional)

Instructions
- Divide students into groups (four or five students per group).
- Ask each group to come up with a scenario about a situation that was difficult to handle. The situation may have been difficult because it involved a socially awkward situation or a situation in which someone did not know how to respond (e.g., someone was trying to join in a game on the playground, but the kids in the group said she could not play with them; someone invited a friend to go to the movies with him, and she told him she was busy, but then he overheard her inviting someone else to go to the movies with her). For

younger students, you may wish to have some scenarios ready, as it may be difficult for them to generate scenarios.

- Each group will do a skit to act out the scenario.
- The other groups can yell, "Freeze!" in the middle of the skit and ask questions to better understand how each person is feeling. They can also offer suggestions for how people in the skit may respond.
- After the skits, spend some time processing them with the students. You may ask discussion questions such as:

    o "Has something like that ever happened to you before?
    o "How did you handle it?"
    o "What did you think was helpful about the way the group handled it?"
    o "Is there anything you would have done differently?"
    o "If that happened to your friend, how would you help him or her?"
    o "If that happened to you, who would you be able to talk to and ask for help?"

Emotion Debit Card (Grades 4–5)

This activity helps students understand the concept of emotional reserves and how certain situations, people, or contexts may either add to or deduct from those reserves. Students will also understand more about how their own behaviors may contribute to their emotional health and well-being or may negatively impact it. As with the scarf activity used for the younger students, this activity offers a metaphor that students may use to describe how they are feeling when it may otherwise be difficult for them to articulate their emotions. For example, a student may indicate to the teacher that he is on a "withdraw" day.

Materials Needed
- 3x5 cards (unlined and, if possible, of different colors)
- Markers

Instructions
- Introduce the concept of the "emotion debit card" to students: "Today we are going to create emotion debit cards. What do you

think an emotion debit card is? Well, let's think about what a debit card is. In the bank, you have money. You can spend it using your card, or you can add to the balance by making a deposit. The emotion debit card works in the same way, except the balance doesn't refer to how much money you have. The balance refers to how much energy, peace, calm, and happiness you have inside you.

"There are certain situations, or even people, that can give you deposits and add to your balance. Things like helping others, doing something that you like to do, and taking care of yourself. Can you think of other examples of situations that may give you deposits? There are also things that may be withdrawals. Can you think of examples of withdrawals?" (Examples might include getting into a fight with someone, getting a bad grade, or losing a family member.)

- Hand out a card to each student and say,
- "Now that you have your card, I want you to write 'Deposit' on one side and 'Withdrawal' on the other side. Make a list of things that are withdrawals and a list of things that are deposits on your card."
- Follow with a discussion:

  o "Let's have a volunteer share his or her withdrawals and deposits."
  o "Did others have similar things listed?"
  o "Did you find anything in common among the things you listed as withdrawals? How about the things you listed as deposits?"
  o "Is there anything that happens in this classroom that is a withdrawal? If there is, how can we change that to increase deposits?"

Domain	Grade	Activity
Understanding Connections Between Thoughts and Emotions	K–5	Bibliotherapy
	4–5	The Emotions Daily

UNDERSTANDING CONNECTIONS BETWEEN THOUGHTS AND EMOTIONS

As discussed in Chapters 2 and 3, emotions are integrally connected to thoughts, behaviors, and relationships. When children are able to understand this connection, it leads to greater self-awareness and ability to manage emotions. As this is an abstract concept, using concrete and fun activities can make this connection more understandable for younger students.

Bibliotherapy (Grades K–5)

It is often difficult for children to use their own experiences as examples for exploring the connection between emotions, thoughts, behaviors, and relationships. However, using the experiences of other characters can be more entertaining and less threatening. Therefore, the use of books (called *bibliotherapy*) to explore this connection between thoughts and emotions can be quite successful.

Materials Needed

Any books that have a social emotional theme. Some suggestions are listed below. These and more books are available through the American Psychological Association's Magination Press (http://www.apa.org/pubs/magination/).

- *Oh, the Places You'll Go* by Dr. Seuss
- *Visiting Feelings* by Lauren Rubenstein
- *A Happy Hat* by Cecil Kim
- *Being Me: A Kid's Guide to Boosting Confidence and Self-Esteem* by Wendy L. Moss

Instructions

- For younger children, you may wish to read the story, then ask open-ended questions to promote discussion about the themes in the book. Encourage children to make connections between their own experiences and the experiences of the characters. Discussion questions may include:

  o "What did [the character] go through in this book?"
  o "How do you think he/she handled it? Why?"
  o "If he/she was your friend, how would you help him her?"
  o "Have you ever gone through something like this?"
  o "Did you do something differently?"

- For older children, you may wish to add more explicit discussion about the connection between emotions, thoughts, behaviors, and relationships. Using the diagram below, you may ask students to identify each section of the diagram and discuss how the story unfolded. You may continue the discussion by asking how the story might have been different if one of the sections of the diagram had been different.

Variation

Ask a student to volunteer a personal experience. The student will go to the board and draw the diagram below. Other students can ask the volunteer questions to better understand his or her experience. Together, they will fill in all parts of the diagram.

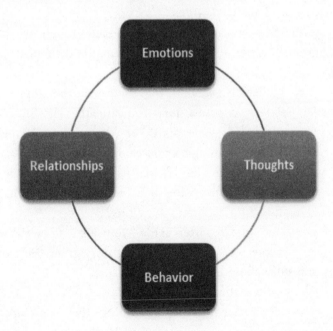

The Emotions Daily (Grades 4–5)

This activity helps students explore a situation to better understand the individual components of the whole. By using a social emotional scenario as a news story, students can break the story down to learn more about how emotions, thoughts, behaviors, and relationships are connected.

Materials Needed
- Pens or pencils
- Four sets of 3x5 cards; one set will have the word "Story" on the cards; the second set will have the word "Reporter" on the cards; the third set will have "Editor" on the cards; and the fourth set will have "Illustrator" on the cards
- Story cards from Appendix E
- Poster board

Instructions
- Introduce the activity to students: "Today we are all going to have jobs working for the *Emotions Daily*, a newspaper that reports on breaking news about emotions."
- Divide the class into four groups. Give each group a set of cards (one group gets the story cards, one group gets the reporter cards, etc.)
- Now give further instruction: "The group with the 'story' cards—your job will be to choose a story. You can either choose one from the two available [see Appendix E], or you can use an experience that one of you went through. Choose one member of your group to act as the person being interviewed. The person who will be interviewed will use the information to act out the story. Use the information to answer the reporter's questions."
- "The group with the 'reporter' cards—your job is to be the reporters who will interview the person in the story group. Find out the breaking story about how the person you are interviewing is feeling. Ask questions about what happened, who was there, and what he or she was thinking, feeling, and doing. Then come up with a headline about the story. For example, Charlie interviewed me ear-

lier. He asked me how I was feeling, what I was thinking, and what I was doing. With all the information I gave him, he came up with this headline: 'Mrs. Lopez is worried she'll never be able to figure out a really hard crossword puzzle.'"

- "The group with the 'editor' cards—your job is to meet with the reporters and write up a small paragraph about the story. Remember, what you write should be able to tell us the full story about what the person was feeling, what he or she was thinking, what he or she did, and how other people may have been involved."

- "The group with the 'illustrator' cards—your job is to work with the reporters and the editors to come up with a picture to go with the story. Make sure your picture captures the emotions discussed in the story."

- Once all the groups have finished, review the headline, the story, and the illustration. Discuss the experience with the students:

  o "What was it like to act out the story?"
  o "Did the information stay the same from the actor, to the reporter, to the editor? What was different?"
  o "Were there other questions you wished the reporters had asked?"
  o "How did the illustrations capture the emotions in the story?"
  o "Now that you know the full story, what suggestions would you have for the people in the stories?"
  o "What do you think Sarah could do to feel better? How would that change her thoughts? Her behaviors? Her relationships? What would you say to Sarah if she came to you for help?"
  o "What do you think Jake could do to feel better? How would that change his thoughts? His behaviors? His relationships? What would you say to Jake if he came to you for help?"

- Use a large poster board and post the article on a corner. Encourage students to write other social-emotional-related stories to post on their "newspaper." Themes for stories may include students being kind to or helping each other, ideas for how to deal with test stress, tips for dealing with returning to school after vacation, and so forth.

Domain	Grade	Activity
Problem Solving	3–5	Problems, Ideas, Plans: Let's Do the PIP!

PROBLEM SOLVING

Problem solving is an important strategy used in the treatment of mental illness and as a coping skill to promote wellness. As mentioned in the previous chapters, children struggling with anxiety and depression often have a hard time with problem solving, given their strong tendency for avoidance as well as their feelings of low self-efficacy and helplessness. Problem solving assists in promoting more active coping and increasing self-efficacy and control.

Problem solving is also an important skill to learn for children who do not struggle with mental illness. Emotional distress and some thought processes, such as rumination (i.e., dwelling on negative feelings), may interfere with optimal problem solving. In this sense, problem solving may be used both as an active coping skill and as a preventive measure to reduce risk factors associated with internalizing disorders (e.g., poor coping, low sense of control and efficacy).

Problems, Ideas, Plans: Let's Do the PIP! (Grades 3–5)*

The PIP is a fun, creative tool for teaching problem-solving skills. It is brief and engaging, and can be used by both children and adults. The PIP promotes the decision-making skills of social emotional learning along with the creative (divergent) and critical (convergent) thinking skills of 21st-century learning. There is a direct link between the skills taught through the PIP and the emotional health skills needed for wellness in children and adolescents. PIP skills include:

- Developing and examining multiple perspectives
- Withholding judgment and criticism in evaluating one's and others' ideas

---

* This activity is based on the creative problem-solving process of the Creative Education Foundation and the Osborn-Parnes Creative Problem Solving Process. It is also based on consultation with Russ Schoen and Gloria Rapport, cofounders of the Creative Youth Leadership Program.

- Cognitive flexibility (generating many ideas and ways of thinking)
- Collaboration
- The use of creativity as it is defined by the individual

Materials Needed
- PIP worksheet (see Appendix F)
- Pencils and markers for each student
- Post-it notes (preferably of different colors)
- Flip chart

Instructions
- Introduce the activity by delivering the following script: *Today we are learning a fun and creative way to solve challenges or problems. Can you give me some examples of challenges or problems you have that you may need help in solving?* (Examples might include how to finish homework on time, how to talk to friends about something, how to find ways to prepare for transitioning to middle school.) *To help us figure out these challenges, we will use the problems, ideas, and plan exercises, or the PIP.*

  When using the PIP, we'll use two different kinds of thinking. One is called divergent thinking. (Use hand gestures to make the point of this, with arms outstretched in a V.) *Divergent thinking is when you come up with as many ideas as you can, without judging any ideas. Don't think, "I won't say that because that could never happen," or "That's a silly idea; I don't want to say that and be embarrassed." All ideas are welcome. Be as bold, brave, loud, and creative as you can! The goal here is to come up with as many ideas as possible, so the more wild and crazy ideas, the better! You can build on each other's ideas, and anything goes!*
- *Are you ready to practice? Let's use an example we can all work on. Our challenge is to come up with ideas for an end-of-the-year party. I'm going to give you markers and Post-it sheets. Using divergent thinking, come up with as many ideas as you can. Write each idea on a separate Post-it sheet, and I'll put them up on our flip chart. Remember, wild and crazy ideas are fantastic. Don't let any restrictions hold you back. Use your imagination!*

- Allow 5 to 10 minutes of divergent thinking. Students often begin a bit slowly here, as they are used to thinking about the feasibility or acceptability of their answers before sharing their ideas. It may take some time for them to stop prejudging their ideas and begin coming up with uncensored ones. To model this nonjudgmental kind of thinking, you may wish to share ideas such as "a party in outer space" or "a party in a floating jumpy house." As students give you their ideas, repeat them for all to hear and place the Post-it notes on the flipchart. Keep going until you have a good number of ideas—remember, the goal here is quantity.

- Encourage your students to reflect on the process so that they realize the flexibility and power that deferring judgment can generate: *That was great! Look at how many ideas we have on the chart! How did that feel?*

- Continue your script: *OK, now let's look at this amazing list of ideas, and let's use* convergent thinking (use hand gestures to convey convergence, bringing your arms together over your head with your palms touching) *to narrow down the ideas and choose the one you like most. When you use convergent thinking, you focus on ideas that seem realistic and helpful. You consider new ways of solving problems and ones that make an improvement on what you've done before. Let's break up into groups.* (Assign groups of three to four students.) *Take five minutes and discuss which ideas you like the most. Let's have each group use convergent thinking and choose the one idea they want to nominate for the end-of-the-year party.*

- Ask each group to present the idea its members chose for the end-of-the-year party. Some students may indicate that the idea they like most is an unrealistic one (e.g., a party with penguins as waiters). If that is the case, encourage students to think about what the "spark" of that idea is and how to turn it into something realistic. Using the penguin example, it is truly unrealistic to have live penguins; however, the "spark" seems to be incorporating penguins somehow. Could it be a penguin-themed party? There were penguin waiters in the movie *Mary Poppins*. Could the party have a Mary Poppins theme? Elicit students' reactions regarding this portion of the process, encouraging them to make connections between collaboration, critical thinking, and finding new perspectives.

The sample challenge chosen, planning the end-of-the-year party, was a group challenge, in which both the divergent and convergent processes happened as a group. In the next section, students will be asked to complete the PIP to solve individual challenges. This involves a slightly different process. First, the students choose their individual challenge and record it on their worksheets. Next, working with a partner, they practice divergent thinking together, first to address one students' challenge and then again to address the other student's challenge. Third, each student goes back to working independently, and the convergent thinking process should happen for the individual alone. Action planning is then completed. Here is a script for guiding students through this part of the PIP:

- *That was fun practicing the PIP as a group! Now let's use the PIP individually to help you find a solution for a real-life situation that is going on for you right now. We'll use divergent and convergent thinking, and we'll also come up with an action plan that you can use starting today.* (Distribute a blank PIP worksheet to each student. Indicate to students that they will be completing each section following your instructions; therefore, they should not try to complete the whole thing ahead on their own.)
- *Take a look at your worksheets. Step 1 asks you to identify your challenge. What's on your mind that you would like help with? Sometimes when we think about problems, we think about something that is too big and may seem hard to solve. It helps to make it smaller, until you find the challenge that you really want to focus on.*
- (Refer here to the upside-down pyramid example in Appendix F; you may wish to write an upside-down pyramid on the board for all students to look at.) *For example, my problem is that I'm too tired. That is too huge* (point to the largest part of the pyramid at the top). *I need to make that smaller. Let's see . . . I want to have more energy . . . it's smaller, but it's still not quite what I want* (point to the second point on pyramid). *How can I make this smaller?* (Ask

students for ideas). *Great ideas; thanks for your help! I can make my challenge this: I want to know how to have more energy during the school day. OK, now think about your individual challenge. Take three minutes to think about this and use your pyramid to make the challenge smaller. Once you decide what your challenge is, write it down in the box.*

- *Now that you have identified your challenge, please find a partner. You and your partner will work together to do some divergent thinking. Do you remember what kind of thinking that was?* (Use of arm gestures here to help students remember, stretching your arms into a large V shape.) *Remember, in this section, to try to come up with as many ideas as possible, and anything goes! You can use Step 2 of your handout to write down your ideas.* (Allow approximately five minutes.)

- *We are moving on to Step 3 now. What kind of thinking do we need to use? That's right—convergent.* (Use arm gestures to help students remember, bringing your arms up above your head with your palms touching.) *Look at the ideas that you and your partner came up with during your divergent thinking, and narrow them down to the one idea or combination of ideas you like most. Write that down for Step 3 of your worksheet. Do this individually. Your partner helped you to come up with ideas for divergent thinking, but only you can be the one to use convergent thinking to choose the solution that feels right for you. Remember what your challenge is and choose an idea that will help you accomplish what you want to do.* (Allow approximately five minutes.)

- *You are doing a great job—really thinking about what the challenge is, thinking of alternatives, and finding the best possible solutions. Now that you've done all this thinking, let's find some actions! We are going to create action plans. This is the part that helps you figure out the steps needed to solve your problem. Take a look at Step 4 on your worksheet. What steps do you need to take to solve your challenge?* (Ask students to volunteer the ideas they chose to solve their challenges so that you can model coming up with action steps). *When coming up with your action steps, think about what specific things you need to do, when you might need to do them, and who might help you. Make sure you find at least one action step that will happen sometime today. If you are able to take your first step in these first 24 hours, you will have a much better chance of completing your whole action plan.* (Again, offer examples so students can understand this. Allow approximately 8 to 10 minutes.)

• When students finish, encourage them to share with the larger group what they have written on their individual worksheets. Ask how the process was helpful in finding potential new solutions. Questions to guide discussion include:

   o "What was it like to come up with a problem and define it?"
   o "What was difficult?"
   o "What did you like about it?"
   o "Why does it make sense to break down large problems into smaller portions?"
   o "What did you come up with for your action plan?"
   o "How does it help to have others as part of your action plan?"
   o "What do they think might happen as you complete each action step?"
   o "How do you think you might feel?"

• Continue your script: *I'm so glad we all had an opportunity to practice this fun way to solve our challenges. Step 5 of your worksheet reminds you that if something doesn't seem to be working, you can always go back and start over. Maybe the challenge needs to be a bit smaller. Maybe it would help to do more divergent thinking. Wherever may need tweaking, remember you have all the tools ready at your fingertips!*

Like other coping and wellness skills, problem solving should be practiced. Students are able to practice the PIP on an online community called Whyville. Whyville (http://www.whyville.net) is the premier educational virtual world for children, embedding simulation-based learning in an engaging and safe collaborative gaming social environment. It was developed by Numedeon, Inc., and has won numerous media and parent awards, including a Gold Award from the National

Parenting Publications Awards (NAPPA). Recently, the Freedman Center for Child and Family Development of the Massachusetts School of Professional Psychology partnered with Whyville to create a destination on the site called the Wellness Center. Within the Wellness Center, students are able to access the PIP, scripts for deep breathing and visualization exercises, journaling exercises, and tips for managing emotional distress as well as for promoting wellness. The content is appropriate for children ages 8 to 15.

Domain	Grade	Activity
Increasing Positive Affect	K–1	Friendship Soup
	2–5	My Strengths

INCREASING POSITIVE AFFECT

Friendship Soup (Grades K–1)

During the early elementary school years, children's friendships are based on common interests, gender, and a mutual liking for one another. For example, Sammy might say, "Matt is my friend because he's nice and we play soccer together." In addition to connecting around common interests, children become increasingly able to understand and acknowledge other children's points of view (Davies, 2011). For example, Sammy may say that playing soccer just for fun during recess is better, but he knows that Matt thinks playing on a team is better. How a child manages differences between his and others' opinions will be reflected in his behavior and, consequently, in his ability to establish and maintain friendships. If Sammy understands that he and Matt don't agree on what's better but can still play together during recess and have fun, then he will continue to act in a friendly manner toward Matt and their friendship will continue, despite their differences in opinions. However, if Sammy thinks, "Matt is wrong—playing on a team isn't fun; it's dumb. I'm not going to play with him anymore unless he takes that back," then he will likely not be friendly to Matt and their friendship will suffer. In this instance, Sammy's inability to cope with differences in opinions will impede his ability to establish and maintain friendships.

This activity helps introduce children to positive qualities of a friendship. Using their developing cognitive abilities to understand and acknowledge others' opinions, it encourages them to think about others' opinions, emotions, and needs in a friendship.

Materials Needed

- A soup pot, a bowl, or a box—anything that may be used as the pot for the friendship soup
- Small pieces of paper

Instructions

- Introduce the activity: *Let's talk about cooking. Who's helped a grown-up make soup before? What kind did you make? How did you make the soup? What did you put in the soup? Great! All that sounds delicious! Today we're going to make a special kind of soup—friendship soup!*

  I have a pot here where we're going to cook our soup. Now, this special soup is going to need some very special kinds of ingredients. What do you think we should put in our soup? Why don't you tell me the ingredients, and I'll write them down on a piece of paper so you can put them in the pot.

  OK, so what should go into making a good friendship? What should our recipe be?
- If prompts are needed, you may suggest things like good listening or taking turns. Write down each ingredient as the students tell you, allowing them to place the pieces of paper into the soup pot.
- Encourage students to share why they think the ingredients they choose should be in the soup.
- A fun continuation of this activity may be to have students create their own "recipe books." The book can include recipes for things such as friendship soup, good- sister/good-brother cake, and careful listener stew.

My Strengths (Grades 2–5)*

A strength-based approach to learning about emotions focuses on how to enhance positive qualities, promote strengths, and increase protective factors. Focusing on strengths allows students to be hopeful by think of possibilities and what they are doing correctly, rather than staying stuck on what they are doing wrong. This activity follows a strengths-based approach and offers an opportunity for students to develop emotion vocabulary and positive behaviors. The activity can be used at least once a day each day.

Materials Needed
- 3x5 cards (preferably of different colors), each with a strength written on it (see Appendix G)
- Box in which to keep the cards

Instructions
- Create a box to hold the strength cards. You may decorate it yourself or ask the students to help you do so.
- Write a strength word on each card, and place all the cards in the box.
- Each day, ideally in the morning, ask a student to choose one of the cards from the box. Once the student has chosen a card, ask him or her to act out the strength without using any words. The other students have to guess what the strength is. Pairing the word with actions helps to create a stronger image and memory of the emotion word.
- Once the strength has been guessed, ask students how they can use that strength during the day. How could they use that strength during difficult times? How could they continue to develop that strength in themselves?
- Throughout the day, notice which students may be using that strength and offer praise for their positive behaviors.

* This activity is based on the "Strengths in a Box" resource from Jane Sleeman and Megan Booth at Hollyhox Positive Resources, Australia.

Variation

Choose a "strength of the week" and write it on a large poster board. Put up the poster board in the room. On the poster board, you may write down the names of students who are exemplifying the strength of the week. Students can also write down the names of peers (or their teacher) when they see them exemplifying the strength of the week.

Domain	Grade	Activity
Active Coping	K–5	Sweet Dreams
	2–5	Surfing the Waves
	3–5	Here's My Card

ACTIVE COPING

Finding active, approach-related ways of coping is a critical aspect of promoting self-regulation. The following set of activities aims to help children develop a repertoire of skills for creating healthy habits, identifying people and ways to help manage their mood, keeping a tangible set of resources, and keeping a record of new skills learned to reference and use in the future.

Sweet Dreams (Grades K–5)

Sleep is essential for good health as well as for mental and emotional functioning. If children do not sleep well, they may experience irritability, moodiness, and disinhibition. With consistent sleep deprivation, they may experience apathy, slowed speech, poor emotional responses, impaired memory, and an inability to problem-solve. This activity introduces children to the importance of sleep and how it impacts their emotional health.

Materials Needed

- A sleep chart for each student (can be structured any way that is convenient for the teacher; critical elements to include are the child's name, the date, the number of hours slept per day, and a space for a parent's or caregiver's signature)
- Handout from Appendix H

Instructions

- Introduce the activity (adjust the language to suit the grade level of your class): *How important do you think sleep is for you? Sleep is so important that if you do not sleep well, it can make you feel tired, cranky, and even sad. Getting only a little bit of sleep can get in the way of your being able to remember things, think of new ideas, and feel good, both physically and emotionally. Do you know how much sleep you should be getting every night? Kids your age need to get 10 or 11 hours of sleep every night. How many of you think you're getting that much sleep?*

  If you think you need to get more sleep, don't worry. We're going to find a fun way to get you all to have more sleep. We are going to have a Sweet Dreams Challenge! During the week, you will keep track of the hours that you're sleeping. If the class reaches our goal of sleep hours for the week, we can have a pajama party (or movie day, or other age-appropriate reward for the class).

- Distribute the sleep chart to each student. Ask them to write down each morning the amount of hours they slept the night before. Have parents sign each day.

- Continue your script: *One of the things that can help us get better sleep is having a good bedtime routine. What is your bedtime routine?* (You can use the handout from Appendix H.) *Are there some things that you do for your bedtime routine that you could teach us?* (Examples might include doing a visualization before bedtime or listening to soothing music.)

- Continue your script: *What are some things that should not be a part of our bedtime?* Encourage conversation about things that may interrupt falling or staying asleep and should be avoided. For example:

  o Don't drink caffeine four to six hours before bed (no soda before bedtime!)
  o Don't eat a big, heavy meal before going to bed
  o Don't watch TV to fall asleep
  o Don't have your phone in your room; you may be tempted to use it!
  o Don't use the computer right before bedtime

Surfing the Waves (Grades 2–5)

In this activity, students learn ways to manage big emotions. Using the image of emotions as waves, students figure out which coping skills can serve as their surfboards. This activity uses a strengths-based approach, where students are encouraged to think of active, positive coping skills they can use not only to manage big emotions but also to increase and maintain a positive mood. The activity promotes self-awareness, self-management, relationship skills, and responsible decision making.

Materials Needed
- For younger students (Grades 1–3), handout from Appendix I
- For older students (Grades 4–5), surfboard cutout from Appendix J
- Large poster board

Instructions for Younger Students (Grades 2 and 3)
- Introduce the activity: *Who has been to the beach before? What was the ocean like? Were there big waves in the water? What happens when there are big waves?* (Encourage discussion around how big waves build up, then come to shore and can knock us over if we are not prepared.) *Have you seen anyone surfing big waves before? How do you think they learned how to surf? Do you think they needed to practice a lot?*

  Sometimes emotions can be like waves—they start to build up inside us and get big, and if we're not ready, they can knock us over. What kinds of big emotions have you had? (Encourage discussion of a wide range of emotions, including surprise, disappointment, frustration, feeling overwhelmed, feeling scared, feeling worried, and so forth.) *Can you think of a time when you had big waves of emotions? What happened? How did your body feel? What kinds of thoughts did you have?*

  At times, it can be tough to figure out what to do when we have big waves of emotions like that. But guess what? Today, we're going to make our very own surfboards that will help us ride those waves of emotions. Ready to build some boards?
- Distribute the handout from Appendix I to each student.

- Continue your script: *OK, now everyone has his or her own ocean and surfboards. Let's start by writing down on the waves the big emotions you might have.* (You may wish to copy the contents of the handout on the board to use as an example so students can better understand the concepts.)
- Using yourself as an example, say something like this: *Today I was feeling a big wave of worry because I thought I was going to be late getting to school in the morning.* (Write down "worry" on the waves.) *Now think of what big emotions you have and write them down on your waves.*
- Walk around and check in with students to make sure they understand the instructions.
- Continue your script: *Great job! Now, let's think of ways that we can deal with those big waves of emotions, and we'll write those down on our surfboards. For my example, who can help me think of a way to deal with worry?* (In this section, you will want to make sure examples such as "Take deep breaths" and "Tell yourself it's OK if you're a little late" are shared.) *Those are great ideas; thank you. I'm going to write down "Take deep breaths" on my surfboard. Now I want you to think of things you can do to deal with your big emotions. Write those ideas on your surfboards.*
- Go around the room to make sure students understand the instructions and are completing the handouts.
- Follow this activity with a discussion:

  - "Who would like to share what you wrote on your handout?"
  - "What did you write on your waves?"
  - "What did you write on your surfboards?"
  - "What other ideas can we think of for our surfboards?"
  - "Do you think it will be easy or tough for us to ride the waves on our surfboards? Why?"
  - "How do you think we can practice riding on our surfboards?"

Instructions for Older Students (Grades 4 and 5)
- Introduce the activity: *How many times a day do you hear someone say they're stressed? Stress is a word we hear all the time, but do we*

really know what stress is? Let's take some time today to learn more about stress and to find ways to manage it.

How would you define stress? (It is important in this discussion to share that stress is a physical and emotional response to a demanding situation.)

How does your body let you know you're feeling stressed? (Examples might include headaches, tiredness, restlessness, sleeping too much or too little, changes in eating habits, stomachaches, or feeling "butterflies" in one's stomach.)

What other feelings or thoughts do you have when you're stressed? (Examples might include feeling nervous, feeling cranky, having difficulty concentrating, forgetting things, worrying, feeling angry, or feeling sad.)

At times when we have stress, it can feel like a big wave of emotions. Unless we're ready to ride those waves, we can end up feeling worse. Let's think of ways that we can manage stress. Let's create our very own surfboards to help us ride the big emotion waves.

- On the board, draw a large surfboard, and inside it write down the stress management ideas students share.
- Continue your script: *Let's build our boards. What are some ways to manage stress?* Below are ideas for stress management skills:

  o Exercise
  o Talk to a friend or a family member
  o Do something fun, such as going outside and playing
  o Take a warm bath
  o Ask for help
  o Break large tasks into small pieces
  o Change negative self-talk to positive self-talk
  o Do some problem solving (what steps do you need to take to succeed?)
  o Listen to music and dance
  o Be flexible; have a backup plan
  o Keep a journal
  o Do something creative
  o Get enough sleep

> ○ Practice deep-breathing exercises
> ○ Practice visualization and guided imagery exercises
> ○ Picture your stress as a monster or imaginary creature; give it a name and picture it shrinking or disappearing when you do something to relieve your stress
> ○ Take a break to "charge your batteries" by disconnecting from technology (i.e., take some time away from phones, iPads, video games, and TVs)

- After students have shared their ideas as a large group, give each student a surfboard handout (see Appendix J).
- Continue your script: *Now that we have a great list of possible ways to ride the big emotion waves, choose five that you like the most and write them down on your surfboard. Keep this list with you to remind you of the positive ways you can manage your stress.*

Supplemental Components (For All Grades)
- Use the surfing theme throughout the day. Pairing a fun and positive theme with discussions of emotions can make the conversation less threatening and more engaging, and it will create more cues for students to remember the material.
- Ask the class to vote on the top three coping skills (or surfboards) they can use in school to ride big emotion waves—for example, before a test, to deal with changes, or to manage interpersonal situations. Write the coping skills on the surfboard, decorate it, and post it in the classroom so students can refer to it daily.

Here's My Card (Grades 3–5)
During times of distress, it may be difficult for a child to quickly or spontaneously remember his or her coping skills, who to go to for help, or scripts to follow for breathing or relaxation exercises. Therefore, having a card with quick prompts and tips can be very helpful in reminding a child of what skills can be used for self-regulation.

Materials Needed
Card from Appendix K

Instructions

- This activity can be done individually with a particular student, or with the whole class.
- You may use this activity at the end of a discussion on emotions, in conjunction with any of the other activities listed in this book, or as part of a regular journaling exercise that you do with your class.
- If you choose to do this activity with the whole class, it is helpful to promote discussion about what students have written on their cards. This prompts open dialogue around emotions as well as the sharing of ideas for positive coping.

Domain	Grade	Activity
Relaxation Skills	K–5	The Chill Zone

RELAXATION SKILLS

"Relaxation training helps [children] recognize that [they] have control over physical reactions" and includes breathing exercises, muscle relaxation, visualization, and guided imagery (Kendall, Furr, & Podell, 2010, p. 48). These techniques are used to help children feel calm and in control and, consequently, to be better able to access their coping skills.

The Chill Zone (Grades K–5)

When children struggle with strong emotions in the classroom, it can be quite difficult for them to practice coping skills while sitting at their desks. Not only is it difficult for them to practice coping, but it can also be difficult for teachers to contain disruptive behaviors associated with emotional dysregulation, such as interrupting, inattentiveness, and aggression. Given the rules of the school setting, such behavioral dysregulation is typically addressed from a punitive perspective. The focus on what the child is doing wrong may lead to guilt or shame in children.

Following a strengths-based perspective, teachers can offer a safe space for children to go when they feel dysregulated. There, children can take a calming break and use coping skills, then return to their desk while not feeling alienated or punished. This technique is based on mindfulness, which involves sitting with and experiencing one's feelings in a safe manner rather than trying to ignore or push them away without acknowledging them or finding a way to manage them. This technique also supports a more positive long-term approach for self-management and self-regulation, as it focuses on what the child is doing right.

Materials Needed

In a space in the room that is away from other desks, create a special location where children can go to have time for calming and soothing themselves when they are upset. It is important not to label this area a "time-out" area, as that has a connotation of punishment. Instead, the space can be described as a "being-kind-to-myself space," a "safe space," or a "calming corner." You may wish to ask the students to help you come up with a name that feels right for the class.

In the calming space, there should be materials that promote regulation and coping. These might include:

- Books
- Headphones for listening to music or books on tape
- Drawing materials
- Clay or Play-Doh
- Stress balls
- Arts and crafts materials
- Laminated scripts for breathing, guided imagery, and muscle relaxation exercises (scripts can be found in Chapter 5)

Instructions

- When a student is expressing distress (verbally or behaviorally), offer him or her an opportunity to go to the calming space for 5 to 10 minutes before returning to the classroom activity. This opportunity for regulation should occur prior to any disciplinary measures.
- For students who have emotional disorders, you may wish to work with the adjustment counselor or mental health clinician of the school to devise an individual plan that includes how often and for how long the calming space may be used.

Notice, Give, Nurture

WHAT CAN I NOTICE?

Children's Strengths

This chapter has focused on building emotional health and wellness following a strengths-based approach. A continued commitment to this approach requires teachers to notice areas of strength or particular talents and interests in their students. Rather than assessing only for risks that may lead to disorder, assessing for strengths capitalizes on children's internal capabilities and taps into their potential for success and hope. Below are areas of strength to assess. This is not an exhaustive list. However, it serves as a starting point for assessing strengths across multiple domains of a child's life.

- Is the child especially attuned to the feelings and needs of others?
- Is the child a good listener?
- Is the child able to communicate effectively and encourage communication in others?
- Do others enjoy the child's company because of his or her kindness and empathy?
- Is the child flexible and able to find creative or novel solutions?
- Is the child able to understand others' perspectives?
- Does the child demonstrate any specific talents (e.g., musical, artistic)?
- Does the child have particular areas of interests (e.g., animals, drawing, building)?
- Is the child involved in extracurricular activities (e.g., sports, drama, clubs)?
- Does the child engage in a particular activity for enjoyment (e.g., dance, poetry)?
- Does the child have meaningful relationships with other peers? With adults?
- Does the child share a common interest and/or activities with family members (e.g., reading about animals with a grandfather)?
- Does the child demonstrate a strong connection to the school?

- Is the child involved in community activities or groups?
- Does the child relate to some aspect of spirituality?
- Is the child involved in any volunteer activities (e.g., delivering meals during Thanksgiving, environmental activities)?

Your Mental Health Literacy

A commitment to student emotional health and wellness also requires reflection on your own understanding and comfort level with respect to mental health. Again, following a strengths-based perspective, mental health literacy is not just about the ability to understand mental health difficulties and make referrals. As Whitley, Smith, and Vaillancourt (2012) indicate, teachers' mental health literacy should also include an understanding of mental health prevention and how to promote social emotional learning. Therefore, teachers are encouraged to notice their own knowledge, skills, and attitudes with respect to social emotional learning.

- Notice opportunities to increase your knowledge about mental health promotion and social emotional learning. These opportunities may come in the form of workshops, books, or special trainings.
- Notice which colleagues may be knowledgeable about the topic and consult with them. Share ideas and tips for infusing your educational curriculum with opportunities for social emotional learning. Professional learning communities and the strong and persistent benefits of teacher collaboration and sharing emerge throughout the literature as excellent ways to gain knowledge and share resources (Whitley et al., 2012).

WHAT CAN I GIVE?

Warm, Supportive Relationships

> Kind words can be short and easy to speak, but their echoes are truly endless.
>
> —Mother Teresa

The echoes of a strong, supportive relationship are also truly endless. Teachers can give supportive and growth-promoting relationships that are "individualized to the child's unique personality style; that build on his or her own interests, capabilities, and initiative; that shape the child's self-awareness; and that stimulate the growth of his or her heart and mind" (National Scientific Council on the Developing Child, 2004, p. 1)

As the National Scientific Council on the Developing Child (2004) reports, relationships "engage children in the human community in ways that help them define who they are, what they can become, and how and why they are important to other people" (p. 1). During times when children have significantly more adverse experiences to deal with, such as neglect, poverty, separation, violence, and abuse, the presence of supportive relationships can buffer some of the negative impact that those adverse life experiences bring to bear. If such nurturing relationships are established early on, they can help shape a child's definition of himself or herself in a positive, hopeful, and meaningful way. A large body of research indicates that supportive teacher–student relationships play a large and long-lasting role in students' connection to school as well as in positive outcomes in the academic and social emotional domains (Cappella et al., 2012; Jennings & Greenberg, 2009). For example, children "who develop warm, positive relationships with their kindergarten teachers are more excited about learning, more positive about coming to school, more self-confident, and achieve more in the classroom." (National Scientific Council on the Developing Child, 2004, p. 2).

Mindful Listening

Mindful listening involves actively listening to another without interruptions. The listener notices, or is mindful of, any emotional reactions he or she may have, but does not act upon them. There are no interruptions, interpretations, advice giving, scolding, problem solving, or judgment. Such listening is by no means simple. I often find myself listening to something one of my sons is telling me and coming up with solutions or advice before he is even finished. The urge to protect, help, and problem-solve for our children is strong, yet if we do not allow them the opportunity to explore and come up with solutions independently, we do not foster self-efficacy, confidence, or trust. By practicing mindful listening, teachers can listen more effectively to their students, be more sensitive to their needs, and respond supportively and calmly during conflict (Jennings, Snowberg, Coccia, & Greenberg, 2011).

WHAT CAN I NURTURE?

Students' Inner Motivational Resources

Teachers can nurture students' inner motivational resources by finding ways to coordinate instructional activities with students' "preferences, interests, sense of enjoyment, sense of challenge, competencies, and choice-making" (Reeve & Jang, 2006, p. 228). Reeve and Jang (2006) identify two types of teaching styles, controlling and autonomy supportive, and posit that an autonomy supportive style is more conducive to nurturing students' inner motivational resources. When following a controlling style, teachers "have students put aside their inner motivational resources and instead adhere to a teacher-centered agenda" (p. 210). In contrast, an autonomy supportive style "revolves around ways to nurture, support, and increase students' inner endorsement of their classroom activity" (Reeve & Jang, 2006, p. 210). While a controlling style may result in students' behavioral compliance, it accomplishes this through externally motivating ways. An autonomy supportive style results in positive behavior and achievement by addressing students' psychological needs. Research demonstrates that students with autonomy supportive teachers, compared to students with controlling teachers, experience "more positive functioning in terms of their classroom engagement, emotionality, creativity, intrinsic motivation, psychological wellbeing, conceptual understanding, academic achievement, and persistence in school" (p. 210). Below are some teacher behaviors that Reeve and Jang (2006) identify as promoting an autonomy supportive style and that nurture students' inner motivational resources:

- Asking what students wants (e.g., allowing choices)
- Allowing students to work in their own way to solve a problem
- Allowing students to talk and express opinions
- Creating purposeful seating arrangements (e.g., inviting students to sit next to learning materials)

- Providing rationales (e.g., indicating why a course of action may be useful)
- Offering praise as informational feedback (i.e., focusing on effort and progress rather than solely on outcome)
- Offering words of encouragement
- Offering process-enabling hints
- Being responsive to student-generated questions
- Communicating perspective-taking statements (i.e., empathic acknowledgment of students' experiences)

Mindfulness Practices for Yourself

Teachers face an incredible amount of stress on a daily basis. The cumulative stress associated with everything from overcrowded classrooms to limited resources, increased testing demands, and difficult student behavior has a negative impact on teachers' health and well-being as well as on the retention rates for the profession. One practice that is increasingly being studied in terms of its impact on reducing teacher stress is mindfulness. As described in Chapter 4, mindfulness is defined as "paying attention in a particular way: on purpose, in the present moment, and nonjudgmentally" (Kabat-Zinn, 1994, p. 4). Research indicates that, for teachers, multiple benefits may accrue following mindfulness training, including a reduction in mental health difficulties, achievement of personally relevant goals, and enhanced ability to cope with the demands of teaching (Gold et al., 2010). Teachers' practicing of mindfulness has also been associated with an overall sense of well-being, teaching self-efficacy, increased ability to manage student behavior, and ability to establish and maintain supportive relationships with students (Meiklejohn et al., 2012).

This chapter has highlighted how teachers can provide opportunities to incorporate the whole child, including his or her emotions, strengths, talents, and gifts, to promote social, emotional, and academic success. The next chapters will address how to engage other important systems in a child's life to further promote emotional health and wellness. Chapter 6 will focus on how to work with parents, and Chapter 7 will discuss how to integrate the concepts discussed throughout the book into the school culture.

CHAPTER SIX

Communicating With Parents About Student Mental Health

From Prevention to Intervention

What a difference it made for Jenna to have Mrs. Goldman as a teacher this year. She really helped us figure out what was getting in the way of Jenna's learning and took the time to get to know us as a family. I feel so grateful for her interest and help.

—Mrs. L, mother of Jenna, fourth-grader

AN EXTENSIVE BODY OF research indicates that healthy parent–child–school relationships and parental engagement are directly linked to a number of positive child outcomes, including those specifically related to the school setting. For example:

- Healthy parenting relationships protect children from the development of later problem behavior in school, even when they are exposed to other risk factors such as stress and poverty (Stormshak et al., 2011).
- When parents assist with homework and monitor grades, achievement scores, and courses, the probability of truancy decreases (Kim & Page, 2013).
- Greater parental involvement in the schooling of their children is associated with better academic achievement and child mental health (Duchnowski et al., 2012).

A unique factor of the parent–school relationship that has been more recently identified is parents' perceptions of teacher responsiveness. According to Christenson (2004), teachers demonstrate responsiveness to children and parents when they meet families where they are. Responsiveness is further demonstrated through communication of openness to new information, suggestions, and feedback, as well as through maintaining a "welcoming, supportive stance toward parents" (Powell, Son, File, & San Juan, 2010, p. 272). Importantly, research indicates that the quality of the parent–teacher relationship, and its subsequent impact on perceived responsiveness, is more strongly associated with child outcomes than the actual amount of parent–teacher interaction (Powell et al., 2010).

As indicated throughout the book, relationships are critical when supporting children's mental health. In this chapter, we will examine how to engage parents in the school setting, specifically around mental health issues, as well as how to foster positive communication and relationships following identification of specific child mental health needs. The material is based on research, evidence-informed practice, and lessons learned from what has gone well (and not so well!) in my own work with schools.

Engaging Parents in the School Setting

A number of factors may interfere with effective or consistent parental engagement with the school. Pragmatic concerns, such as multiple jobs, lack of transportation, or childcare, may impede parents' visits to the school. Emotional concerns, such as negative previous experiences with schools or mental illness, may also inhibit parents' participation in school events. It may be tempting to say such factors are largely, if not wholly, responsible for parents' lack of engagement; however, it is important to remember that engagement is a bidirectional process, and the burden of engagement cannot rest solely upon the parents. Therefore, it is important for schools to engage in a process of self-reflection and examination of current practices to help identify those factors that may be limiting parental engagement.

SELF-REFLECTION: WHAT ARE YOUR STRATEGIES FOR PARENT OUTREACH?

Consider the following questions when assessing your school's outreach plans and protocols.

- *What methods are you currently using to contact families?*

  While some families may respond consistently to emails or weekly newsletters, some families may need to be contacted multiple times and in multiple ways to receive messages from schools. In addition to electronic communication, do you use other forms of communicating with parents? Alternatives include flyers sent home in the child's backpack, notices sent home in the mail, phone calls, or home visits. Wegmann, Powers, and Blackman (2013) advocate home visits, noting that such an approach may be a particularly helpful way to build relationships with parents who do not feel comfortable coming to the school.

- *Does your school culture encourage and welcome parent participation?*

  Small gestures can convey large messages when it comes to developing a school culture that encourages and welcomes parent participation. For example, are there signs that say "Welcome, parents!" in the school, or do teachers regularly and openly invite parents to set up meetings or to come volunteer? During open-house nights, do administrators and teachers encourage parent participation and share acceptable and helpful ways for them to be involved? Methods for easy communication with teachers, such as regular parent-teacher conferences, email exchanges, and invitations for feedback, also convey a strong interest in parent communication and engagement.

- *Do you have a specific strategy for parent outreach?*

  In some schools, a particular team may be assigned to parent outreach, and that team plans regular yearly events to engage parents. In some schools, the strategy may involve identifying particular a particular topic based on a needs assessment and then organizing large parent events to focus on that topic. For example, based on a student questionnaire, the school identifies stress as a topic of focus, then offers parent workshops to help parents understand how to support their children. Regardless of the specific strategy employed, having a rationale and specific plan driving outreach efforts leads to greater success.

  Another important strategic consideration involves communication among the school staff. For example, if there is a team whose job it is to focus on parent outreach, how does this team communicate with teachers? If the teachers are the ones directly responsible for parent outreach efforts (e.g., offering workshops or leading parent-teacher coffee meetings), it is important to discuss these plans with administrators. Initiating conversations with parents around child mental health is of utmost importance, yet parents may have different reactions, ranging from relief and acceptance to fear and anger, to the fact that these topics are being discussed in the school setting. A coordinated effort among administrators, school mental health staff, and teachers can help to anticipate and manage different parent reactions.

• *Do you have a way of helping families overcome logistical barriers, such as lack of childcare and/or transportation, and language difficulties?*

Sometimes parents very much want to participate in school events but are unable to do so given logistical complications. Providing assistance that helps overcome these barriers can be very helpful and can help to build parents' trust in and connection to the school. For example, many parents may not be able to read English-language notices about upcoming events or meetings. Offering flyers in different languages can help increase the likelihood that not just English-speaking and -reading parents will be able to attend. Offering translation services during parent events can also be helpful.

• *Do you have regular communication with parents to share positive news and updates, or do you contact parents only when there are behavioral or academic difficulties?*

Parents may be more reluctant to engage with school staff if their perception is that they will be contacted only when something is wrong. Following a strengths-based perspective, teachers are encouraged to reach out to parents to share positive updates, good news, and child successes. For parents whose children struggle with behavioral issues or with mental illness, it may feel discouraging to receive information only about what is going wrong. Such communication may also reinforce the worry that parents may have about their children being seen only in light of their illness, rather than in light of other aspects of who they are. For parents whose children struggle behaviorally and emotionally, receiving updates of successes and positive changes and admiration of positive qualities instills a sense of hope and reassurance.

• *Do you give up after a specific number of attempts to reach parents?*

As Herman, Reinke, Frey, and Shepard (2014) indicate, "Can you persist too much when attempting to access a parent? No, not really" (p. 30). Although it may feel somewhat intrusive, or perhaps even bothersome, to repeatedly attempt to contact a parent, frequent outreach conveys caring and commitment. Perhaps families are going through a particularly stressful time (e.g., loss of a loved one or a separation), or perhaps parents' work schedules do not allow communication with teachers during regular hours. More persistent efforts for outreach increase the possibility of connecting with families despite such barriers. Be sure to include alternative ways or times that they can contact staff personnel, or offer strategies for communication (e.g., by letter) that do not rely on specific schedules.

SELF-REFLECTION: HOW ARE YOU CONSIDERING CULTURE?

Cultural differences and expectations play a significant role in how engaged and connected parents may be to the school system. For example, many parents of Latino heritage believe that schools are wholly responsible for all aspects of the child's education. They tend to be less engaged and do not initiate interactions, not due to lack of interest but out of deference and respect for the expertise of the school staff (Ortiz, 2012). You may wish to consider the following questions when reflecting about how culture is considered in parent outreach efforts.

• *Are school staff encouraged to recognize and identify any biases or stereotypes regarding members of other cultures?*

Conversations about culture may be difficult to have, as teachers may feel shy to share their potential biases or stereotypes. While the dialogue may initially feel awkward, if teachers feel safe having the conversations, it can lead to greater understanding and self-reflection. If teachers do not feel safe having these conversations, however, there is a strong likelihood either that culture will be discussed only superficially, or that parents of other cultures may not feel fully understood or welcomed at the school. Therefore, it is critical for school administrators to foster an environment of psychological safety where difficult conversations are not only had, but strongly encouraged. Teachers must feel safe to share their personal ideas and potential biases, and administrators must model a method of communication and information sharing that leads to productive conversation rather than to shaming or repercussions.

• *Do you have a sense of how students feel about the climate for different cultural groups?*

Even young children in elementary school can sense how different cultural groups are viewed and treated. It is important to have a sense of how children feel about the climate for different groups. Do they feel other cultures are represented? Accepted? Are there any children that are left out or treated differently based on culture?

• *Do you provide parent materials in different languages? Do you provide translation services?*

Although it may not be possible to account for all languages represented in your school, offering parent materials in a range of different languages helps to include parents that may not speak or read English. A few years back, our office received a request to lead a parent workshop at a school that was experiencing increased instances of bullying among its students. The school had a predominantly Latino population, and many of the parents did not speak English. However, it was English-speaking parents from the Parent Teacher Organization (PTO) that requested the workshop. A colleague and I worked together and decided to offer a bilingual version of the workshop. My colleague presented the material in English, and I presented the material in Spanish. Although the workshop took longer, given the two languages, we were able to accommodate many more parents and were also able to unite the parents in a common mission of learning how to stop bullying in the school.

• *When planning events, do you consider specific cultural factors, such as nonverbal language, time orientation, levels of formality used in social contexts, view of school responsibilities, and understanding of educational structure?*

When planning parent events where multiple cultures are represented, it is important to consider cultural factors that may impact how welcome and included parents may feel. This is also important when inviting staff members or other speakers who may not be familiar with the cultures to lead the activities. For example, what is the time orientation of the culture? For some cultures, arriving at the exact time an activity is scheduled for is critical, yet for others the time may feel more flexible. Therefore, parents may arrive a bit later than the identified start time, not due to lack of interest or respect but due to a different time orientation. Nonverbal language cues also differ by culture. For example, for some Asian cultures, staring into someone's eyes for too long may be seen as disrespectful, whereas for other cultures it is viewed as conveying interest and engagement. Cultures also differ in terms of the levels of formality used in social contexts. For example, for some cultures, a hug may seem appropriate, whereas for others, only a handshake conveys the proper formality.

• *Do you have access to consultation if you are unsure how to handle a question related to culture?*

It is important to remember that there are as many intragroup differences among cultural groups as there are intergroup differences. For example, although they are all considered Latinos, a family from El Salvador will be very different from a family from Puerto Rico. Not all culturally related questions will be simple to answer. Asking the family about their culture in a respectful, nonjudgmental way can be very helpful in further understanding their needs. However, when asking a family is not possible, consider seeking consultation with someone who may be able to help with culturally related questions or dilemmas.

Mental Health Activities for Parents: A Prevention and Strengths-Based Approach

The self-reflection questions in the previous section apply to all parent engagement efforts. We now turn our attention to engaging parents specifically around the topic of mental health. While parents may be quite willing to attend a parent meeting focusing on how to improve a child's grades or on how to make a child a better athlete, they may be more hesitant to attend a workshop that focuses on depression in the family. The reluctance to attend may not necessarily be due to lack of interest, but may instead be due to the fear that such a topic may evoke, or to the stigma associated with attending the meeting (i.e., if you go to that meeting, either you or your child must be depressed, and either scenario is bad). Indeed, education efforts around mental health have traditionally followed a deficit or illness model, where the symptoms and negative effects are most salient. Parent activities using this model are traditionally very poorly attended.

A more engaging model focuses on strengths and positive outcomes, using mental health (rather than mental illness) as a framework. Mental health is defined as "a state of successful performance of mental function, resulting in productive activities, fulfilling relationships with other people, and the ability to adapt to change and cope with adversity" (U.S. Department of Health and Human Services, Substance Abuse and Mental Health Services Administration, Center for Mental Health Services, 2007, p. 6). Herman and colleagues (2014) suggest offering parent services and activities that focus on promoting child health and wellness and avoid language such as "treatment" and "intervention" (p. 25).

In my work as director of a depression prevention initiative, it was quite difficult to circumvent the topic of depression. Although parents were very interested in depression and wanted to know how to identify it in their children, workshops with the word *depression* in the title just seemed too intimidating. I felt quite frustrated when, after multiple requests to lead parent workshops focusing on childhood and adolescent depression, only a few brave souls would appear. One solution I found to be very helpful in engaging parents was using titles for the workshops that were more interesting, normalizing, and hopeful. For example, during a workshop titled "Finding the Strength Within: Fostering Emotional Wellness," while we still discussed depression, we did so through the larger lens of prevention and wellness promotion.

In addition to positive and strengths-based titles, activities that follow a scaffolding model are helpful when engaging parents around mental health topics. One format that I have found helpful is as follows:

1. During open house, introduce parents to the connection between emotional well-being and learning. Let them know that the school

is as equally committed to promoting student emotional health as it is to promoting academic progress. Also during this time, introduce any mental health providers, adjustment counselors, and guidance counselors in the school. Let parents know how to reach the staff.

2. Conduct a workshop in the fall around a strengths-based topic, such as promoting resilience; raising happy, healthy children; or promoting student success. During this workshop, include warning signs to look for that may indicate that a child may be having a hard time emotionally. Again, offer resources and information on how to contact mental health staff. Indicate that during the winter or spring, there will be a follow-up workshop for parents who are interested in learning more about how to help their children develop emotional coping skills. Consider having teachers make phone calls to parents to personally invite them to attend the workshop. Teachers may endorse the information presented in the workshop as helpful and something they use in their own work with children.

3. During the follow-up workshop, address specific difficulties children may experience, including anxiety and mood disorders. Offer resources for obtaining mental health services and information about how to contact mental health staff at the school.

Sometimes multiple meetings are not possible. When only one meeting is possible or feasible, it is important to think about what format may best encourage parent participation. Below are some possible options for parent activity formats. As always, it is important to match the format to the needs and culture of the school.

- *Parent coffee meetings.* A parent coffee meeting is a more informal way of sharing information about a particular topic or a new program for children, or to have parents meet a consultant who will be working with the school.
- *Regularly scheduled PTO meetings.* Like parent coffee meetings, PTO meetings offer a less formal way to share information with a group of people who meet regularly. This is a good setting for sharing updates, asking parents to engage other parents in future activities, or to distribute resource information.

- *Panel discussions.* Panel discussions can be a very effective way to discuss a topic from multiple perspectives. For example, I recently participated in a panel discussion where we discussed how mindset (growth vs. fixed; see Chapter 1) is related to learning and coping. Also present in the panel were teachers, the principal, the head of the guidance department, and the school psychologist. Each person discussed the concept from his or her perspective and gave a tip on how it might be used to promote engagement in learning and healthy emotional coping.
- *Collaboration with community organizations or places of worship.* Hosting an event outside the school setting and outside the traditional school schedule may elicit increased attendance from a broader range of parents. Meetings may be held at a local community center or at local houses of worship, with school and community staff working together to indicate how the school, home, and community might work together to promote child mental health and wellness. The increased familiarity with and respect for some of the community center personnel or religious leaders may lead to parents experiencing less stigma and more willingness to initiate action. This is also a perfect place for parents to share different community resources, meet mental health providers, and meet families from other schools.

Tools for Teacher–Parent Collaboration

UNDERSTANDING THE CHILD'S PSYCHOSOCIAL CONTEXT

If discussing children's emotional health and wellness is a normative part of teacher–parent communication, then bringing up a particular question, situation, or concern related to emotional health will not seem threatening or out of context.

In order to better understand a child's psychosocial context, teachers may wish to offer a questionnaire that can be initially used as an entry interview with parents. This information can be revisited during the year should any changes occur. At the end of the year, the questionnaire may be used to review progress and successes and also to contribute to the information used for planning for teacher selection for the next academic year.

Parents may not be used to sharing such information with teachers, or they may wonder why it is relevant for the teacher to have. Teachers may wish to share with parents that factors discussed in the questionnaire have been found to impact child functioning in the domains of self-regulation, academics, and emotional health. Therefore, having this information can be extremely helpful in devising a plan to maximize learning and support for the child. A sample questionnaire is found in Appendix L of this book.

COMMUNICATING ABOUT MENTAL HEALTH CONCERNS: REFERRALS AND PARENT MEETINGS

If you are concerned about a student and believe he or she would benefit from mental health services, the next step is to initiate a referral as quickly as possible. Most schools have a mental health referral protocol they follow. For example, the student's name is given to a guidance or adjustment counselor or other mental health clinician in the building. That person then initiates the conversation with parents about the referral for services. Different schools may follow different practices for referral protocols, so it will be important to become familiar with the specific one used in your school.

Regardless of who initiates the referral conversation with parents, it is very likely that they will want to speak to the teacher directly to better understand the teacher's observations and the child's presentation in the classroom. Having that initial conversation with parents, where you are raising concerns about possible mental health difficulties in their child, can seem daunting. At this time, it will be important to remember that you are acting on the child's behalf and for his or her best interest. It is equally important to remember that parents' responses to your conversation will be based on a combination of factors, including any past experiences they may have had with the mental health field, any emotions prompted by their own mental illness, and any number of emotions (including sadness, disappointment, guilt, fear, shame, anger) they may feel about their child's emotional functioning. These factors will impact how receptive they will be to your initial outreach and conversation (Herman et al., 2014). Below are some suggestions for navigating initial and subsequent conversations with parents around their children's mental health.

Share direct observations about the child's behaviors that prompted the concern.

When first conveying your impressions about a child's potential mental health issues, it is important to share clear behavioral observations of what prompted your concern. For example, you might say, "I noticed that Joey stays alone at the playground during recess and does not play with any of the other kids," or "I noticed that Maddie has been crying during the school day. She becomes very upset and is not able to share what made her cry." Indicate how these behaviors may be different than how the child typically behaved, as well as the duration of the new behaviors.

Be mindful of culture and how mental health is understood.

Research indicates that cultural differences account for differences in perception of the causes, nature, onset, and symptom expression of different mental disorders (Stewart, Simmons, & Habibpour, 2012). For example, many people of Haitian descent espouse beliefs of supernatural forces. Illness, including mental illness, is often induced spiritually by an offended *lwa* (a spiritual god). Treatment, therefore, is sought from spiritual healers and traditional remedies such as herbal teas and religious ceremonies (Nicolas & Schwartz, 2012). When conveying concerns to parents about possible mental illness in their children, it will be important to be receptive to parents' interpretation, questions, and help seeking, especially considering that their approach may not follow traditional Western-medicine approaches.

Share positive observations about the child.

It can be very difficult for parents to first hear of their child's struggles. They may worry that the child is struggling with everything related to school, very quickly envisioning the worst possible scenarios. Therefore, it is important to share what is positive about the child, including any accomplishments or successes. Hopeful and positive observations are especially powerful, such as, "He is a very good friend to others in the classroom," or "He was able to learn the breathing exercises I taught him." For parents who are aware of their children's struggles, hearing about the child's successes and accomplishments can be helpful in a different way. Children often "let down their guard" at home and are at their most irritable or difficult, as they have expended so much emotional energy at school trying to maintain control. Understanding the effort the child is putting forth in school and hearing about any areas of competence or progress can be very helpful and hopeful for parents.

Be an active listener.

If parents do not agree with your observations, question your knowledge of the subject, or simply refuse to engage in the conversation, it can be very difficult to remain engaged and listen attentively. Try to quiet the chatter in your own mind and listen carefully to what the parents may be saying. Stay focused on the conversations and words of the moment rather than trying to figure out what to do or how to fix the situation. Rushing to problem solving or giving advice may make parents feel forced into action or may make them defensive. Reflect back on what you heard parents say to make sure you understood them correctly. Use open-ended questions to encourage more clarification and understanding. Avoid yes/no questions that limit conversation. Parents' initial reactions may be due to prior experiences with mental health providers or agencies. Rather than insisting that treatment is the only way for the child to get better, acknowledge that there are different experiences and possibilities. If the parents seem receptive, inquire about their previous experiences with questions such as, "Have you received mental health services before? What was that experience like for you? What can we do to work together to find the best possible therapeutic fit for your family?"

Discuss possible worries and concerns parents may have.

Parents may have many worries related to your conversation about their child's mental health, but they may not feel comfortable bringing up their worries. A helpful technique is to discuss any potential worries you think they may have and invite them to share other worries or concerns. You may say something like, "I wonder if you have any concerns about our discussion of your son's mental health. When I've talked to other parents about their children's mental health, they've raised worries about how this information will be shared. Other parents have expressed questions about how much information the school needs to have about the child's treatment. Do you have any of these, or other, worries?"

Common worries parents have around mental health issues center around confidentiality. They may have concerns that information such as the child's diagnosis, family psychiatric history, or family secrets will be shared among school staff. Alternatively, parents may worry that if the child receives a mental health diagnosis, he or she will be "labeled" and may be signaled out or treated differently. Yet other parents worry that the school will insist on a particular kind of treatment, such as medication. Letting parents know that these are worries that other parents have expressed will reassure them that they are not the only ones with such worries. Your initiation of this conversation will let parents know that you feel comfortable discussing these topics with them.

Convey optimism about finding help for the child and working together with the parents.

Herman and colleagues (2014) highlight the importance of conveying optimism and building "the perception that something can be done to improve the situation" (p. 78). It is not sufficient to simply raise concerns. Parents will feel most supported when you let them know that you are willing to collaborate with them to find the best possible resources for the child. You do not need to have all the answers, nor do you need to be an expert in mental health. Typically, what parents value most is the willingness to listen and offer help without judgment. The next section of this chapter offers ideas on how to help parents access mental health services.

Facilitating Mental Health Services

Navigating the mental health system can be challenging and, quite often, frankly frustrating. Parents seeking mental health supports for their children may receive outdated lists from insurance companies, or they may hear about a provider only to find out that the provider has a four-month waiting list. For these reasons, it is important to help parents become more empowered consumers of the mental health system. It is also important to create opportunities for them to access services more easily.

- Help parents understand their insurance coverage.

    o Insurance benefits and coverage are typically different for mental health needs than for medical needs. Encourage parents to call their insurance company to ask specifically about mental health benefits. How many visits are covered per calendar year, whether a referral from the pediatrician is needed, what fees are not covered by insurance, and what the options are for out-of-network providers are critical pieces of information to gather. The American Academy of Child and Adolescent Psychiatry (n.d.) has a one-page resource sheet guiding parents on how to better understand their insurance benefits.

- Help parents identify the resources available to find mental health providers.

    o *Pediatricians.* Pediatric practices may have a list of providers with whom they have collaborated over the years and may facilitate a referral through this relationship. Additionally, some pediatric practices have either a consulting or an in-house mental health provider who may offer direct services.
    o *Schools.* School personnel, including guidance and adjustment counselors, as well as school mental health professionals, may have a list of providers they know from the community.
    o *Referral services.* Professional organizations, such as the American Psychological Association (www.apa.org) and the National Association of Social Workers (www.socialworkers.org), have referral services that can assist in finding an appropriate referral.
    o *Local hospitals and community mental health centers.* Large

children's hospitals often have outpatient psychiatry departments where children may be seen for either urgent care appointments of for regularly scheduled outpatient appointments. Community mental health centers often also have outpatient psychiatric departments. This type of setting may be particularly useful in promoting conversations among providers if the child is already receiving medical care in the center.

• Help parents communicate effectively with potential mental health providers.

  o Working with children and families requires particular expertise and experience. Parents may wish to "interview" potential providers to determine the goodness of fit between the provider and their child. Questions to ask of potential providers include:

  ☐ "Are you a licensed mental health practitioner?"
  ☐ "What insurances do you take?"
  ☐ "How long have you been in practice?"
  ☐ "What is your experience in working with children?"
  ☐ "What are your areas of expertise"? (e.g., depression, anxiety, ADHD)
  ☐ "Are you affiliated with a group practice, clinic, or hospital?"
  ☐ "What is your policy around including parents in treatment?"
  ☐ "Do you offer any school-based services?"
  ☐ "Do you offer psychological testing?"
  ☐ "If you recommend medication, do you work with a colleague in the practice that would serve as the prescriber, or do I need to find a prescriber on my own?"
  ☐ "What is your policy around communicating with the child's school?"
  ☐ "If I have a question or concern to share and call you about it, is this considered a session and billed accordingly, or do you have a different policy for phone calls?"

□ "Who provides coverage for you when you are on vacation or unavailable?"

• Help parents identify other sources of support.

○ Parents often feel isolated when managing their children's mental health needs. Stigma related to mental health remains strong, often silencing families during a time when they need help the most. Shame, guilt, and a worry that they are the only ones experiencing an emotional crisis may also prevent parents from seeking additional support. Teachers can help parents identify other sources of support, apart from mental health providers, that can help parents manage the day-to-day difficulties associated with mental illness in the family. These include:

□ *Religious communities.* Many places of worship offer workshops, meetings, and groups related to mental health issues, including how to care for loved ones with mental illness.

□ *After-school programs.* Programs offering recreational activities, additional academic support, or a safe place for children to be after school are important sources of additional support.

□ *Mentoring programs.* Children benefit tremendously from mentoring relationships that focus on the child's strengths and that foster nurturing relationships.

□ *Specific support groups.* A child's emotional distress may be related to a broader family system issue, such as alcohol or drug addiction, postpartum depression, grief and bereavement, or trauma. Groups addressing these different topics (e.g., GriefShare, www.griefshare.org; the American Foundation for Suicide Prevention, www.afsp.org; Postpartum Support International, www.postpartum.net; Trauma Survivors Network, www.traumasurvivorsnetwork.org) can serve as additional sources of support to family members.

o *Peer-to-peer parent support.* As part of the family support movement in children's mental health, new models of service delivery have emerged, including "direct peer-to-peer support provided by parents or caregivers of children who are raising or have raised a child with identified mental health needs to parents or caregivers" (Cavaleri, Olin, Kim, Hoagwood, & Burns, 2011, p. 400). Given their life experience, parent peer support specialists are able to establish trusting relationships with parents and are able to guide them in how to become active participants in their children's mental health services (Cavaleri et al., 2011). Hoagwood and colleagues indicate what may be particularly helpful about peer-to-peer parent support services is that they are "designed to assist parents in clarifying their own needs or concerns, reducing their sense of isolation, stress, or self-blame, and empowering them to take an active role in their children's services" (Hoagwood et al., 2009, p. 17). The National Alliance on Mental Illness (www.nami.org) offers family-to-family support groups.

Working Together

Mental health support for children requires a well-coordinated, comprehensive approach where all of the relevant systems in a child's life are communicating and working together. For example, research supports the helpfulness of frequent communication between mental health providers and parents, citing that therapeutic interventions "in which parents can help provide support, model new behavior, and help generalize skills to the home and other contexts, are likely to be particularly beneficial during childhood" (Tompson, Boger, & Asarnow, 2012, p. 361). Similarly, communication between parents and teachers around what interventions are helpful for the child can maximize treatment outcomes.

Once you have completed the referral, communicated with parents around your concerns, and, if appropriate, helped parents access mental health services, it will be important to maintain open communication and collaboration to best support the child's progress. For example, children dealing with school-related anxiety disorders often engage in avoidance behaviors as a way to manage their distress. In the mornings, they may complain of feeling ill and may plead with their parents, making deals or bargains (e.g., "I won't ask for any new toys," "I'll stay home and not watch TV," "I'll be good for the rest of the week"). It can be very difficult for a parent to see his or her child in such distress, and he or she may therefore accede to the child's going to school late or not at all that day. Close communication with teachers and school personnel in this regard is invaluable. When parents have the same goals and intervention approaches as the teachers, they can work together to prevent, rather than reinforce, the avoidant behavior. In this example, parents and teachers would agree on whom to contact at the school if the child is having a hard time in the morning, where is the best place for the child to go in the school if he or she arrives late, what information will be given the child when encouraging attendance, and what interventions will be used in the classroom to promote attendance throughout the day. Follow-up communication, such as an email from the teacher letting the parents know the child is doing well or staying in the classroom, can also be helpful, especially in giving the parent reassurance and hope that the collaborative efforts are working. Furthermore, following such struggles with a child to attend school, parents can feel distressed and worried. A reassuring phone call or email can help the parents remember that they are not alone in this endeavor and have the support of the school.

Teachers can also work effectively with parents by creating a joint vision about what leads to effective child mental health treatment. For example, mental health treatment should not be considered to be solely those interventions that occur when the child is in acute distress. Mental health treatment should also include maintenance, or regularly scheduled follow-ups, even in the absence of symptoms (Beardslee, Gladstone, & O'Connor, 2012). Such follow-up can maintain treatment gains as well as anticipate any alterations in the treatment regimen due to development or specific circumstances. Parents and teachers can plan together how these follow-up visits may coincide with school-related changes. For example, teachers and parents can have a check-in at the beginning of each semester as well as at the beginning of each new academic year to review current treatment recommendations and to determine whether any changes to classroom-based accommodations or strategies need to be made.

In communicating around this joint vision of treatment, teachers and parents should also anticipate together how to handle any potential setbacks or crises that may arise. Potential questions to discuss in this regard may include the following:

- What is the best way to communicate with the parents if the child develops a new symptom or a more severe manifestation of an existing symptom?
- What is the protocol around contacting the child's mental health provider?
- If the child needs a psychiatric hospitalization, how will the child's absence be explained?
- How do the parents feel about their child's wanting to share information about his or her diagnosis, treatment, or hospitalization with other students?
- What is the school protocol around sharing of such information?

Finally, teachers can further work together with parents by sharing resources and psychoeducation around child mental health. The next section offers tools to use with parents in supporting child mental health, ranging from prevention to intervention.

Tools for Parents

The following sections offer topic-based psychoeducation ranging from prevention (how to foster communication) to crisis intervention (what to do if a child is suicidal). This information can be used as helpful talking points when consulting with parents, or it may be copied as handouts to distribute to parents.

"WHAT CAN I DO TO FOSTER COMMUNICATION WITH MY CHILD?"

- *The best talking time.* Children have different times in the day when they are typically most receptive to having a conversation. Observe your child and see if there is a pattern regarding when he or she is most and least likely to talk. Offer invitations to talk often (e.g., "If there is something on your mind, I'd love to hear all about it"), and do not be discouraged if the invitations are not readily accepted. While they may not be acknowledged, they are heard. You may wish to have alternative ways of initiating communication, such as by writing notes or leaving Post-it messages in places where the child is certain to see them. Sometimes the time your child chooses to talk may not feel so convenient—for example, right before bedtime. Although you may be tired, do not let this opportunity pass. When a child initiates a conversation and it is immediately and readily accepted, it reinforces the notion that parents are interested and ready to talk.

- *Step into my office.* Young children feel safe with routines and boundaries and may therefore appreciate the creation of a special place to talk about how they are feeling. In this place, they will come to know and feel that it is safe to talk. For some children, this space may be their bedroom, a playroom, or even a bathroom where they feel there will be no interruptions. The actual location is not as important as making sure that that place is used consistently and that the ability to have an uninterrupted, private conversation is present.

- *Listening ears.* Active listening is very important when communicating with children. If possible, try to listen more than you talk. Be sure to let your child finish talking before you begin. Instead of immediately offering advice or problem-solving, offer empathic remarks, such as "That sounds difficult" or "It sounds like you are struggling with a lot right now." Such remarks let the child know that you've heard what he or she is saying and that you are able to help him or her sit with the emotions. Encourage interpretation of the situation that includes the child's narrative rather than solely your own interpretation or conclusions. Children will feel unheard or may give up trying to explain how they feel if the response they receive includes criticism, judgment, or lecturing. When talking together about what the child can do, elicit his or her input as well. For example, you may wish to ask things such as, "What do you think would be helpful? Has this happened before? What did you do then? Was there something that helped you feel better?" The child's participation in problem solving increases his or her sense of control and efficacy in solving difficulties.

- *Do as I do.* Sharing your own stories about challenges and successes during the day gives the child a template for communicating with others. For example, you might say, "I had a tough situation today at work. I was feeling pretty frustrated, but then I remembered that deep breathing can help me feel better."

- *Getting to know you.* Spend time learning about your child's interests in friends, videogames, movies, music, sports, books, and hobbies. Talking about an area of interest may generate more conversation that will then lead to other topics. You can find your own creative way to find out about your child's interest. For example, you can have a family jeopardy game where family members have to guess about each other's interests.

- *Get moving.* For many children, sitting down for a one-to-one conversation can be quite daunting. Sustaining attention, eye contact, and perhaps discussing emotions may prove difficult. Talking while doing activities helps to relieve some of the additional stress of face-to-face conversation. Engaging your child in a conversation while in the car, while riding a bike, while playing a game, or while drawing together may help facilitate more sharing.

- *Turn it off.* Multitasking seems to be a core requirement of parenting. We must attend to dinner, make sure homework is completed, drive to sports practices, and many other things. However, when trying to engage in conversation with your child, that multitasking button should be turned off. Putting everything down, sitting down to be at the child's level, and letting the child know verbally and nonverbally that you are attentive and listening are important.

- *What is this bringing up for me?* Engage in frequent self-reflection. Sometimes particular conversations or situations bring up strong feelings. Try to understand where your reactions are coming from (Were you angry about something else before? Does this conversation remind you of a painful time for you? Is your reaction more about you than about your child?). This process of self-reflection is important not only in giving you more information about your reaction, but also in helping you to figure out how to best manage those reactions.

- *Acting time!* Children may struggle to communicate about situations they find scary or difficult because they feel as if they do not know how to handle those situations. Identifying difficult situations and role-playing solutions can be helpful. For example, for a child struggling with depression, it may be difficult for her to explain to friends why she does not want to join them at an outing. Allowing the child to role-play (by playing herself and her friends) may offer her a calm, safe space to gain perspective, better understand others' perspectives, generate solutions, and develop a repertoire of skills to use.

- *Let's play!* Through play, children release energy, express feelings, explore how to get along with others, relieve frustration, and simply enjoy themselves by letting imagination be their guide. Child-directed play, in particular, is helpful in fostering open communication with children. This type of play creates a comfortable space to interact with a parent or caregiver in a way that reinforces the safety and strength of the relationship. In this type of play, the child takes the lead in how the play will unfold, while the parent observes, reflects on what is happening, and participates as he or she is invited. The parent does not dictate rules or structure for the play.

WHAT CAN I DO IF I AM WORRIED ABOUT MY CHILD'S EMOTIONAL WELL-BEING?

- Set up an appointment with your child's pediatrician. It is important to determine whether any physical symptoms the child reports (e.g., stomachaches, headaches) are due to a medical condition rather than assuming that such symptoms are psychologically based.

- Keep a record of changes you notice in your child. Take particular note of things such as regressions in functioning (e.g., not wanting to sleep alone anymore) or changes in sleep and appetite, in social interactions (e.g., not wanting to play with friends), and in school functioning.

- Ask your child how he or she is feeling. Approach him or her during a calm time, when others are not around and when there is no time pressure. Phrases such as "I noticed you've been having a really hard time in the morning" or "It seems like something is on your mind; do you want to talk about it?" can be a good way to ask children about their feelings. Asking questions that give concrete examples may be necessary, especially for younger children. For example, you might say, "Sometimes our bodies let us know when we're not feeling so great. Is your body telling you anything? Sometimes my tummy gets all grumbly and tight, and that's how my body tells me when I'm feeling a little scared or nervous. Does that ever happen to you?" Use words and examples that are comfortable for you and your child. It is important to remember that children may be internally experiencing these feelings but may not be able to articulate them. Don't become frustrated if your child is not able to tell you right away how he or she is feeling. Continue to ask gently and invite him or her to express those feelings through other means, such as through drawing or playing.

- Contact your child's teacher and share your observations and concerns. Ask about your child's functioning in the classroom. Have social interactions changed? How is he or she doing academically? Has the teacher noted any changes in your child? If your child participates in sports or other activities, communicate with the adults supervising these activities and ask them whether they have noted any changes in your child.

- If you are concerned that your child is struggling emotionally, a prevention-based approach is recommended. In other words, if you notice symptoms, it is best to act quickly rather than wait until symptoms worsen or a crisis arises. Sometimes parents worry that seeking mental health supports might be overwhelming or will mean that the child will be in long-term treatment. There are a range of options for treatment, including short-term interventions that have been proven to be very effective with children. The type of treatment will depend on the child's current functioning. Setting up a consultation meeting can be a good way to begin the process and determine what may be most helpful for your child. In a consultation meeting, parents go without the child to an appointment with a mental health provider. During that time, parents can share their observations and concerns, and together with the mental health provider they will determine whether further evaluation or treatment is necessary.

WHAT CAN I DO IF MY CHILD IS ANXIOUS ABOUT SCHOOL?

- Although some children may express excitement about a new school year, remember that it is still something new. It is understandable and normal for all children to be a little nervous when anticipating something new. This is a great time to talk about expectations for the new school year. A helpful question to initiate conversation with your child might be, "What are you expecting this year to be like?" This open-ended question will help you get a sense of your child's perceptions and expectations.

- In a well-meaning effort to ease a child's distress, we may simply encourage him or her to "just not think about it," or we might say, "Don't worry; it will be fine." For children with mild anxiety, it is not easy to simply not think about the anxiety. In fact, asking the child not to think about it may paradoxically make him or her think about it more. Instead of not talking about the anxiety, give your child some tools for talking about the main components of it: emotions, bodily symptoms, and thoughts.

- If your child reports feelings of worry or anxiety, listen and respond empathically. This is a good time to ask with curiosity, "What is that like for you? When do you feel calmest? When do you feel the most worried/stressed/anxious?" Be patient and calm; it is often difficult for children to articulate the feelings and thoughts associated with anxiety.

- Help your child recognize and identify signs of nervousness or anxiety in his or her body. Stomachaches, headaches, GI distress, racing heart, sweaty palms, and reports of tiredness are physical symptoms typically reported by children experiencing anxiety. A helpful question might be, "Where in your body do you feel it when you are worried or nervous?"

- Help your child recognize and identify negative thoughts associated with anxiety. Children might express thoughts such as "I'm never going to make any friends" or "I won't know what to do if I get nervous." A helpful question might be, "When you get worried or nervous, what thoughts pop up in your head?" Gently confront the negative thoughts; for example, if a child says, "I always mess up!" you can respond with, "Is it true that you always mess up? Let's think of a time when you did a great job." (Hint: Have a time when he or she did a great job ready in your mind, as your child might say, "I can't think of one.")

- Teach your child different ways to relax and target those negative thoughts. Allow your child time to practice these skills in a calm, relaxed setting. Deep breathing, muscle relaxation, and imagery are all wonderful ways for children to learn how to relax. Ask your child's teacher for scripts you can use for these exercises.

- Problem solving and role playing together with your child can be a wonderful way to target negative thoughts. Help your child think about worrisome situations in advance (e.g., making new friends, asking the teacher a question). Encourage him or her to come up with as many alternatives as possible. Encourage your child to not prejudge his or her solutions. Have fun and be creative—laughter and humor can be very therapeutic! A helpful way to initiate this process might be, "How might we handle _____?"

- While your child is learning relaxation techniques and new problem-solving skills, praise him or her often for any efforts and partial successes. Strive for participation, not perfection. In this situation, the process is just as important as the outcome. A helpful thing to say might be, "Great job figuring out what was making you nervous this morning—I can tell that you are trying very hard to feel more relaxed!"

- If your child is avoiding school, support a prompt return to school. The longer a child is out of the school setting, the more difficult it can be to resume a routine. Again, involve your child to the extent possible in this. A helpful question might be, "What would help you feel comfortable in returning to school?" Be kind but firm in stating that staying home is not an option.

- Communicate with your child's teacher and inform him or her of what is helpful in reducing your child's anxiety (e.g., bringing in a special picture from home, squeezing a stress ball) and ask how this may be used in the classroom. Using consistent techniques across settings is helpful.

- Sometimes working on the child's anxiety and restoring normal routines becomes the focus of all the attention. It is important to keep a balance for the child. Remember the child's strengths and interests and who he or she is apart from the anxiety. Encourage participation in activities of interest, and allow play and rest time.

- It might be helpful to seek professional help if the following is true for your child: (a) Your child is exhibiting school avoidance that lasts for two weeks or longer; (b) regardless of the interventions you try, your child's mood seems different and is negatively impacting school, social, and family life; and (c) your child's academic functioning is declining.

WHAT SHOULD I DO IF MY CHILD IS SUICIDAL?

- Suicidal thoughts and behaviors signal an emotional crisis. People who are suicidal do not necessarily want to die; instead, they feel hopeless and think death might be the only way to stop the negative feelings they are experiencing.
- While rare, it is possible for young children to experience suicidal thoughts.
- If your child expresses any suicidal thoughts, take him or her seriously. If a child indicates, "I want to die" or "I want to kill myself," ask him or her directly how he or she would do that. Having such a conversation is heartbreaking and difficult, but critical. It is important to understand what plans a child might have, as this will allow you to understand potential risk. For example, if a child says he would run out into traffic, this is an accessible means and therefore a high risk.
- Do not dismiss or downplay the child's emotional state by saying things such as, "You don't really mean that" or "Don't say things like that." This indicates to the child that it is not safe to express how he or she feels.
- Trust your parental instincts. If you are worried about your child and feel he or she may be in danger, act immediately. Immediate guidance can be obtained through the National Suicide Prevention Lifeline (http://www.suicidepreventionlifeline.org) or 1–800–273–TALK. You can also take your child to the local emergency room for a psychiatric evaluation.
- Witnessing your child's extreme distress is very difficult; however, for the child's sake, it is important to remain calm as well as available, both physically and emotionally. Being physically available means not leaving the child alone. Also, take steps to make sure you remove any dangerous items (e.g., weapons, knives, prescription medicine, poisons) from the child's access. Being emotionally available means listening to what the child has to say. It also means tolerating the discussion, listening carefully, and not rushing to convince the child out of his or her feelings. Let your child know you will be there for him or her no matter what.

- After the immediate crisis, be sure to follow up with the recommended treatment. Although the child may no longer have suicidal thoughts, it is important to continue to address the risk factors and emotional state that led to the suicidal thoughts. Communicate with the school and let them know what is happening for the child, as well as how to best support him or her in the classroom.
- Seek additional supports. Mental illness does not impact just the child experiencing it; it impacts the family as a whole. Be sure to seek support for yourself and other children in the family.

Resources for Parents

There are a wealth of resources available for parents that offer guidance on how to identify symptoms of mental illness in their children, how to access resources, and how to connect with other parents who are facing similar difficulties with their children.

Ideally, teachers and mental health professionals at the school should compile a list of national as well as state-specific resources that may be offered to parents. Examples of such resources include:

The American Academy of Child and Adolescent Psychiatry (www. aacap.org). This website offers a number of resources, including family and youth resources, research, provider information, and suggestions for advocacy.

The American Psychological Association (www.apa.org). "The American Psychological Association is the largest scientific and professional organization representing psychology in the United States."

The Balanced Mind Foundation (thebalancedmind.org). "The Balanced Mind Foundation guides families raising children with mood disorders to the answers, support and stability they seek. The Balanced Mind Foundation envisions a world where children living with mood disorders thrive because their families have the resources, community and support they need."

Military Families Near and Far (www.familiesnearandfar.org/ login). "Military Families Near and Far is a website where families can create, communicate, and stay connected. Developed for military families, the site provides new ways for preschool and school-aged children to express themselves and communicate within their own family networks. New interactive tools for creating art, music, videos, letters, cards, and notebooks help kids explore their emotions and encourage communication. Materials from Sesame Street's ongoing Talk, Listen, Connect initiative and new materials from The Electric Company provide resources for parents and caregivers to help children cope with challenging transitions. Parents and caregivers can find information and multimedia resources on the topics of military deployments, multiple deployments, home-comings, changes, grief, and self-expression."

A number of books addressing child and adolescent mental health topics are also available. The following are recommended as particularly helpful resources:

- *The Parents' Guide to Psychological First Aid: Helping Children and Adolescents Cope with Predictable Life Crises*, edited by Gerald P. Koocher and Annette M. LaGreca (2011)
- *Out of the Darkened Room: Protecting the Children and Strengthening the Family When a Parent Is Depressed* (2002)
- *Helping Your Troubled Teen* by Cynthia S. Kaplan (2007)
- *If Your Adolescent Has an Anxiety Disorder: An Essential Resource for Parents* by Edna B. Foa and Linda Wasmer Andrews (2006)
- *If Your Adolescent Has Depression or Bipolar Disorder: An Essential Resource for Parents* by Dwight L. Evans, and Linda Wasmer Andrews (2005)
- *The Modern Dad's Handbook* by John Badalament (2008)

This chapter has focused on how to work with parents, specifically around child mental health. Prevention-based strategies focusing on parent engagement and education have been offered, as well as specific tools for helping parents through the referral process and in seeking supports for their children. The next chapter focuses on how to promote a prevention strategy for school-based mental health as well as how to become an advocate for children's mental health.

CHAPTER SEVEN

A Broader View of Children's Mental Health

Schoolwide Efforts and Advocacy

We found that integrating social emotional lessons into our curriculum was critical—our students are facing too many stressors to manage on their own. It's our responsibility to give them skills to address their learning as well as their emotional well-being.

—Elementary school principal

THE PRIMARY OUTCOMES OF prevention, mental health promotion, and social emotional learning are improved self-regulation, strong interpersonal skills, strong emotional functioning, school adjustment and achievement, and resilience—in essence, life skills that promote emotional health and wellness. There is one important caveat, however. Promoting student emotional health and wellness is a long-term investment. Single presentations, lessons, or workshops—what I call "one-shot deals"—are not effective. Promoting resilience and wellness needs to follow a holistic approach that involves not just the child, but the systems in which he or she lives. This type of attention to student wellness calls for comprehensive schoolwide efforts that involve school, family, and community stakeholders (Leadbeater, Gladstone, Yeung Thomson, Sukhawathanakul, & Desjardins, 2012; Nelson, Schnorr, Powell, & Huebner, 2012). In this chapter, we focus our attention on engaging the school system in integrating mental health programming into their ecology.

As Merrell and Gueldner (2010) indicate, "mental health programs implemented in a school ecology will be most successful when pertinent ecological factors are considered" (p.112). Such factors include school community needs, cultural issues, training and professional development for educators, school mental health practitioners and other staff (e.g., paraprofessionals), parental involvement, use of evidence-based interventions, and community partnerships (Merrell & Gueldner, 2010). While the inclusion of these factors in the development of school mental health programming is important, their inclusion is not a guarantee for successful implementation. A careful examination of the readiness for the school system to change existing practices, mobilize resources differently, and integrate new processes into its culture must first be conducted. The topic of school readiness around integration of mental health programs for students is an important one to address, as program dissemination may either succeed or fail based on readiness and preimplementation processes (Leadbeater et al., 2012).

The next section of this chapter focuses on assessing school readiness around mental health programming.

School Mental Health Readiness

A process of self-reflection around school readiness promotes examination of how a school may or may not have the factors pertinent to successful mental health programming. This process also allows for individualization to best meet a specific school context rather than adhering to a "one-size-fits-all" model. The self-reflection questions below are offered as suggestions for topics to address.

Do we have a mental health leadership team?

A mental health leadership team is one that takes primary responsibility for structuring and implementing initiatives related to schoolwide mental health efforts. Such initiatives include:

- Conducting needs assessments related to school readiness, mental health needs, and stakeholder opinions (at all levels of the school) and disseminating this information.
- Researching programs and curricula that may be helpful for the school.
- Disseminating information to all staff related to mental health protocols and procedures.

- Creating mechanisms to disseminate information to parents about school mental health programming (e.g., letters, email newsletters, open-house events).
- Facilitating professional development opportunities for teachers and staff.
- Organizing parent and community events hosted by the school.
- Participating in an iterative process of evaluation of schoolwide mental health efforts.

Ideally, the leadership team comprises staff representing different positions within the school, including administrative, counseling (including guidance), student support, and health and nursing staff; teachers; and parent representatives. Additionally, if there is an existing partnership or relationship with outside mental health agencies or community programs, a representative from those organizations should be a participating member of the mental health leadership team.

While members of the mental health leadership team may be appointed due to their respective roles in the school, it is also very helpful to encourage participation by self-selected advocates, or champions, of mental health programming. Often, these advocates are staff members who have personal reasons for promoting mental health programming, (e.g., personal experience, a particular passion for working with kids from a social emotional perspective, experience of success with a specific curriculum), and their passion and experience can be very influential in engaging others around new initiatives related to student mental health.

Do we have an atmosphere of emotional safety among staff (including administration) that allows us to discuss difficult topics in a way that is supportive and helpful rather than blaming and punitive?

One out of every four people is affected by mental illness (American Psychiatric Association, 1994). This means that the topic will be very relevant and directly meaningful for many of the school personnel. In this case, emotional safety refers to the perceived sense of safety staff feel about discussing both their own and their students' experiences with mental illness. If there is a low sense of emotional safety, there may be worries regarding the potentially negative implications of sharing personal information (e.g., stigma, judgment, shame). Understanding how staff members feel about this is critical, as not only does the general sense of safety (or lack thereof) impact staff's own comfort in participating in schoolwide mental health efforts, but it also has an influence on the explicit and implicit messages the students receive from staff about the acceptability of discussing emotions. A staff exercise to initiate this conversation is found in Appendix M.

Emotional safety also refers to the sense of safety that staff feel around voicing their opinions, having difficult conversations (in general), and communicating with each other around conflicting viewpoints. Discussing mental health will most certainly raise difficult conversations. Therefore, another aspect of self-reflection in this domain includes asking questions, such as:

- Is the communication between staff respectful?
- Is communication and reflection among staff valued and promoted?
- Do administrators feel comfortable initiating and facilitating difficult conversations?
- Is there a process whereby staff may voice their concerns, not as complaints, but as observations and considerations for possible change?

What are the beliefs in our school community about the relationship between student social emotional functioning and learning?

Many schoolwide mental health efforts rest on these assumptions: that social emotional health is as important as academic success, that there are internal resources (i.e., teachers and other staff) within all schools that can take an active role in promoting emotional wellness in students, and that dedication (i.e., participation and time) to efforts aimed toward promotion of mental health will yield positive results. It is important to note, however, that not all school personnel endorse these assumptions. For some, there is a clearer delineation between social and academic functioning, and their professional belief is that social emotional endeavors should not be part of the school's responsibility. While it is not realistic to expect to shift everyone's viewpoints, it is important to understand how staff feel about this issue to best determine what dissemination plans will look like as well as what expectations about teacher participation may be most appropriate for your school.

What are the most salient mental health issues in our community?

Typically, schoolwide mental health efforts are prevention based. However, prevention may not necessarily be the correct approach for all schools. Understanding the particular school's circumstances and needs is essential before implementing any program. For example, for a school that has recently experienced a traumatic event (e.g., death of a teacher or student, school shooting, suicide, natural disaster), crisis intervention to deal with the aftermath of the trauma is indicated prior to implementing broader prevention efforts.

A careful assessment of the most salient mental health issues in the school community is therefore important in guiding schoolwide efforts. Questions that may be asked around this area include:

- What issues do school staff see as impacting students most? (e.g., trauma, bullying, depression, anxiety, loss, disruptive behavior)
- What issues do parents see as most salient?
- What issues do students see as most salient?
- How responsive do the different groups (i.e., staff, parents, students) feel that the school is in responding to these issues?
- What additional consultation or resources are needed to best understand the issues in general, and more specifically, how they manifest in our school?

What training opportunities are available for our staff around student mental health?

Training school staff around student mental health should focus on two related yet distinct constructs: knowledge and comfort. A teacher, for example, may feel knowledgeable about the etiology of anxiety disorders in children, or about specific statistics related to different childhood diagnoses. However, this factual knowledge does not translate into comfort in directly working with children struggling with anxiety disorders. The teacher's low sense of comfort may be related to a lack of understanding about what the parameters of her role are (i.e., is she expected to diagnose? Is she expected to implement a behavioral intervention?). Her lack of comfort may also be due to a lack of knowledge about what she can do in the classroom to best support her students' mental health needs.

Opportunities for staff training should therefore include:

- Specific information about the particular staff member's role within the larger schoolwide mental health program
- The school's mental health protocols, including communication, referrals, and crisis intervention
- Specific information about the developmental presentation of mental illness related to the student population (e.g., elementary vs. high school students)
- Practical tools for supporting student mental health in the classroom and how this should be integrated into the academic curriculum
- Tools for supporting teachers' own mental health and wellness
- Information about how to seek consultation or support

Administrators are encouraged to create opportunities for staff to access training as part of their professional development days to avoid additional burden on the staff to seek such opportunities during their own time or at their own expense.

What current resources do we have available for student mental health programming?

Schools may already have in place particular aspects of mental health programming that could be enhanced by combining them with either topic-specific or more general social emotional learning curricula. For example, some schools may be part of a district that uses Positive Behavioral Interventions and Supports (PBIS; www.pbis.org). PBIS is a schoolwide system that follows "a data-oriented approach to school discipline and behavior management that is based on behavior principles" (Merrell & Gueldner, 2010, p. 12). PBIS efforts are well complemented and enhanced by adding social emotional learning (SEL) curricula, as

"SEL has the potential to expand the reach of PBIS efforts by moving beyond a basic behavioral focus and into the realm of students' cognitions, emotions, goals, problem-solving abilities, resilience, and relationship concerns" (Merrell & Gueldner, 2010, p. 14).

Other examples of evidence-based programs that offer excellent SEL curricula include Tools of the Mind (for kindergarten and first grade), Promoting Alternative Thinking Strategies (PATHS), Incredible Years, and the PAX Good Behavior Game.

Do we have any community partnerships that can support our mission of increasing access to treatment?

Partnerships or collaborations with mental health providers from community agencies (e.g., hospitals, community mental health clinics) can offer additional resources for meeting the mental health needs of students in a variety of ways. From a consultation perspective, mental health providers can support school staff in creating and evaluating schoolwide programs as well as in providing professional development. From a direct service perspective, mental health providers can support program implementation as well as offer therapeutic services for individual students. Wegmann, Powers, and Blackman (2013) indicate that "although it may be difficult for schools to allocate space for in-house mental health resources, it is an investment that makes services far more accessible to students, school staff, and families" (p. 307).

What process of evaluation do we have for new programming?

Evaluation should be an integral and ongoing part of schoolwide mental health efforts. This iterative process can offer an understanding of what works, as well as how it works, thereby identifying factors that support a sustainable program. Evaluation efforts should be conducted at multiple levels, including the following:

- How effective are efforts to disseminate information about the mental health programming?
- Is there enough training for all staff involved?
- How does the mental health programming impact specific problem areas? (e.g., bullying, depression)

- How does the programming target potential risk factors general to all children and those specific to your student population?
- How does your program promote protective factors at the student, adult, and school community levels?
- What qualitative information (i.e., narratives or themes obtained through open-ended questions, interviews, or focus groups) can be collect to guide your evaluation?
- What quantitative information (i.e., validated questionnaires, surveys, rating scales, or student data) can be collected to guide your evaluation?

Advocacy

The majority of this book has focused on interventions at the individual, home, and school levels. We now turn our attention to more *macro-level* interventions. According to ecological theory, macro-level interventions are those that aim to change broader systems, including economic policy, educational policy, and social legislation (Bronfenbrenner, 1977). This broader perspective is critical when efforts center on improving child mental health, as we know that "child and youth outcomes are multidetermined and that various levels of influence impact developmental trajectories" (Greenberg, 2006, p. 140).

The work we do individually with children is of utmost importance. In order for children to fully thrive, however, we must also create nurturing environments at a broader level that will support the work done at homes and schools and continue to foster children's well-being. Given the multiple risk factors children face and the potential for those risks to lead to significant impairment into adulthood, it is critical to develop a comprehensive public health movement that mobilizes all important figures of a child's life and capitalizes on all possible intervention points to create nurturing environments from the microsystemic to the macrosystemic level (Biglan, Flay, Embry, & Sandler, 2012; Greenberg, 2006; Jacka et al., 2013). For example, the negative impact of children living in poverty is an urgent public health issue. In a longitudinal study conducted by Blair and Raver (2012), the authors found that high risk as associated with living in poverty was directly associated "with reduced delay of gratification, increased learned helplessness, greater psychological distress, and reduced working memory in children, indicating links among poverty, stress physiology, and self-regulation (Blair & Raver, 2012, p. 312). Despite our best efforts to intervene individually with children once they are in school, if we do not take action to address the larger social issues impacting childhood outcomes, we are not creating opportunities for children to fully thrive emotionally and academically.

Below is a list of topics directly related to children's mental health. I urge you to examine each topic, considering how you can be involved in advocacy and give the children and families with whom you work voice and power.

Advocacy of efforts to address student mental health at the earliest levels of schooling and continuing through high school graduation

Durlak, Weissberg, Dymnicki, Taylor, and Schellinger (2011) reported that from a national sample of 148,189 sixth- to twelfth-graders, only 29% of students surveyed indicated that their school provided a caring, encouraging environment. Furthermore, by the time they reach high school, as many as 60% of students become chronically disengaged from school (Durlak et al., 2011).

The statistics are indeed dismaying. Stagman and Cooper (2010) present the following data regarding outcomes for children with mental health issues:

- In the course of the school year, children with mental health problems may miss as many as 18 to 22 days.
- Up to 14% of youth with mental health problems receive mostly Ds and Fs (compared to 7% of all children with disabilities).
- Up to 44% drop out of high school.
- The percentage of children who receive mental health services is very small. Within that small percentage, significant racial disparities exist, with 31% percent of White children and youth receiving mental health services and 13% percent of children from diverse racial and ethnic backgrounds receiving mental health services.

If the children are telling us directly about their disengagement from school, and outcome data are telling us that mental health outcomes are poor, why are we waiting so long to intervene? Why is it that crisis intervention seems to be the predominant approach, rather than a comprehensive, developmentally based approach?

One potential solution is to create nurturing environments that intentionally integrate social emotional learning into their programming. Preschools offer excellent settings for such programs. In a study assessing self-regulation of children living in poverty, Raver and colleagues found that "preschool teachers in high poverty schools who received training, coaching, and consultation improved in their management of behavior and provision of emotional support; and, children increased their self-regulation skills and academic performance beyond the skills and performance of comparison children" (Cappella et al., 2012, p. 598).

Nurturing environments can serve as protective factors against the negative effects of stressful life circumstances, such as poverty. The protection these environments offer has positive effects across different domains, including brain development (e.g., by reducing stress levels and constant vigilance for threat, thereby reducing negative impact on brain structures that regulate emotions) and social emotional functioning. Furthermore, gaps in test scores across socioeconomic groups appear to be in part due to lack of attention to social emotional needs (Heckman, 2006). By advocating nurturing environments, we can leverage these settings to support the self-regulation and academic success of young students (Blair & Raver, 2012; Raver, 2012).

Advocacy for social emotional learning training for teachers as a formal part of their graduate school curriculum

Social emotional learning is fundamentally based on a relational context. This means that SEL approaches rely on both teachers' and students' self-regulation and interactions to develop a learning environment where members feel safe sharing their emotions, cooperate out of a sense of unity and responsibility, and demonstrate internal motivation (Jennings, Snowberg, Coccia, & Greenberg, 2011). If teachers are to promote this regulation, both in themselves and their students, they must be given the opportunities and support to learn about child development, mental illness in students, and how to implement SEL programming (National Scientific Council on the Developing Child, 2004).

Currently, teachers do not consistently receive such training as a regular part of their graduate work. Once out on the workforce, new teachers are faced with taxing expectations about student testing outcomes while simultaneously trying to figure out how to promote learning for a large number of students whose mental health needs interfere with academic progress. This takes a significant toll on their own emotional well-being as well as on their relationships with their students.

Training should not occur only during graduate studies. Opportunities for continued professional development are important in broadening teachers' knowledge of child mental health needs. The goal of such professional development should not be to make teachers mental health clinicians, but to give them the skills to identify students at risk and to implement programming that supports children's emotional development more generally. Research indicates that teachers are indeed interested in gaining a clearer understanding of the nature of student mental health difficulties as well as strategies for managing such difficulties in the classroom (Whitley, Smith, & Vaillancourt, 2012).

As Raver (2012) indicated, providing easily accessible training and support for teachers has an impact at two important levels: (a) increasing teacher knowledge of child mental health issues, thereby promoting early intervention and treatment access; and (b) promotion of teacher and student self-regulation, thereby creating nurturing and emotionally safe learning environments. Furthermore, this offers important insights for advocacy and policy. Training and support for teachers may lower turnover, may lead to benefits for teachers' emotional health, and may create new avenues for researching specific aspects of the relational impact of adult and child self-regulation (Raver, 2012).

Advocacy around the need for integration of physical and emotional well-being

There is a strong mind–body connection when it comes to emotional health, and self-regulation in particular. Diamond and Lee (2011) report that "stress, loneliness, and not being physically fit impair prefrontal cortex function and [executive functions]" (p. 963). Prefrontal cortex function and executive functions are critical structures underlying children's self-regulation. The most successful approaches to improving executive functions and school outcomes are those that offer emotional coping skills and engage student interests. However, addressing these domains alone is not sufficient. Most effective programming offers opportunities for emotional and social development paired with opportunities for children's physical development (such as vigorous aerobics, yoga, and martial arts; Bryck & Fisher, 2012; Diamond & Lee, 2011).

Advocacy to preserve play as an integral component of children's learning

Young children's making sense of the world relies significantly on play and imagination, and play is a primary vehicle for their social emotional learning and for the process of self-regulation (Nicolopoulou, 2010). Because play offers scaffolding for self-regulation and social competence, it is therefore strongly related to school readiness. In middle childhood (6–11 years), play continues to fulfill the functions that dramatic play did for the preschooler: pleasure, imagined fulfillment of wishes, exploration of reality, imagining oneself in more advanced roles, rehearsal of actions and plans, and understanding the emotions and perspectives of others through identification and role playing (Davies, 2011, p. 350). Again, these are aspects of social competence that promote self-regulation. As self-regulation is related to school readiness in preschoolers, it is related to academic achievement in elementary school children.

With strong expectations for academic outcomes, however, more of the day is often spent on training in academic skills and less time is spent on focusing on developmentally appropriate play opportunities for children. Some educational systems have even proposed elimination of recess in order to fit more instructional time into the school day. It is critical for teachers to advocate the protection of play opportunities for children. At the preschool level, educational practices that "can systematically integrate the play element into the preschool curriculum" are critical (Nicolopoulou, 2010, p. 2). At the elementary school level, engaging children around their continued development of mastery and social skills through play is also critical.

A Public Health Movement to Improve Children's Mental Health

Parents and school staff, though tremendously influential in children's development, cannot be the sole individuals responsible for addressing children's mental health. A public health movement is needed to put into practice what the research tells us about what influences child development. At one level, we need to create nurturing environments that promote health for the family, even before birth. We also need to create programs that are based on sound developmental research and that integrate the key participants in children's lives. We need to create funding sources that will support early childhood work, as well as continuity of mental health support and programming for children until the end of high school. This is not sufficient, however. We need to address the societal issues of cultural inequalities in mental health care, poverty, and lack of resources for children.

Heckman (2006) highlights the salience of this movement and its potential for long-term impact for the individual and for society at large:

> Investing in disadvantaged young children is a rare public policy initiative that promotes fairness and social justice and at the same time promotes productivity in the economy and in society at large. Early interventions targeted toward disadvantaged children have much higher returns than later interventions such as reduced pupil teacher ratios, public job training, convict rehabilitation programs, tuition subsidies, or expenditure on police. At current levels of resources, society overinvests in remedial skill investments at later ages and underinvests in the early years. (p. 1902)

This public health movement needs to shift away from a focus on pathology and individual problems and instead shift toward the creation of coordinated efforts informed by research and prevention science. Teachers are in a unique role that includes shaping early childhood experiences and interactions, acting as a first-line responder, and being an advocate for students. I encourage you to leverage this important and unique role you hold to become a part of the public health movement that will improve children's health and well-being.

Appendix A

Thought Bubble

Appendix B

The Roadblock Crew

What is the situation?

_____

_____

_____

Who is the construction worker? (circle one)

Anger   Worry   Frustration

Fear   Sadness   Other:

_____

What do the roadblocks say?

_____

_____

_____

How do I get over the roadblocks?

_____

_____

_____

Appendix C

Anger Management Plan (Grades K–3)

How does my body let me know I'm feeling mad?

_____
_____
_____
_____

How bad is the mad?

a little mad   pretty mad   super mad

What can I do?

_____
_____
_____
_____

GREAT JOB!

Appendix D

Anger Management Plan (Grades 4–5)

Where in my body am I feeling the anger?

_____

_____

_____

_____

_____

How strong is my anger right now?

1 – I have little or no anger

2 – I have some anger, but I can stay focused

3 – I'm angry and starting to feel it all over

4 – I'm very angry

5 – I'm so angry I can't think straight
   and I can't focus on anything else

HOW ANGRY?

BOILING MAD

What else am I feeling?

_____

_____

_____

What can I do at this moment to feel better?

_____

_____

_____

_____

Appendix E

The Emotions Daily: Story Cards

Story #1: Sarah needs surgery.

Sarah is very athletic. She is on the travel soccer team and is also a dancer. She is in a dance company and always participates in recitals. She has always been very proud of her speed, strength, and agility. Last week when she was playing soccer, her knee started hurting. She kept playing, but the pain got worse. During halftime she noticed that her knee was quite swollen. By the end of the game, her knee was hurting so much that she could barely walk. The following week, the doctor told her she needed knee surgery and could not play soccer or dance until after recovery from her surgery. Sarah was very disappointed that she would miss the recital scheduled for the end of the month. Although she was very upset, she did not share this with her friends. When she was at home, she worried that while she was out of the dance company, other girls might get better or that when she returned, she would not be given the same lead parts. She often worried that she would not be the same person after the surgery. She wondered what it would be like not to be an athlete and what people would say.

Story #2: Jake's parents are getting a divorce.

Jake is kind of a quiet kid, but he's a good student and has a group of friends. His parents told him last week that they're getting a divorce. Jake feels relieved that he won't hear all the arguing anymore, but he's also sad that his parents will be living in different houses. Jake's been having a hard time focusing at school because he's worried about everything that's going on at home. He wonders if he should have done something different, like not tell his parents that he hated all their arguing. He doesn't want to tell his teacher what's happening because he thinks he should be able to pull himself together. His friends know what's going on, but Jake keeps telling them "it's no big deal." Jake gets angry sometimes and isn't sure why. Sometimes he feels like crying too, but he tries not to so he won't upset his little brother. Jake wants to say so many things to his parents, but when he tries to talk to them, the words just don't come out right and he gets really frustrated and just ends up going to his room. He feels like a loser because he can't figure out what to do to feel better.

Appendix F

Problems, Ideas, Plans: Let's do the PIP!

Step 1: What's on your mind? What problem would you like to solve? Think about how to narrow it down into something you can work on.

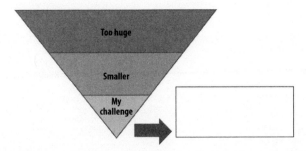

Step 2: Divergent thinking time! Come up with as many ideas as you can to solve the problems. Be creative! Have fun! Use your imagination and don't leave anything out! Ask others for help and build on ideas.

Step 3: Convergent thinking time! From the list that you just came up with, choose the idea that you would like to use.

I choose: _____
_____
_____

Step 4: Action plan! What steps will you take to reach your solution? When will you do this? Who will help? Let's find out!

Step 5: Check it out! How is your action planning going? Do you need to tweak anything? Remember that you can always go back to any step to fix your plan.

What will I do?	When will I do this?	Do I need some help? Who can help?

Here's a hint! For your first action step, find something that you can do right away, or at some time today. If you do something right away, it will help you stay on track. Best of all, it will help you find success!

Appendix G

Box of Strengths

Suggested Strengths

- Helpful
- Hopeful
- Playful
- Friendly
- Kind
- Respectful
- Responsible
- Determined
- Graceful
- Energetic
- Excited
- Curious
- Creative
- Flexible
- Strong
- Musical
- Generous
- Cooperative
- Honest
- Hardworking
- Cheerful
- Forgiving
- Sensitive
- Confident
- Patient
- Organized
- Bold
- Calm
- Grateful
- Fair
- Gentle
- Considerate
- Observant
- Caring
- Assertive
- Compassionate
- Funny
- A good listener
- Understanding
- Optimistic
- Spiritual

Appendix H

Sweet Dreams

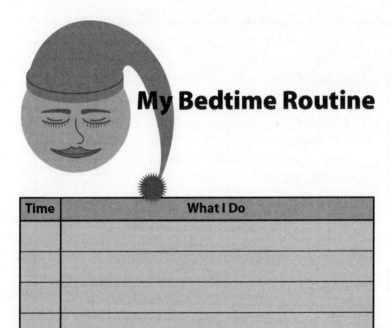

Time	What I Do

Appendix I

Surfing the Waves (Grades 2–3)

What's on your waves?

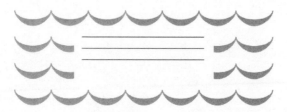

Build your surfboards!

Great job! Keep practicing your surfing!

Appendix J

Surfing the Waves (Grades 4–5)

Appendix K

Here's My Card

Name: _____

When I'm stressed, here are three things that make me
feel better right away:

1. _____

2. _____

3. _____

When I need help, here are people I can talk to:

1. _____

2. _____

3. _____

A calm body leads to a clam mind and calm actions.
Here is my favorite relaxation exercise to help me
feel calm.

_____

_____

_____

_____

_____

Appendix L

Parent Questionnaire

Name: _____

Age: _____   Grade: _____

How would you describe your child?

What are his or her areas of strength?

Does your child have any difficulties in learning?

How do you think your child learns best?

What types of situations are easiest for your child?

What types of situations are most difficult for your child?

What does your child like to do?

Who are your child's role models?

How does your child let you know he or she is happy?

How does your child let you know he or she is upset?

Who does your child seek for comfort?

What does your child find most comforting?

Is your child able to establish and maintain friendships?

Has your child experienced any recent changes? If so, which ones and when? (e.g., divorce, move to a new home, birth of a sibling, move to a new school, loss of a friend)

Have there been any deaths in the family? (including pets)

Have there been any significant financial changes in the household that have impacted your child?

Does your child have a history of trauma?

Does your child have a history of abuse?

Does your child have a physical or mental illness?

Does your child need any special assistance or accommodations in the classroom?

What is the best way for me to communicate and collaborate with you around your child's progress?

Appendix M

Staff Activity: Assumptions and Attributions Related to Mental Illness*

Understanding child mental health is difficult. Grappling with the fact that young children can experience emotional pain is not easy, and in an attempt to find an explanation for the cause, we often seek out the answers by looking at the role of adults in a child's life. Sometimes, this look at the adults' roles can turn to fault finding and blaming, however, leading to the shame and stigma families often feel related to their struggles with mental illness. Stigma is broadly related to this sense of blame and shame, and eventually shapes larger organizational and societal assumptions related to mental illness. During this exercise, participants will examine their personal assumptions and attributions about mental illness. The goal of the activity is twofold: first, to identify factors that may perpetuate stigma in the school, and second, to discuss ways to target these factors so that students and staff alike feel more comfortable openly discussing issues related to mental illness. This exercise is ideally conducted in a small-group setting to allow for in-depth discussion. All members should be strongly encouraged to participate in order to gather as many different viewpoints as possible.

Alternative Adaptation

Conducting this exercise as part of a group discussion assumes that there is at least a moderate level of emotional safety that group members feel in sharing their personal information and opinions. If the group members do not know each other well, or if there is a low level of emotional safety, you may wish to conduct this activity as an individual exercise not to be openly discussed, but individually considered. The

---

* This exercise was adapted from Reilly, N. N. (2006). *Preventing depression: A toolkit from schools.*

information may be used for self-reflection or as a part of a more private discussion with a member of the mental health leadership team.

Materials Needed
- Easel and paper or dry-erase board and markers
- Prepared script*
- Copy of school referral protocol
- Resource information for teachers and staff should they wish to pursue their own mental health referral, including information about specific referral sources and about the teachers' employee assistance program and its related mental health supports

Instructions
- Arrange chairs in an open circle so that everyone is able to see others in the group.
- Deliver the following script:

    Welcome everyone. The purpose of this exercise is to explore our own feelings about mental illness and the possible assumptions we might make about people struggling with mental illness. We will listen to a vignette, then together discuss the thoughts and ideas we have related to the characters. It is not always comfortable to discuss our assumptions and beliefs related to mental illness. Therefore, to make this discussion as safe as possible for everyone participating, I ask that you please listen to each other with curiosity and respect and refrain from questioning or judging others' beliefs. I ask that you also please respect each other's confidentiality. All of us are affected by mental illness—either directly or indirectly. It makes sense that these experiences color our beliefs and ideas about mental illness. As we bring our own experiences into this discussion, please respect each other's privacy and be sure to not share with others any information you hear during our time together.

- Choose an audience member to read the script below.

    I am a mother of two children. My daughter is 16 and my son is 11.

---

* The script in this exercise is a sample. Presenters should modify the script to best fit the needs of their schools.

I am a consultant and my job of requires a lot of traveling. I feel constantly stressed and overwhelmed by the demands of my family and my job. My son has been struggling with depression and recently revealed to his guidance counselor that he has thoughts about suicide. His guidance counselor called me and we went to the emergency room, where we sat for hours. They sent him home and I don't know what to do.

• Once the script has been read, facilitate a discussion about what emotions, thoughts, and assumptions the script evoked for the group members. You may use the following questions as guides for the discussion:

  o "What are your impressions of this woman?"
  o "What do you think the family composition is like? Where do they live? Why?"
  o "What assumptions do you have of her as a mother?"
  o "What conclusions do you draw about her parenting skills?"
  o "What other information would you like to have about the family?"
  o "What was your first gut reaction about what led to the son's suicidal thoughts?"
  o "What do you think the son is like? What might his future be like?"
  o "If this boy were a student in your school, would you feel comfortable talking to him about his depression? About his suicidal thoughts?"
  o "Would you feel comfortable talking to the mom?"
  o "If you as a parent were in this situation, how would you talk to your own child about his or her depression?"
  o "If you were in this (or a similar) situation, how would you talk to your own family, friends, and coworkers about what happened?"
  o "Would you tell them what happened?"
  o "How often do you think situations like these come up for our students and families?"
  o "How well do you think we as a school respond to students' and families' mental health needs?"

o "What can we do to improve communication and help for families?"

- As the group members provide responses, record these on the board. A diagram, such as the one found below, can be drawn to record the responses. The center circle represents the child, and outside circles represent responses to the discussion questions. Once everyone has responded, highlight, with a different color marker, the themes relevant to schoolwide mental health efforts (e.g., current stigma, areas of "difficult conversations," concerns about talking to parents and/or students about mental illness, ideas about how to improve services for children and families). Here is an example:

Continue your script: *As you can see, when any conversation about mental illness is initiated, individuals bring with them fears, assumptions, and questions. Our students and families share very similar ideas and fears, and these are what often perpetuate stigma associated with mental illness and make people hesitant to share their experiences. Understanding and acknowledging these issues among ourselves will facilitate more open, frank discussions with*

each other, our students, and their parents. Within our school, can you identify particular factors, expectations, and assumptions that might perpetuate the stigma associated with mental illness? Can we generate some solutions for this? What messages do we explicitly or implicitly give that say that it is healthy and acceptable to discuss mental health? How can we make these messages more explicit, consistent, and frequent?

References

Abela, J. R. Z., & Hankin, B. L. (2008). Cognitive vulnerability to depression in children and adolescents: A developmental psychopathology perspective. In J. R. Z. Abela & B. L. Hankin (Eds.), *Handbook of depression in children and adolescents* (pp. 35–78). New York, NY: Guilford Press.

American Academy of Child and Adolescent Psychiatry. (n.d.). *Understanding your mental health insurance.* Retrieved from http://www.aacap.org/AACAP/ Families_and_Youth/Facts_for_Families/Facts_for_Families_Pages/ Understanding_Your_Mental_Health_Insurance_26.aspx

American Psychiatric Association. (1994). *Mental illness (an overview review).* Retrieved from http://www.psych.org/public_info/overview.cfm

American Psychiatric Association. (2013). *Diagnostic and statistical manual of mental disorders* (5th ed.). Arlington, VA: Author.

Amstadter, A. (2008). Emotion regulation and anxiety disorders. *Anxiety Disorders, 22,* 211–221.

Anderson, E. R., & Mayes, L. C. (2010). Race/ethnicity and internalizing disorders in youth: A review. *Clinical Psychology Review, 30,* 338–348.

Ang, R. P., Lowe, P. A., & Yusof, N. (2011). An examination of the RCMAS-2 scores across gender, ethnic background, and age in a large Asian school sample. *Psychological Assessment, 23*(4), 899–910.

Angelkovska, A., Houghton, S., & Hopkins, S. (2012). Differential profiles of risk of self-harm among clinically referred primary school aged children. *School Psychology International, 33*(6), 646–660.

Ansari, T. L., & Derakshan, N. (2011). The neural correlates of impaired inhibitory control in anxiety. *Neuropsychologia, 49,* 1146–1153.

Atkins, M. S., Hoagwood, K. E., Kutash, K., & Seidman, E. (2010). Toward the integration of education and mental health in schools. *Administration and Policy in Mental Health, 37*(1–2), 40–47.

Auerbach, R. P., Bigda-Peyton, J. S., Eberhart, N. K., Webb, C. W., & Ringo Ho, M. (2011). Conceptualizing the prospective relationship between social support, stress, and depressive symptoms among adolescents. *Journal of Abnormal Child Psychology.* doi: 10.1007/s10802-010-9479-x

Auerbach, R. P., & Ringo Ho, M.-H. (2012). A cognitive-interpersonal model of adolescent depression: The impact of family conflict and depressogenic cognitive styles. *Journal of Clinical Child and Adolescent Psychology, 41*(6), 792–802.

Banducci, A. N., Gomes, M., MacPherson, L., Lejuez, C. W., Potenza, M. N., Gelenter, J., & Amstadter, A. A. (2014). A preliminary examination of the relationship between the *5-HTTLPR* and childhood emotional abuse on depressive symptoms in 10–12-year-old youth. *Psychological Trauma: Theory, Research, Practice, and Policy, 6*(1), 1–7.

Bandura, A., & Schunk, D. H. (1981). Cultivating competence, self-efficacy, and intrinsic interest through proximal self-motivation. *Journal of Personality and Social Psychology, 41,* 586–598.

Beardslee, W. R., Gladstone, T. R. G., & O'Connor, E. E. (2012). Developmental risk of depressive disorders: Experience matters. *Child and Adolescent Clinics of North America, 21,* 261–278.

Beesdo-Baum, K., & Knappe, S. (2012). Developmental epidemiology of anxiety disorders. *Child and Adolescent Psychiatric Clinics of North America, 21,* 457–478.

Biederman, J., Hirshfeld-Becker, D. R., Rosenbaum, J. F., Herot, C., Friedman, D., Snidman, N., . . . Faraone, S. V. (2001). Further evidence of association between behavioral inhibition and social anxiety in children. *American Journal of Psychiatry, 158,* 1673–1679.

Biglan, A., Flay, B. R., Embry, D. D., & Sandler, I. N. (2012). The critical role of nurturing environments for promoting human wellbeing. *American Psychologist, 67*(4), 257–271.

Birmaher, B., & Brent, D. (2007). Practice parameters for the assessment and treatment of children and adolescents with depressive disorders. *Journal of the American Academy of Child and Adolescent Psychiatry, 46*(11), 1503–1526.

Blair, C. (2002). School readiness: Integrating cognition and emotion in a neurobiological conceptualization of children's functioning at school entry. *American Psychologist, 57*(2), 111–127.

Blair, C., & Raver, C. C. (2012). Child development in the context of adversity:

Experiential canalization of brain and behavior. *American Psychologist, 67*(4), 309–318.

Blair, C., & Razza, R. P. (2007). Relating effortful control, executive function, and false belief understanding to emerging math and literacy ability in kindergarten. *Child Development, 78*(2), 647–663.

Brent, D. A., & Maalouf, F. T. (2009). Pediatric depression: Is there evidence to improve evidence-based treatments? *Journal of Child Psychology and Psychiatry, 50*(1–2), 143–152.

Bridgett, D.J., Oddi, K.B., Laake, L.M., Murdock, K.W, & Bachman, M.N. (2013). Integrating and differentiating aspects of self-regulation: Effortful control, executive functioning, and links to negative affectivity. *Emotion, 13*(1), 47-63.

Bronfenbrenner, U. (1977). Toward an experimental ecology of human development. *American Psychologist, 32*(7), 513–531.

Brooks, B. L., Iverson, G. L., Sherman, E. M. S., & Roberge, M. C. (2010). Identifying cognitive problems in children and adolescents with depression using computerized neuropsychological testing. *Applied Neuropsychology, 17*, 37–43.

Bruffaerts, R., Borges, G., Maria Haro, J., Chiu, W. T., Hwang, I., Karam, E., . . . Nock, M. K. (2010). Childhood adversities as risk factors for onset and persistence of suicidal behaviors. *British Journal of Psychiatry, 197*, 20–27.

Bryck, R. L., & Fisher, P. A. (2012). Training the brain: Practical applications of neural plasticity from the intersection of cognitive neuroscience, developmental psychology, and prevention science. *American Psychologist, 67*(2), 87–100.

Bubrick, K., Goodman, J., & Whitlock, J. (n.d.). *Non-suicidal self-injury in schools: Developing and implementing school protocol.* Retrieved from http://www.selfinjury.bctr.cornell.edu/documents/schools.pdf

Burkhouse, K. L., Uhrlass, D. J., Stone, L. B., Knopik, V. S., & Gibb, B. E. (2012). Expressed emotion-criticism and risk of depression onset in children. *Journal of Clinical Child and Adolescent Psychology, 41*(6), 771–777.

Calkins, S. D., & Hill, A. (2007). Caregiver influences on emerging emotion regulation. In J. J. Gross (Ed.), *Handbook of emotion regulation* (pp. 229–248). New York, NY: Guilford Press.

Campbell-Sills, L., & Barlow, D.H. (2007). Incorporating emotion regulation into conceptualizations and treatments of anxiety and mood disorders. In J.J. Gross (Ed.), *Handbook of emotion regulation* (pp. 542-559). New York, NY: Guilford Press.

Cappella, E., Hamre, B. K., Kim, H. Y., Henry, D. B., Frazier, S. L., Atkins, M. S.,

& Schoenwald, S. K. (2012). Teacher consultation and coaching within mental health practice: Classroom and child effects in urban elementary schools. *Journal of Consulting and Clinical Psychology, 80*(4), 597–610.

Cartwright-Hatton, S., Roberts, C., Chitsabesan, P., Fothergill, C., & Harrington, R. (2004). Systematic review of the efficacy of cognitive behavior therapies for childhood and adolescent anxiety disorders. *British Journal of Clinical Psychology, 43*(4), 421–436.

Cavaleri, M. A., Olin, S. S., Kim, A., Hoagwood, K. E., & Burns, B. J. (2011). Family support in prevention programs for children at risk for emotional/behavioral problems. *Clinical Child and Family Psychology Review, 14*(4), 399–412.

Center on the Developing Child at Harvard University. (2011). *Building the brain's "air traffic control" system: How early experiences shape the development of executive function* (Working Paper No. 11). Retrieved from http://developingchild.harvard.edu/index.php/resources/reports_and_working_papers/working_papers/wp11/

Christenson, M. A. (2004). Teaching multiple perspectives on environmental issues in elementary classrooms: A story of teacher inquiry. *Journal of Environmental Education, 35*(4), 3–16.

Cohen, J. R., Young, J. F., & Abela, J. R. Z. (2012). Cognitive vulnerability to depression in children: An idiographic, longitudinal examination of inferential styles. *Cognitive Therapy and Research, 36*(6), 643–654.

Cole, D. A., Cho, S.-J., Martin, N. C., Youngstrom, E. A., March, J. S., Findling, R. L., . . . Maxwell, M. A. (2012). Are increased weight and appetite useful indicators of depression in children and adolescents? *Journal of Abnormal Psychology, 121*(4), 838–851.

Collaborative for Academic, Social, and Emotional Learning. (n.d.). *Social and emotional learning core competencies.* Retrieved September 25, 2014, from http://www.casel.org/social-and-emotional-learning/core-competencies

Creveling, C. C., Varela, R. E., Weems, C. F., & Corey, D. M. (2010). Maternal control, cognitive style, and childhood anxiety: A test of a theoretical model in a multi-ethnic sample. *Journal of Family Psychology, 24*(4), 439–448.

Cummings, C. M., Caporino, N. E., & Kendall, P. C. (2013). Comorbidity of anxiety and depression in children and adolescents: 20 years after. *Psychological Bulletin,* advance online publication. doi: 10.1037/a0034733

Cummings, E. M., Cheung, R. Y. M., & Davies, P. T. (2013). Prospective relations between parental depression, negative expressiveness, emotional insecurity, and children's internalizing symptoms. *Child Psychiatry and Human Development, 44,* 698–708.

Davies, D. (2011). *Child development: A practitioner's guide* (3rd edition). New York, NY: Guilford Press.

DeBoo, G. M., & Spiering, M. (2010). Pre-adolescent gender differences in associations between temperament, coping, and mood. *Clinical Psychology and Psychotherapy, 17,* 313–320.

Denham, S. A., Blair, K. A., DeMulder, E., Levitas, J., Sawyer, K., Auerbach-Major, S., & Queenan, P. (2003). Preschool emotional competence: Pathway to social competence?. *Child development, 74*(1), 238–256.

Dennis, T. A. (2010). Neurophysiological markers for child emotion regulation from the perspective of emotion–cognition integration: Current directions and future challenges. *Developmental Neuropsychology, 35*(2), 212–230.

Diamond, A. (2010). The evidence base for improving school outcomes by addressing the whole child and by addressing skills and attitudes, not just content. *Early Education Development, 21*(5), 780–793.

Diamond, A., & Lee, K. (2011). Interventions shown to aid executive function development in children 4–12 years old. *Science, 333*(6045), 959–964.

Dobson, C. E., & Byrne, M. W. (2014). Original research: Using guided imagery to manage pain in young children with sickle cell disease. *American Journal of Nursing, 114*(4), 26–36.

Domitrovich, C. E., Bradshaw, C. P., Greenberg, M. T., Embry, D., Poduska, J. M., & Ialongo, N. S. (2010). Integrated models of school-based prevention: Logic and theory. *Psychology in the Schools, 47*(1), 71–88.

Dozois, D. J. A., Seeds, P. M., & Collins, K. A. (2009). Transdiagnostic approaches to the prevention of depression and anxiety. *Journal of Cognitive Psychotherapy: An International Quarterly, 23*(1), 44–59.

Duchnowski, A. J., Kutash, K., Green, A. L., Ferron, J. M., Wagner, M., & Vengrofski, B. (2012). Parent support services for families of children with emotional disturbances served in elementary school special education settings: Examination of data from the Special Education Elementary Longitudinal Study. *Journal of Disability Policy Studies.* doi: 1044207312460889

Durlak, J. A., Weissberg, R. P., Dymnicki, A. B., Taylor, R. D., & Schellinger, K. B. (2011). The impact of enhancing students' social and emotional learning: A meta-analysis of school-based universal interventions. *Child Development, 82*(1), 405–432.

Dweck, C. S. (2006). *Mindset: The new psychology of success.* New York, NY: Ballantine Books.

Eckshtain, D., & Gaynor, S. T. (2011). Combining individual cognitive behavior therapy and caregiver–child sessions for childhood depression: An open trial. *Clinical Child Psychology and Psychiatry.* doi: 10.1177/1359104511404316

Ehrenreich-May, J., & Bilek, E. L. (2012). The development of a transdiagnostic, cognitive behavioral group intervention for childhood anxiety disorders and co-occurring depression symptoms. *Cognitive and Behavioral Practice, 19*(1), 41–55.

Eisenberg, N., Hofer, C., & Vaughan, J. (2007). Effortful control and its socio-emotional consequences. In J. J. Gross (Ed.), *Handbook of emotion regulation* (pp. 287–306). New York, NY: Guilford Press.

Elkins, R., McHugh, R., Santucci, L. C., & Barlow, D. H. (2011). Improving the transportability of CBT for internalizing disorders in children. *Clinical Child and Family Psychology Review, 14*(2), 161–173.

Espelage, D. L, Hong, J. S., Rao, M. A., & Low, S. (2013). Associations between peer victimization and academic performance. *Theory Into Practice, 52*(4), 233–240.

Essau, C. A. (2005). Use of mental health services among adolescents with anxiety and depressive disorders. *Depression and Anxiety, 22,* 130–137.

Essau, C. A., Conradt, J., Sasagawa, S., & Ollendick, T. H. (2012). Prevention of anxiety symptoms in children: Results from a universal school-based trial. *Behavior Therapy, 43,* 450–464.

Essex, M. J., Klein, M. H., Slattery, M. J., & Hill, H. (2010). Early risk factors and developmental pathways to chronic high inhibition and social anxiety disorder in adolescence. *American Journal of Psychiatry, 167*(1), 40–46.

Eysenck, M. W., & Derakshan, N. (2011). New perspectives in attentional control theory. *Personality and Individual Differences, 50,* 955–960.

Festa, C. C., & Ginsburg, G. S. (2011). Parental and peer predictors of social anxiety in youth. *Child Psychiatry and Human Development, 42,* 291–306.

Fjell, A. M., Beate Walhovd, K., Brown, T. T., Kuperman, J. M., Chung, Y., Hagler, D. J., Jr., . . . Dale, A. M. (2012). Multimodal imaging of the self-regulating developing brain. *Proceedings of the National Academy of Sciences, 109*(48), 19620–19625.

Fox, N. A., & Pine, D. S. (2012). Temperament and the emergence of anxiety disorders. *Journal of the American Academy of Child and Adolescent Psychiatry, 51*(2), 125–128.

Frattaroli, J. (2006). Experimental disclosures and its moderators: A meta-analysis. *Psychological Bulletin, 132,* 823–865. doi: 10.1037/0033-2909.132.6.823

Galand, B., & Hospel, V. (2013). Peer victimization and school disaffection: Exploring the moderation effect of social support and the mediation effect of depression. *British Journal of Educational Psychology, 83,* 569–590.

Garber, J. (2006). Depression in children and adolescents linking risk research and prevention. *American Journal of Preventive Medicine, 1*(6S1), 104–125.

Garber, J., & Weersing, V. R. (2010). Comorbidity of anxiety and depression in youth: Implications for treatment and prevention. *Clinical Psychology, 17*(4), 293–306.

Ginsburg, G. S., Kendall, P. S., Sakolsky, D., Compton, S. N., Piacentini, J., Albano, A. M., . . . March, J. (2011). Remission after acute treatment in children and adolescents with anxiety disorders: Findings from the CAMS. *Journal of Consulting and Clinical Psychology, 79*(6), 806–813.

Gold, E., Smith, A., Hopper, I., Herne, D., Tansey, G.. & Hulland, C. (2010). Mindfulness-based stress reduction (MBSR) for primary school teachers. *Journal of Child and Family Studies, 19,* 184–189.

Goldman, S. (2012). Developmental epidemiology of depressive disorders. *Child and Adolescent Psychiatric Clinics of North America, 21,* 217–235.

Gomez, R., Vance, A., & Miranjini Gomez, R. (2014). The factor structure of anxiety and depressive disorders in a sample of clinic-referred adolescents. *Journal of Abnormal Child Psychology, 42,* 321–332.

Gonzalez, A., Boyle, M. H., Kyu, H. H., Georgiades, K., Duncan, L., & MacMillan, H. L. (2012). Childhood and family influences on depression, chronic physical conditions, and their comorbidity: Findings from the Ontario Child Health Study. *Journal of Psychiatric Research, 46,* 1475–1482.

Gould, L. F., Dariotis, J. K., Mendelson, T., & Greenberg, M. T. (2012). A school-based mindfulness intervention for urban youth: Exploring moderators of intervention effects. *Journal of Community Psychology, 40*(8), 968–982.

Graziano, P.A., Reavis, R.D., Keane, S.P., & Calkins, S.D. (2007). The role of emotion regulation in children's early academic success. *Journal of School Psychology, 45,* 3-19.

Gravel, E. (2013). *How do you doodle? Drawing my feelings and emotions.* Washington, DC: Magination Press.

Greenberg, M. T. (2006). Promoting resilience in children and youth: Preventive interventions and their interface with neuroscience. *Annals of the New York Academy of Sciences, 1094,* 139–150.

Grills-Taquechel, A. E., Fletcher, J. M., Vaughn, S. R., Denton, C. A., & Taylor, P. (2013). Anxiety and inattention as predictors of achievement in early elementary school children. *Anxiety, Stress and Coping: An International Journal, 26*(4), 391–410.

Guan, K., Fox, K. R., & Prinstein, M. J. (2012). Nonsuicidal self-injury as a time-invariant predictor of adolescent suicide ideation and attempts in a diverse community sample. *Journal of Consulting and Clinical Psychology, 80*(5), 842–849.

Guerry, J. D., & Hastings, P. D. (2011). In search of HPA axis dysregulation in child and adolescent depression. *Clinical Child and Family Psychology Review, 14,* 135–160.

Guerry, J. D., Reilly, N. N., & Prinstein, M. J. (2011). Suicide risk and self-injury. In G. P. Koocher & A. M. LaGreca (Eds.), *The parents' guide to psychological first aid for parents: Helping children and adolescents cope with predictable life crises* (pp. 323–332). New York, NY: Oxford University Press.

Hankin, B. L., Badanes, L. S., Abela, J. R. Z., & Watamura, S. E. (2010). Hypothalamic pituitary adrenal axis dysregulation in dysphoric children and adolescents: Cortisol reactivity to psychosocial stress from preschool through middle adolescence. *Biology Psychiatry, 68*(5), 484–490.

Heckman, J. J. (2006). Skill formation and the economics of investing in disadvantaged children. *Science, 312,* 1900–1902.

Hella, B., & Bernstein, G. A. (2012). Panic disorder and school refusal. *Child and Adolescent Psychiatric Clinics of North America, 21,* 593–606.

Herman, K. C., Reinke, W. M., Frey, A. J., & Shepard, S. A. (2014). *Motivational interviewing in schools: Strategies for engaging parents, teachers, and students.* New York, NY: Springer.

Herts, K. L., McLaughlin, K. A., & Hatzenbuehler, M. L. (2012). Emotion dysregulation as a mechanism linking stress exposure to adolescent aggressive behavior. *Journal of Abnormal Child Psychology, 40*(7), 1111–1122.

Herzig-Anderson, K., Colognori, D., Fox, J. K., Stewart, C. E., & Warner, C. M. (2012). School-based anxiety treatments for children and adolescents. *Child and Adolescent Psychiatric Clinics of North America, 21,* 655–668.

Hiebert-Murphy, D., Williams, E. A., Mills, R. S. L., Walker, J. R., Feldgaier, S., Warren, M., . . . Cox, B. J. (2011). Listening to parents: The challenges of parenting kindergarten-aged children who are anxious. *Clinical Child Psychology and Psychiatry, 17*(3), 384–399.

Hoagwood, K. E., Cavaleri, M. A., Olin, S. S., Burns, B. J., Slaton, E., Gruttadaro, D., & Hughes, R. (2009). Family support in children's mental health: A review and synthesis. *Clinical Child and Family Psychology Review, 13,* 1–45.

Howell, A. J., Keyes, C. L. M., & Passmore, H.-A. (2013). Flourishing among children and adolescents: Structure and correlates of positive mental health, and interventions for its enhancement. In C. Proctor & P. A. Linley (Eds.), *Research, applications, and interventions for children and adolescents* (pp. 59–79). Dordrecht: Netherlands: Springer.

Hughes, A. A., Lourea-Waddell, B., & Kendall, P. C. (2008). Somatic complaints in children with anxiety disorders and their unique prediction of poorer academic performance. *Child Psychiatry and Human Development, 39,* 211–220.

Hughes, E. K., Gullone, E., Dudley, A., & Tonge, B. (2010). A case-control study of emotional regulation and school refusal in children and adolescents. *Journal of Early Adolescence, 30*(5), 691–706.

Hughes, E.K., Gullone, E., & Watson, S.D. (2011). Emotional functioning in children and adolescents with elevated depressive symptoms. *Journal of Psychopathology and Behavioral Assessment, 33,* 335–345.

Ialongo, N., Edelsohn, G., Werthamer-Larsson, L., Crockett, L., & Kellam, S. (1995). The significance of self-reported anxious symptoms in first grade children: Prediction to anxious symptoms and adaptive functioning in fifth grade. *Journal of Child Psychology and Psychiatry, 36*(3), 427–437.

Immordino-Yang, M. H., & Damasio, A. (2007). We feel, therefore we learn: The relevance of affective and social neuroscience to education. *Mind, brain, and education, 1*(1), 3-10.

Jacka, F. N., Reavley, N. J, Jorm, A. F., Toumbourou, J. W., Lewis, A. J., & Berk, M. (2013). Prevention of common mental disorders: What can we learn from those who have gone before and where do we go next? *Australian and New Zealand Journal of Psychiatry, 47*(10), 920–929.

Jennings, P. A., & Greenberg, M. T. (2009). The prosocial classroom: Teacher social and emotional competence in relation to student and classroom outcomes. *Review of Educational Research, 79*(1), 491–525.

Jennings, P. A., Snowberg, K. E., Coccia, M. A., & Greenberg, M. T. (2011). Improving classroom learning environments by cultivating awareness and resilience in education (CARE): Results of two pilot studies. *Journal of Classroom Interaction, 46*(1), 37–48.

Juang, L. P., Syeng, M., & Cookston, J. T. (2012). Acculturation-based and everyday parent–adolescent conflict among Chinese American adolescents: Longitudinal trajectories and implications for mental health. *Journal of Family Psychology, 26*(6), 916–926.

Kabat-Zinn, J. (1994). *Mindfulness meditation for everyday life.* New York, NY: Hyperion.

Kalpidou, M. D., Power, T. G., Cherry, K. E., & Gottfried, N. W. (2004). Regulation of emotion and behavior among 3- and 5-year-olds. *Journal of General Psychology, 131*(2), 159–178.

Kawabata, J., Crick, N. R., & Hamaguchi, Y. (2010). The role of culture in relational aggression: Associations with social-psychological adjustment problems in Japanese and US school-aged children. *International Journal of Behavioral Development, 34*(4), 354–362.

Kearney, C., & Albano, A. M. (2007). *When children refuse school: A cognitive-behavioral therapy approach* (2nd ed.). Oxford, UK: Oxford University Press.

Kendall, P. C., Furr, J. M., & Podell, J. L. (2010). Child-focused treatment of anxiety. In J. R. Weisz & A. E. Kazdin (Eds.), *Evidence-based psychotherapies for children and adolescents* (2nd ed., pp. 45–60). New York, NY: Guilford Press.

Kim, H., & Page, T. (2013). Emotional bonds with parents, emotion regulation, and school-related behavior problems among elementary school truants. *Journal of Child and Family Studies, 22*(6), 869–878.

Kingery, J. N., Roblek, T. L., Suveg, C., Grover, R. L., Sherrill, J. T., & Bergman, R. L. (2006). They're not just "little adults": Developmental considerations for implementing cognitive-behavioral therapy with anxious youth. *Journal of Cognitive Psychotherapy: An International Quarterly, 20*(3), 263–273.

Kinniburgh, K. J., Blaustein, M., & Spinazzola, J. (2005). Attachment, self-regulation, and competency: A comprehensive intervention framework for children with complex trauma. *Psychiatric Annals, 35*(5), 424–430.

Kitts, R. L., & Goldman, S. J. (2012). Education and depression. *Child and Adolescent Psychiatric Clinics of North America, 21,* 421–446.

Kovacs, M., Joormann, J., & Gotlib, I. H. (2008). Emotion (dys)regulation and links to depressive disorders. *Child Development Perspectives, 2*(3), 149–155.

Kovacs, M., & Lopez-Duran, N. L. (2012). Contextual emotion regulation therapy: A developmentally based intervention for pediatric depression. *Child and Adolescent Psychiatric Clinics of North America, 21,* 327–343.

LaGreca, A. M., & Harrison, H. M. (2005). Adolescent peer relations, friendships, and romantic relationships: Do they predict social anxiety and depression? *Journal of Clinical Child and Adolescent Psychology, 34,* 49–61.

Lau, J. Y. F., Pettit, E., & Creswell, C. (2013). Reducing children's social anxiety symptoms: Exploring a novel parent-administered cognitive bias modification training intervention. *Behaviour Research and Therapy, 51,* 333–337.

Leadbeater, B. J., Gladstone, E., Yeung Thomson, R. S., Sukhawathanakul, P., & Desjardins, T. (2012). Getting started: Assimilatory processes of uptake of mental health promotion and primary prevention programmes in elementary schools. *Advances in School Mental Health Promotion, 5*(4), 258–276.

Lee, J., Semple, R. J., Rosa, D., & Miller, L. (2008). Mindfulness-based cognitive therapy for children: Results of a pilot study. *Journal of Cognitive Psychotherapy, 22*(1), 15–28.

Leflot, G., van Lier, P. A. C., Onghena, P., & Colpin, H. (2010). The role of teacher behavior management in the development of disruptive behaviors: An intervention study with the Good Behavior Game. *Journal of Abnormal Child Psychology, 38,* 869–882.

Liew, J. (2012). Effortful control, executive functions, and education: Bringing self-regulatory and social-emotional competencies to the table. *Child Development Perspectives, 6*(2), 105–111.

Loades, M. E., & Mastroyannopoulou, K. (2010). Teachers' recognition of children's mental health problems. *Child and Adolescent Mental Health, 15*(3), 150–156.

Lonigan, C. J., & Philips, B. M. (2001). Temperamental influences on the development of anxiety disorders. In M. W. Vasey & M. R. Dadds (Eds.), *The developmental psychopathology of anxiety* (pp. 60–85). New York, NY: Oxford University Press.

Lynch, T. R., Chapman, A. L., Rosenthal, M., Kuo, J. R., & Linehan, M. M. (2006). Mechanisms of change in dialectical behavior therapy: Theoretical and empirical observations. *Journal of Clinical Psychology, 62*(4), 459–480.

Maalouf, F. T., & Brent, D. A. (2012). Child and adolescent depression intervention overview: What works, for whom and how well? *Child and Adolescent Psychiatric Clinics of North America, 21,* 299–312.

Madigan, S., Atkinson, L., Laurin, K., & Benoit, D. (2013). Attachment and internalizing behavior in early childhood: A meta-analysis. *Developmental Psychology, 49*(4), 672-689

Maeda, N., Hatada, S., Sonoda, J., & Takayama, I. (2012). School-based intensive exposure therapy for school refusal behavior. *Clinical Case Studies, 11*(4), 299–311.

March, J. S. (2011). Looking to the future of research in pediatric anxiety disorders. *Depression and Anxiety, 28,* 88–98.

Martinez, W., Polo, A. J., & Smith Carter, J. (2012). Family orientation, language, and anxiety among low-income Latino youth. *Journal of Anxiety Disorders, 26,* 517–525.

Maslowsky, J., Mogg, K., Bradley, B. P., McClure-Tone, E., Ernst., M., Pine, D. S., & Monk, C. S. (2010). A preliminary investigation of neural correlates of treatment in adolescents with generalized anxiety disorder. *Journal of Child and Adolescent Psychopharmacology, 20*(2), 105–111.

Maughan, B., Collishaw, S., & Stringaris, A. (2013). Depression in childhood and adolescence. *Journal of the Canadian Academy of Child and Adolescent Psychiatry, 22*(1), 35–40.

McClelland, M. M., & Cameron, C. E. (2012). Self-regulation in early childhood:

Improving conceptual clarity and developing ecologically valid measures. *Child Development Perspectives, 6*(2), 136–142.

McClelland, M. M., Cameron, C. E., McDonald Connor, C., Farris, C. L., Jewkes, A. M., & Morrison, F. J. (2007). Links between behavioral regulation and preschoolers' literacy, vocabulary, and math skills. *Developmental Psychology, 43*(4), 947–959.

McCloud, C. (2006). *Have you filled a bucket today? A guide to daily happiness for kids.* Northville, MI: Ferne Press.

Meiklejohn, J., Phillips, C., Freedman, M. L., Griffin, M. L., Biegel, G., Roach, A., . . . Saltzman, A. (2012). Integrating mindfulness training into K–12 education: Fostering the resilience of teachers and students. *Mindfulness.* doi: 10.1007/s12671-012-0094-5

Mennuti, R. B., & Christner, R. W. (2012). An introduction to cognitive-behavioral therapy with youth. In R. B. Mennuti, R. W. Christner, & A. Freeman (Eds.), *Cognitive-behavioral interventions in educational settings: A handbook for practice* (2nd ed., pp. 3–24). New York, NY: Routledge.

Menzies, V., & Jallo, N. (2011). Guided imagery as a treatment option for fatigue: A literature review. *Journal of Holistic Nursing, 29*(4), 279–286. doi: 10.1177/0898010111412187

Merikangas, K. R., He, J.-p., Burstein, M., Swanson, S. A., Avenevoli, S., Cui, L., . . . Swendsen, J. (2010). Lifetime prevalence of mental disorders in U.S. adolescents: Results from the National Comorbidity Study–Adolescent Supplement (NCS-A). *Journal of the American Academy of Child and Adolescent Psychiatry, 49*(10), 980–989.

Merrell, K. W., & Gueldner, B. A. (2010). *Social and emotional learning in the classroom: Promoting mental health and academic success.* New York, NY: Guilford Press.

Miller, D. N., & Eckert, T. L. (2009). Youth suicidal behavior: An introduction and overview. *School Psychology Review, 38*(2), 153–167.

Miller, L. D., Gold, S., Laye-Gindhu, A., Martinez, Y. J., Yu, C. M., & Waechtler, V. (2011). Transporting a school-based intervention for social anxiety in Canadian adolescents. *Canadian Journal of Behavioural Science, 43*(4), 287–296.

Min, H. J., Jon, D.-I., Jung, M. H., Hong, N., Song, M. A., Kim, Y. S., . . . Hong, H. J. (2012). Depression, aggression, and suicidal ideation in first graders: A school-based cross-sectional study. *Comprehensive Psychiatry, 53*, 1145–1152.

Muris, P., Mayer, B., Kramer Freher, N., Duncan, S., & van den Hout, A. (2010). Children's internal attributions of anxiety-related physical symptoms:

Age-related patterns and the role of cognitive development and anxiety sensitivity. *Child Psychiatry and Human Development, 41,* 535–548.

Muris, P., vanBrakel, A. M. L., Arntz, A., & Schouten, E. (2011). Behavioral inhibition as a risk factor for the development of childhood anxiety disorders: A longitudinal study. *Journal of Child and Family Studies, 20,* 157–170.

Mychailyszyn, M. P., Beidas, R. S., Benjamin, C. L., Edmunds, J. M., Podell, J. L., Cohen, J. S., & Kendall, P. C. (2011). Assessing and treating child anxiety in schools. *Psychology in the Schools, 48*(3), 223–232.

Najman, J. M., Hayatbakhsh, M. R., Clavarino, A., Bor, W., O'Callaghan, M. J., & Williams, G. M. (2010). Family poverty over the early life course and recurrent adolescent and young adult anxiety and depression: A longitudinal study. *American Journal of Public Health, 100*(9), 1719–1723.

National Scientific Council on the Developing Child. (2004a). *Children's emotional development is built into the architecture of their brains* (Working Paper No. 2). Retrieved from http://developingchild.harvard.edu/index.php/resources/reports_and_working_papers/working_papers/wp2/

National Scientific Council on the Developing Child. (2004). *Young children develop in an environment of relationships* (Working Paper No. 1). Retrieved from http://developingchild.harvard.edu/index.php/resources/reports_and_working_papers/working_papers/wp1/

National Scientific Council on the Developing Child. (2005/2014). *Excessive stress disrupts the architecture of the developing brain* (Working Paper No. 3. Updated Edition). Retrievedf from http://developingchild.harvard.edu/index.php/resources/reports_and_working_papers/working_papers/wp3/

National Scientific Council on the Developing Child. (2010). *Persistent fear and anxiety can affect young children's learning and development* (Working Paper No. 9). Retrieved from http://developingchild.harvard.edu/index.php/resources/reports_and_working_papers/working_papers/wp9/

National Scientific Council on the Developing Child. (2012). *Establishing a level foundation for life: Mental health begins in early childhood* (Working Paper No. 6, updated ed.). Retrieved from http://developingchild.harvard.edu/index.php/resources/reports_and_working_papers/working_papers/wp6/

Nelson, R. B., Schnorr, D., Powell, S., & Huebner, S. (2012). Building resilience in schools. In R. B. Mennuti, R. W. Christner, & A. Freeman (Eds.), *Cognitive-behavioral interventions in educational settings: A handbook for practice* (2nd ed., pp 643–682.). New York, NY: Routledge.

Neuenschwander, R., Röthlisberger, M., Cimeli, P., & Roebers, C. (2012). How do different aspects of self-regulation predict successful adaptation to school? *Journal of Experimental Child Psychology, 113,* 353–371.

Nicolas, G., & Schwartz, B. (2012). Culture first: Lessons learned about the importance of the cultural adaptation of cognitive behavior treatment interventions for Black Caribbean youth. In G. Bernal & M. M. Domenech Rodríguez (Eds.), *Cultural adaptations: Tools for evidence-based practice with diverse populations* (pp. 71-90). Washington, DC: American Psychological Association.

Nicolopoulou, A. (2010). The alarming disappearance of play from early childhood education. *Human Development, 53,* 1–4.

O'Connell, M. E., Boat, T., & Warner, K. E. (Eds.). (2009). *Preventing mental, emotional, and behavioral disorders among young people: Progress and possibilities.* Washington, DC: National Academic Press.

O'Connor, E., & McCartney, K. (2007). Examining teacher–child relationships and achievement as part of an ecological model of development. *American Educational Research Journal, 44*(2), 340–369.

Ortiz, S. O. (2012). Multicultural issues in school mental health. In R. B. Mennuti, R. W. Christner, & A. Freeman (Eds.), *Cognitive-behavioral interventions in educational settings: A handbook for practice* (2nd ed., pp. 53–80). New York, NY: Routledge.

Peterson, C., & Park, N. (2007). Explanatory style and emotion regulation. In J. J. Gross (Ed.), *Handbook of emotion regulation* (pp. 159–179). New York, NY: Guilford Press.

Pina, A. A., Little, M., Wynne, H., & Beidel, D. C. (2013). Assessing social anxiety in African American youth using the Social Phobia and Anxiety Inventory for Children. *Journal of Abnormal Child Psychology.* doi: 10.1007/s10802-013-9775-3

Posner, M. I., & Rothbart, M. K. (2000). Developing mechanisms of self-regulation. *Development and Psychopathology, 12,* 427–441.

Postert, C., Dannlowski, U., Müller, J. M., & Konrad, C. (2012). Beyond the blues: Towards a cross-cultural phenomenology of depressed mood. *Psychopathology, 45,* 185–192.

Powell, D. R., Son, S. H., File, N., & San Juan, R. R. (2010). Parent–school relationships and children's academic and social outcomes in public school pre-kindergarten. *Journal of School Psychology, 48*(4), 269–292.

Raver, C. (2012, November). Low-income children's self-regulation in the classroom: Scientific inquiry for social change. *American Psychologist.* doi: 10.1037/a0030085

Reeve, J., & Jang, H. (2006). What teachers say and do to support students' autonomy during a learning activity. *Journal of Educational Psychology, 98*(1), 209–218.

Reilly, N. (Ed.). (2011). *Break free from depression.* Boston, MA: Children's Hospital.

Rimm-Kaufman, S. E., Pianta, R. C., & Cox, M. J. (2000). Teachers' judgments of problems in the transition to kindergarten. *Early Childhood Research Quarterly, 15*(2), 147–166.

Roeser, R. W., Skinner, E., Beers, J., & Jennings, P. A. (2012). Mindfulness training and teachers' professional development: An emerging area of research and practice. *Child Development Perspectives, 6*(2), 167–173.

Röll, J., Koglin, U., & Petermann, F. (2012). Emotion regulation and childhood aggression: Longitudinal associations. *Child Psychiatry and Human Development.* doi: 10.1007/s10578-012-0303-4

Semple, R. J., Reid, E. G., & Miller, L. (2005). Treating anxiety with mindfulness: An open trial of mindfulness training for anxious children. *Journal of Cognitive Psychotherapy, 19*(4), 379–392.

Shaffer, A., Suveg, C., Thomassin, K., & Bradbury, L. L. (2012). Emotion socialization in the context of family risks: Links to child emotion regulation. *Journal of Child and Family Studies, 21*(6), 917–924.

Shapiro, S. L., Carlson, L. E., Astin, J. A., & Freedman, B. (2006). Mechanisms of mindfulness. *Journal of Clinical Psychology, 62*(3), 373–386.

Silk, J. S., Sheeber, L., Tan, P. Z., Ladouceur, C. D., Forbes, E. E., McMakin, D. L., . . . Ryan, N. D. (2013). "You can do it!": The role of parental encouragement of bravery in child anxiety treatment. *Journal of Anxiety Disorders, 27,* 439–446.

Silverman, W. K., Kurtines, W. M., Ginsburg, G. S., Weems, C. F., Lumpkin, P., & Carmichael, D. (1999). Treating anxiety disorders in children with group cognitive-behavioral therapy: A randomized clinical trial. *Journal of Consulting and Clinical Psychology, 67*(6), 995–1003.

Silverman, W. K., Pina, A. A., & Viswesvaran, C. (2008). Evidence-based psychosocial treatments for phobic and anxiety disorders in children and adolescents. *Journal of Clinical Child and Adolescent Psychology, 37*(1), 105–130.

Sportel, B. E., Nauta, M. H., deHullu, E., deJong, P. J., & Hartman, C. A. (2011). Behavioral inhibition and attentional control in adolescents: Robust relationships with anxiety and depression. *Journal of Child and Family Studies, 20,* 149–156.

Stagman, S. M., & Cooper, J. L. (2010). *Children's mental health: What every pol-*

icymaker should know. New York, NY: Columbia University, National Center for Children in Poverty.

Stark, K. D., Streusand, W., Krumholz, L. S., & Patel, P. (2010). Cognitive-behavioral therapy for depression: The ACTION treatment program for girls. In J. R. Weisz & A. E. Kazdin (Eds.), *Evidence-based psychotherapies for children and adolescents* (2nd ed., 93–109). New York, NY: Guilford Press.

Stegge, H., & Meerum Terwogt, M. (2007). Awareness and regulation of emotion in typical and atypical development. In J. J. Gross (Ed.), *Handbook of emotion regulation* (pp. 269–286). New York, NY: Guilford Press.

Stein, G. L., Gonzalez, L. M., & Huq, N. (2012). Cultural stressors and the hopelessness model of depressive symptoms in Latino adolescents. *Journal of Youth and Adolescence, 41,* 1339–1349.

Stewart, S. M., Simmons, A., & Habibpour, E. (2012). Treatment of culturally diverse children and adolescents with depression. *Journal of Child and Adolescent Psychopharmacology, 22*(1), 72–79.

Stormshak, E. A., Connell, A. M., Véronneau, M. H., Myers, M. W., Dishion, T. J., Kavanagh, K., & Caruthers, A. S. (2011). An ecological approach to promoting early adolescent mental health and social adaptation: Family-centered intervention in public middle schools. *Child Development, 82*(1), 209–225.

Strawn, J. R., Wehry, A. M., DelBello, M. P., Rynn, M. A., & Strakowski, S. (2012). Establishing the neurobiologic basis of treatment in children and adolescents with generalized anxiety disorder. *Depression and Anxiety, 29,* 328–339.

Suárez, L. M., Bennett, S. M., Goldstein, C. R., & Barlow, D. H. (2008). Understanding anxiety disorders from a "triple vulnerability" framework. In M. M. Anthony & M. B. Stein (Eds.), *Oxford handbook of anxiety and related disorders* (153–172). New York, NY: Oxford University Press. doi: 10.1093/oxfordhb/9780195307030.013.0013

Szapocznik, J., & Williams, R. A. (2000). Brief strategic family therapy: Twenty-five years of interplay among theory, research and practice in adolescent behavior problems and drug abuse. *Clinical Child and Family Psychology Review, 3*(2), 117–134.

Telzer, E. H., & Vasquez Garcia, H. A. (2009). Skin color and self-perceptions of immigrant and US-born Latinas: The moderating role of racial socialization and ethnic identity. *Hispanic Journal of Behavioral Sciences, 31*(3), 357–374.

Thomassin, K., Morelen, D., & Suveg, C. (2012). Emotion reporting using electronic diaries reduces anxiety symptoms in girls with emotion dysregulation. *Journal of Contemporary Psychotherapy, 42,* 207–213.

Thompson, R. A., & Meyer, S. (2007). Socialization of emotion regulation in the family. In J. J. Gross (Ed.), *Handbook of emotion regulation* (pp. 249–268). New York, NY: Guilford Press.

Tominey, S. L., & McClelland, M. M. (2011). Red light, purple light: Findings from a randomized trial using circle time games to improve behavioral self-regulation in preschool. *Early Education and Development, 22*(3), 489–519.

Tompson, M. C., Boger, K. D., & Asarnow, J. R. (2012). Enhancing the developmental appropriateness of treatment for depression in youth: Integrating the family in treatment. *Child and Adolescent Psychiatric Clinics of North America, 21*(2), 345–384.

Tunnard, C., Rane, L. J., Wooderson, S. C., Markopoulou, K., Poon, L., Fekadu, A., . . . Cleare, A. J. (2013). The impact of childhood adversity on suicidality and clinical course in treatment-resistant depression. *Journal of Affective Disorders.* doi: 10.1016/j.jad.2013.06.037

U.S. Department of Health and Human Services, Substance Abuse and Mental Health Services Administration, Center for Mental Health Services. (2007). *Promotion and prevention in mental health: Strengthening parenting and enhancing child resilience* (DHHS Publication No.CMHS-SVP-0175). Rockville, MD: Author.

Valiente, C., Swanson, J., & Eisenberg, N. (2012). Linking students' emotions and academic achievement: When and why emotions matter. *Child Development Perspectives, 6*(2), 129–135.

Valiente, C., Swanson, J. & Lemery-Chalfant, K. (2012). Kindergartners' temperament, classroom engagement, and student-teacher relationship: Moderation by effortful control. *Social Development, 21*(3), 558–576

Varela, R. E., & Hensley-Maloney, L. (2009). The influence of culture on anxiety in Latino youth: A review. *Clinical Child and Family Psychology Review, 12*, 217–233.

Verboom, C.E., Sijtsema, J.J., Verhulst, F.C., Pennix, B.W.J.H., & Ornel, J. (2014). Longitudinal associations between depressive problems, academic performance, and social functioning in adolescent boys and girls. *Developmental Psychology, 50*(1), 247–257.

Vervoot, L., Wolters, L. H., Hogendoorn, S. M., Prins, P. J., de Haan, E., Boer, F., & Hartman, C. (2011). Temperament, attentional processes, and anxiety: Diverging links between adolescents with and without anxiety disorders? *Journal of Clinical Child and Adolescent Psychology, 40*(1), 144–155.

von Suchodoletz, A., Gestsdottir, S., Wanless, S. B., McClelland, M. M., Birgisdottir, F., Gunzenhauser, C., & Ragnarsdottir, H. (2013). Behavioral self-regulation and relations to emergent academic skills among children in Germany and Iceland. *Early Childhood Research Quarterly, 28,* 62–73.

Walsh, B. (2006). *Treating self-injury: A practical guide.* New York: Guilford Press.

Warner, C. M., Colognori, D., Kim, R. E., Reigada, L. C., Browner-Elhanan, K. J., Saborsky, A., . . . Benkov, K. (2011). Cognitive-behavioral treatment of persistent functional somatic complaints and pediatric anxiety: An initial controlled trial. *Depression and Anxiety, 28,* 551–559.

Wegmann, K. M., Powers, J. D., & Blackman, K. (2013). Supporting vulnerable families through school-based mental health services: Results of caregiver and teacher focus groups. *Journal of Family Social Work, 16*(4), 297–313.

Whitley, J., Smith, J. D., & Vaillancourt, T. (2012). Promoting mental health literacy among educators: Critical in school-based prevention and intervention. *Canadian Journal of School Psychology, 28*(1) 56–70.

Whitlock, J., Muehlenkamp, J., Eckenrode, J., Purington, A., Baral Abrams, G., Barreira, P., & Kress, V. (2013). Nonsuicidal self-injury as a gateway to suicide in young adults. *Journal of Adolescent Health, 52,* 486–492.

World Health Organization. (2003). Investing in mental health.

Zelazo, P. D., & Carlson, S. M. (2012). Hot and cool executive function in childhood and adolescence: Development and plasticity. *Child Development Perspectives, 6*(4), 354–360.

Zelazo, P. D., & Lyons, K. E. (2012). The potential benefits of mindfulness training in early childhood: A developmental social cognitive neuroscience perspective. *Child Development Perspectives, 6*(2), 154–160.

Zhou, Q., Chen, S. H., & Main, A. (2012). Commonalities and differences in the research on children's effortful control and executive function: A call for an integrated model of self-regulation. *Child Development Perspectives, 6*(2), 112–121.

Index

The following abbreviations are used in this index: *f* for figure.

student interests incorporated into,
138
classroom interventions
factors to consider in using, 143
overview of, 142–43f
questions regarding success of,
135–36
single student interventions versus,
142
See also specific activities
classroom rules, 209, 210
clearances. *See* health clearances
Clue, 147–48
cognition. *See* anterior cingulate
cortex (ACC); executive
functions; thoughts
cognition and emotions, 17–18, 17f
cognitive behavioral therapy (CBT),
70–71, 73, 122
cognitive distortions, 101–2
cognitive-processing abilities, 103,
118
cognitive restructuring, 122
cognitive restructuring activities,
149–157
Collaborative for Academic, Social,
and Emotional Learning
(CASEL), 6–7, 23, 206, 210, 216
Collishaw, S., 83
Colpin, H., 164
communication
among school staff, 250–51
cultural sensitivity in, 251, 253–54
of parents with treatment
providers, 263–64
use of multiple means of, 250, 252
See also language; special
signals; teacher-parent

communication; teacher-student
relationships; treatment provider
communication
community mental health centers,
263
community partnerships, 257, 282,
286
comorbidity
anxiety disorders and, 63, 65, 70
depressive disorders and, 65, 70,
85, 116, 118
competence. *See* self-efficacy;
self-esteem
competition. *See* cooperation versus
competition
compliment cards, 32
compulsions, 64
concentration, 118, 119
See also attentional control
conduct disorder, 118
confidentiality, 193, 197, 261
See also self-disclosure
connections between thoughts and
emotions activities, 222–25, 223f
contingency management activities,
157–160
control. *See* attentional control;
effortful control; sense of control
controlling teaching style, 246
convergent thinking, 228
conversations, opportunities for, 79,
130–31, 268–69
cooperation versus competition, 35
coping skills
active versus passive strategies,
90–91
categories of, 43–44
effortful control and, 89

insecure attachment and, 45, 92
of parents, 46
stress response system and, 40
See also depressive disorders
internal shame, 98–99
interpersonal therapy (IPT), 122
interpretation. *See* negative
    interpretation
IPT. *See* interpersonal therapy (IPT)
irritability, 106, 109, 112
    See also Deescalating Anger
"I" statements, 130–31

Jang, H., 246
joint vision creation, 266–67
Journaling, 173–75
Juang, L., 58
judgmental responses, 79
    See also criticism, parental

Kabat-Zinn, J., 33, 179
Kagan, J., 41
Keane, S., 20
Kearney, C., 67
Kendall, P., 150
khyâl, 57
kindergarteners, 9, 20, 37–38, 55,
    173–75, 211
kindness, acts of, 32
Knappe, S., 72

labeling, 102, 151
language
    importance of developmentally
      appropriate, 199
    person-first, 78, 130
    positive use of, 210, 255, 256,
      259–260

use of metaphors in, 217, 220, 237
    See also person-first language;
      power of language
Latino children and youth, 57
Latino culture
    communication with parents of,
      253
    mental illness and, 56, 57
    school engagement and, 252
    somatic complaints and, 107
    symptoms of depressive disorders
      in, 108
learning, 35, 67–70, 119–120, 283–84
    See also academic achievement
learning disabilities, 103, 106
Lee, K., 214, 290
Leflot, G., 164, 201
legal problems, 84
life satisfaction factors, 206
listening, 199–200, 245–46, 260,
    268–69
long-term assignments, 138
low socioeconomic status, 287–88
    See also poverty effects
lwa, 259

macro-level interventions, 287
Madigan, S., 93
Magination Press, 203
maintenance therapy, 120
    See also follow-up therapy
major depressive disorder, 110–12
maladaptive behavior reinforcement,
    164–65, 200–201
    See also contingency management
      activities
maltreatment. *See* abuse and trauma
    history

teacher-parent communication
(*continued*)
strategies for improving, 250–52
strengths-based approach in, 251–52, 259–260
worries during, 260–61
teachers, 9, 244, 289–290
teacher self-care, 136, 203, 247, 290
See also staff training
teacher-student relationships
academic achievement and effects of, 20, 107, 133
anxiety disorders and, 56
depressive disorders and, 106, 131
empathic communication within, 199–202
importance of, 244–45
long-lasting effects of nurturing in, 80
maladaptive behavior reinforcement in, 158, 164–65
personal factors affecting, 200–201
self-regulation and effects of, 21
suicidal behavior and, 198
See also conversations, opportunities for; "Nurture" approach
teacher support, as precursor to student support, 136
teaching styles, 246
team approach, 134, 136, 194, 196, 250–51
temperament, anxiety disorders and, 41–42, 45
temperament, depressive disorders and, 87–89
temperament-based approach, 13–14

temper tantrums, 109
A Terrible Thing Happened: A Story for Children Who Have Witnessed Violence or Trauma (Holmes), 204
test accommodations, 141
test anxiety, 119
test scores, 289
Thank-You Notes, 167–68
thinking errors. *See* cognitive distortions
Thomassin, K., 174
Thompson, R., 79
Thought Bubble, 150–52, 293
thoughts, 24, 51–53, 100–104
See also connections between thoughts and emotions activities
thought stopping. *See* cognitive restructuring activities
threats, 40, 42, 68
timed tests, 140
time orientation, 254
TLC, 202
tools
emotional and behavioral, 141–44, 142–43*f*, 207, 208*f*
psychoeducation for parents, 267–277
questions regarding success of, 135–36
See also book resources; curriculum resources
Tools of the Mind, 286
touch. *See* gentle touch
training. *See* staff training
transdiagnostic treatment framework, 134

Wishing Wellness: A Workbook for Children of Parents With Mental Illness (Clarke), 204
withdrawal, 15, 99
"won't" versus "can't," 141–42
words, self-awareness of emotions and, 24–25
work functioning, 84
working memory, 12
World Health Organization (WHO), 84
worries, parental, 260–61, 264–65, 271–72
worry
  anxiety disorders and, 59, 63, 64

depressive disorders and, 102–3
instruction reflection and, 139
lack of control and, 51–52
Latino children and youth and, 57
peer sharing of, 170
See also rumination
worry management, 187
Worry Stones, 178–79
worship places, 257, 264
worthlessness, 110
writing. *See* Journaling

"You Can Do It" Messages, 190–91